The Life of Henrietta Anne

The Life of Henrietta Anne

Daughter of Charles I

Melanie Clegg

PEN & SWORD
HISTORY

First published in Great Britain in 2017 by
Pen & Sword History
an imprint of
Pen & Sword Books Ltd
47 Church Street
Barnsley
South Yorkshire
S70 2AS

ISBN 978 1 47389 311 5

A CIP catalogue record for this book is available from the British
Library

Typeset in Ehrhardt by
Mac Style Ltd, Bridlington, East Yorkshire
Printed and bound in the Great Britain by TJ International Ltd.
Padstow, PL28 8RW

Pen & Sword Books Ltd incorporates the imprints of Pen & Sword
Archaeology, Atlas, Aviation, Battleground, Discovery, Family
History, History, Maritime, Military, Naval, Politics, Railways, Select,
Transport, True Crime, Fiction, Frontline Books, Leo Cooper,
Praetorian Press, Seaforth Publishing and Wharncliffe.

For a complete list of Pen & Sword titles please contact
PEN & SWORD BOOKS LIMITED
47 Church Street, Barnsley, South Yorkshire, S70 2AS, England
E-mail: enquiries@pen-and-sword.co.uk
Website: www.pen-and-sword.co.uk

Contents

Acknowledgements		vi
Chapter 1	Portrait of a Family	1
Chapter 2	A Child of War	11
Chapter 3	The Exiled Court	21
Chapter 4	The Widowed Queen	34
Chapter 5	The Palais Royal	48
Chapter 6	Colombes	61
Chapter 7	Restoration	72
Chapter 8	Whitehall	83
Chapter 9	Madame	96
Chapter 10	Vardes	112
Chapter 11	War	126
Chapter 12	The Chevalier	141
Chapter 13	The Secret Treaty	157
Chapter 14	Homeward Bound	174
Chapter 15	Madame est Morte	192
Bibliography		201
Index		203

Acknowledgements

This book has been a true labour of love for me and I hope that it will be as much of a treat to read as it has been to research and write. Henrietta Anne Stuart, youngest daughter of Charles I and Henrietta Maria, was reputedly one of the most charming, charismatic and bewitchingly delightful women of her time, adored by (almost) all who knew her and deeply respected not just for her sweet nature and gift for friendship but also for her keen intelligence and formidable political acumen. Even though nearly three hundred and fifty years have passed since her death in 1670, she still continues to enchant and fascinate historians and writers today as much as she delighted her contemporaries and it has been a rare pleasure to become better acquainted with her over the past twelve months.

Although writing is an essentially solitary business, I couldn't have completed this book without the seemingly endless support and encouragement of my blog's readers as well as my amazing friends, who have had to endure more than their fair share of cancelled plans, drunken rantings and self-pitying Facebook posts as the book's deadline rapidly approached. They have all been wonderful and I thank them from the bottom of my heart. I also promise not to make as much of a fuss when the next deadline begins to loom.

As always, writing a book is a group effort and I'd really like to thank Kate Bohdanowicz for her sterling work at the very start of this project, Lauren Burton of Pen and Sword Books for all of her help, encouragement and kindness when personal calamity made finishing the book rather more of an uphill task than it needed to be and Carol Trow for making the often hideous editing process much less painless than usual and for being the very first person to read the finished article. I just hope that everyone else who reads it agrees with your assessment! I'd also really like to thank the wonderful Desmond Shawe-Taylor and Karen Lawson of the Royal Collection for granting me permission to use the illustrations in this book. I am so very grateful to you all.

Above all though, I would like to thank the very lovely Simon Hayden, to whom this book is dedicated, for being the most excellent, accommodating, helpful and uncomplaining companion that any writer could ever wish to have and for all the endless and usually sadly forgotten and untouched cups of tea that he provided while I was working on this book.

Chapter One

Portrait of a Family

1625–1643

Seventeenth century visitors fortunate enough to be admitted to the magnificent state apartments of Whitehall Palace would have been hard pressed not to stop and admire, if only for a few minutes, the huge portrait of King Charles I, his French wife Henrietta Maria and their two eldest children, Charles, Prince of Wales and Mary, Princess Royal that hung in one of the vast reception rooms. This spectacular work, known as 'The Greate Peece', was the first portrait commissioned from Anthony van Dyck after he accepted the position of Royal Painter in 1632 and it remains one of the finest examples of his virtuoso talent. The thirty-two-year-old King Charles, dressed in his court finery and with the blue Order of the Garter ribbon around his neck looks sternly, even reprovingly, at the viewer, while his young wife, dressed in an amazing confection of buttercup yellow satin trimmed with blue silk ribbon bows and the finest lace, gazes lovingly across at him, their infant daughter in her arms. Their eldest son, Charles, who was just two years old and still dressed in skirts, stands proudly at his father's knee, anxiously playing with his own fingers as he solemnly scrutinises anyone impertinent enough to stop and stare, while at his feet one of the royal pet spaniels gambols and makes a bid for attention. It's a charming depiction of a happy family, albeit one surrounded by the trappings of majesty but although one immediately knows that one is in the presence of royalty, as the state crown, sceptre and orb sitting ignored at the King's elbow confirm, there is no stately otherness on display here but rather affection, trust and familial warmth of a nature never before seen in royal portraiture.

However, all was clearly not well in the world of Van Dyck's painting, as evidenced by the overcast and bleak sky behind the royal family. In the distance, the viewer can just make out the shadowy towers of Parliament House and Westminster Hall looming over the Thames while overhead, the storm threatens to break. This dismal background gives the painting, which would otherwise be a riot of rich colours and sensuously detailed fabrics, an air of foreboding, which of course seems all the more poignant today when we know that just seventeen years after posing for Van Dyck, King Charles would stand trial for his life in Westminster Hall while the family that he was so proud of would find themselves scattered all across Europe, lost to him forever. In 1632 though, when the painting was first commissioned, no one could ever possibly have imagined just how this most happy of royal marriages would eventually end, although the seeds of rebellion had already quietly been sown as early as 1629 when Charles peremptorily dissolved his parliament and imprisoned several members for questioning his policies. He then began to rule without parliamentary interference, a period known variously as the Personal Rule or the Eleven Years Tyranny depending on your loyalties, causing a deep rift between himself and his political opponents, who became increasingly and then overwhelmingly numerous over the next decade.

Although the royal couple were now a picture of marital felicity, things had not always gone so smoothly between them – they had heartily disliked each other for the first few years of their marriage, their quarrels exacerbated by Charles' devotion to his Master of the Horse, the Duke of Buckingham and Henrietta Maria's insistence upon publicly participating in Roman Catholic rites and her refusal to participate in the Protestant ceremony of Charles' coronation or part with the French household that had accompanied her from Paris. Although he was nine years older than his impetuous and hot headed little wife, who was just fifteen when they married in 1625, Charles behaved with just as much immaturity, allowing himself to be drawn into childish quarrels on an almost daily basis and behaving with excessive severity, particularly in the matter of the French household, because he lacked the emotional maturity or wisdom to negotiate with her as a more experienced and confident man might have done. Driven to despair, Henrietta Maria wrote to her brother Louis XIII and mother Marie de Medici, begging them to let her return home to France but to no avail – her presence in England was necessary to maintain at least the appearance of an Anglo-French alliance even if her husband's favourite, Buckingham, threatened this delicate status quo with his support of the Huguenots at La Rochelle in 1627.

It was only after Buckingham's assassination in August 1628 that Charles and Henrietta Maria began to draw closer, as evidenced by the fact that she conceived for the first time just a few months after the Duke's death, giving birth to a stillborn son in March 1629. By the time their next child, Prince Charles, was born in May 1630, the couple had, seemingly against all odds, fallen deeply in love and all their quarrels were, for now at least, at an end. Charles was followed in November of the following year by a sister, Mary and then at regular intervals by four more siblings; James, Elizabeth, Anne and Henry. Another baby, Catherine, was born dead in January 1639. The ever-increasing royal family kept Van Dyck busy throughout the 1630s as his patrons commissioned numerous portraits of themselves and their children, most notably the 1637 masterpiece depicting the five eldest children grouped around a massive dog. The eldest boy, Charles, was now seven years old and no longer the anxious toddler of the earlier painting but instead a confident, solemn miniature adult dressed in red silk and clearly very certain of his prominent position within the family dynamic as he stands centre stage amidst his siblings. To his right stand his delightful sister Mary and brother James, both of whom have clearly inherited the auburn-haired good looks of their Stuart forebears, including their great grandmother Mary Queen of Scots, while Charles, like his first cousin Louis XIV of France, is a throwback to his swarthy, dark haired Medici ancestors. The Victorian artist Sir David Wilkie said of the work's young sitters that:

'the simplicity of inexperience shows them in most engaging contrast with the power of their rank and station, and like the infantas of Velasquez, unite all the demure stateliness of court, with the perfect artlessness of childhood'.

This then was the royal family in the 1630s – happy, charming, good looking, affectionate and apparently wearing the burden of their royal heritage and responsibilities extremely lightly. It is no wonder that when, almost exactly two centuries later, the young Queen Victoria was looking for a way to erase the embarrassingly scandalous recent memory of her Georgian predecessors on the throne, she cast her eyes back to the comely, charming, close-knit Stuarts and commissioned paintings of her own family that projected the same apparently artless combination of majesty and cosy, domestic bliss. Although, naturally, this idealistic revision of Charles I reign ignored the political and personal tensions that simmered behind the scenes in the richly decorated state rooms and private closets of the Stuart royal palaces as Charles' period of personal rule became increasingly unpalatable to his subjects and rebellious whispers and secret plots rapidly turned into open insurrection and defiance.

Van Dyck painted Charles and Henrietta Maria for the last time at the end of the 1630s – less than ten years had passed since he completed the Greate Peece but the still relatively youthful royal couple now looked rather older than their years, despite the best efforts of Van Dyck's famously flattering brush and were clearly depressed and worried by the ever-worsening political strife, which was exacerbated by the recall of Parliament in April 1640, and saddened by the stillbirth of a baby princess in January 1639 and the death of the three year old Princess Anne in December 1640. It was not all doom and gloom, however – one of Van Dyck's last commissions before his premature death at the age of just forty-two in 1641 was a splendid double portrait of Mary, Princess Royal with her new husband Prince William of Orange. The little bride was just nine years old but looks every inch the princess in her cloth of silver wedding gown while her steady, self-assured gaze suggests a strength of purpose that her beleaguered father might have done well to emulate. Her marriage to the eldest son and heir of the Stadtholder of the United Provinces had been something of a step down for her parents, who had hoped to see their favourite daughter married to one of the crowned heads of Europe, perhaps even one of her first cousins Louis of France or Balthasar Charles of Spain. However, their pressing need for money and support from the Netherlands put a peremptory end to Charles and Henrietta Maria's grander ambitions, especially as the Stadtholder Frederick Henry handed over an enormous amount of money for the privilege of allying his family to that of the English ruling house.

Due to Princess Mary's extreme youth, almost a year passed before she was deemed ready to leave for the Netherlands and her new life, her going away expedited by secret diplomatic negotiations between her father and father-in-law, who was encouraged to demand her presence as a cover for the departure of her mother Henrietta Maria, who would be accompanying her. It was well known throughout the country that the strong willed and opinionated French born queen completely dominated her weaker, indecisive husband – a state of affairs that naturally inspired consternation and suspicion, all inflamed of course by the royal couple's enemies in Parliament, who already saw Henrietta Maria's Catholicism, which they reminded each other had even led to her refusal to be crowned alongside her husband, as reason enough to distrust her, as if her reputed loyalty to French interests was not already bad enough. When rumours reached the royal court that certain Parliamentarians had been eagerly scouring old documents in the Westminster archives in search of precedents that would enable them to have the queen arrested and put on trial for treason, Charles decided that it was time for his wife to leave the country; the upcoming departure of their eldest daughter seemed like the perfect opportunity to put this plan into motion. For good measure, they also put it about that as well as accompanying her daughter to The Hague, the queen would also be travelling to Spa in Belgium for health reasons, the implication being, of course, that Parliament's threatening behaviour had sent her into such a state of nervous anxiety that she needed to take the waters.

Although Henrietta Maria, who believed that her place must always be beside her husband in his hour of need, was largely resistant to the plans being made on her behalf, she had no real option but to submit and even endured the humiliation of having her personal doctor, Sir Théodore de Mayerne, called to Parliament in order to answer questions about her health and justify the need for a trip abroad, which he manfully attempted to do in the face of overwhelming hostility. Parliament's resistance to the queen's departure was only increased when it became known that she would be taking a large amount of plate and some of the crown jewels with her, obviously in order to sell them abroad. Naturally, it was not in Parliament's interests for the royal party to find themselves in possession of large sums of money, so objections were made to this and measures were taken to ensure that the crown jewels could not be secretly smuggled out of the country, which naturally incensed Henrietta Maria, who began to feel more than ever as though she was being persecuted for no good reason. Her fears of eventual impeachment and arrest were only increased by Parliament's reminder that, as she had so rudely snubbed the opportunity to be crowned alongside her husband in 1626, she was therefore little more than a subject of the crown just like everyone else and therefore subject to all the same laws and restrictions. Naturally, this was a calculated slap in the face to a woman who had always prided herself on her elevated and hitherto untouchable status and derived an enormous amount of satisfaction from her position as both daughter and wife of kings.

Despite Parliament's objections to Henrietta Maria's departure, she nonetheless defied them and in February 1642 took sail from Dover with Princess Mary, having said goodbye to her other children at Greenwich a few days earlier. King Charles accompanied his wife and daughter to the coast, where the trio clung together weeping for quite some time before the king felt able to tear himself away. As Henrietta Maria and Mary departed on the *Lion* with their entourage of loyal courtiers and, hidden in the hold, a secret stash of jewels to sell on the continent, they stood on the deck and watched as Charles rode along the cliffs above, jauntily waving his feathered hat above his head in farewell. It was the last time that Princess Mary would ever see her father, while, for Henrietta Maria, well over a year would pass before she was reunited with her husband, during which time the Royal Standard was raised at Nottingham in August 1642, calling those loyal to the king to his side, the first battle of the war was fought at Edgehill two months later and the royal headquarters were set up in the university town of Oxford after the court was forced to leave London.

Henrietta Maria landed at Bridlington Bay on the Yorkshire coast in February 1643 but although she immediately wrote to her beleaguered husband to assure him that she was 'in the greatest impatience in the world' to join him, several months would pass before she was able to leave the north of England for the makeshift royal court in Oxford as her route was impeded by Parliamentarian forces. In the meantime, the queen moved to York and there oversaw the northern campaign of the Royalist forces, who were engaged in trying to wrest the important port of Hull out of Parliamentarian hands. It must have been quite a change in pace for Henrietta Maria as this pampered, frivolous French princess took a seat at councils of war and wrote a regular stream of despatches to her husband, keeping him informed of the activities of his armies in the north. Dismissed by her enemies as unintelligent, ignorant and fatuous, Henrietta Maria surprised everyone with her commitment to her husband's cause and genuine interest in army manoeuvres and strategy. Whereas once her letters to Charles would have been filled with all the latest court gossip and very little else, now they contained lengthy passages about the army movements, sieges, skirmishes, victories and failures that now preoccupied her time. Meanwhile, keen to have her at his side again, Charles did his best to clear her route to Oxford until finally it was judged safe for her to make the journey.

The valiant little queen eventually left York at the start of June, accompanied by a small army of several thousand foot soldiers and cavalry. If her letters are to be believed, this was to be one of the happiest periods in Henrietta Maria's life as she proudly rode out at the head of her men, camped alongside them and enjoyed picnics with the officers in sun dappled meadows along the way. Dubbing herself their 'She-Majesty Generalissima', Henrietta Maria clearly revelled in her new role as a warrior queen, a part that, pleasingly, offered far more for this accomplished actress to get her teeth into than her previous rather milquetoast roles in the court masques in the banqueting house of Whitehall Palace. Although eyebrows were naturally raised at her close camaraderie with her troops and her pretensions to being a seasoned military leader, Henrietta Maria's courage could not be disputed and even her many enemies were forced to concede that there was something valiant, perhaps even heroic about this woman that they had previously dismissed as a silly, petulant and vapid little French chatterbox. In fact, so alarmed were they by reports of Henrietta Maria's progress south and her unexpected popularity both with her troops and the general populace that she was charged with high treason and efforts were made to apprehend her, the most serious of which was foiled by her husband's nephew, Prince Rupert, at Chalgrove, which left the way clear for him to rendezvous with her at Stratford then accompany her for the rest of her journey.

Henrietta Maria was eventually reunited with her husband and two eldest sons in the village of Kinerton on 13 July 1643, just over five months after she first landed back in England. The political situation had already been dire before her departure but now it was absolutely catastrophic and there was not a single household in the country that had not been affected in some way by the conflict between her husband and his Parliament, with many other women having lost fathers, husbands, brothers and sons in the fighting. Even the royal family was not left unscathed – the king's distant cousin, Lord George Stewart, handsome and dashing younger brother of the Duke of Richmond and Lennox, had been killed leading a cavalry charge during the conflict's inaugural battle at Edgehill, leaving behind a young widow and two small children, while Lord George's two younger brothers, Lord John and Lord Bernard Stewart, whose splendid double portrait by Van Dyck is perhaps the most quintessential depiction of the wealthy young gentlemen of the court who were now being sneeringly referred to by their enemies as 'Cavaliers', would also both die in battle in the next few years.

A few days after the emotional reunion in Kinerton, the royal party arrived back in Oxford where they were greeted by cheering crowds, the jubilant ringing of the city's many church bells and lengthy welcoming speeches from the Oxford town and gown dignitaries. Although the war had taken its toll, there was still much to celebrate that summer as the king's armies soundly defeated their opponents at Adwalton Moor near Bradford and Roundway Down in Wiltshire and Prince Rupert took control of the key port of Bristol. As Henrietta Maria and her entourage settled into their new rooms in the Warden's Lodgings of beautiful Merton College, there was every reason to believe that the war might still go their way and the royal family and court would soon be able to return to London and resume their lives. In the meantime, the arrival of the queen and her ladies definitely did much to lift the spirits of what remained of the royal court, particularly as she had managed to raise over £2 million for the war effort while on the continent. If the Generalissima was disappointed to find herself sidelined by her husband's military advisors and expected to concentrate solely on the more traditional queenly activities of looking decorative, embroidering standards and organising masques, banquets and picnics then she showed very little sign of it, although it must have rankled on some level.

Although Henrietta Maria did her best to lighten the heavy mood that had abounded in Oxford until her arrival, she still had to prevail against the petty jealousies of her husband's closest and most experienced advisors, who regarded her presence at his side as a threat to their own ascendancy over the king. Even the most loyal of his supporters, such as his own nephew, Prince Rupert of the Rhine, had long regarded Henrietta Maria as Charles' evil genius, working always to her own personal agenda, allowing her private likes and dislikes to cloud her judgement and employing the enormous influence that she wielded over the king in order to lead him astray with flawed advice. As well as being the temporary home of the royal court, Oxford was also functioning as a military headquarters, providing a base for the king's officers and entertaining a constant stream of diplomats, including the French ambassador Harcourt, who reported back to Paris that Charles was struggling to keep order amongst his own supporters, whose incessant quarrelling, jostling for power and jealousy of the queen were all effectively doing as much to undermine Charles' authority as the Parliamentarian rebellion that had first set the war in motion.

Behind the scenes, though, the king continued to regard his wife as his main support and continued to go to her for advice just as he had always done, frequently making his way to her from his own apartments in splendid Christ Church College, where he could attend services in the adjoining cathedral while Henrietta Maria performed her devotions in a Catholic chapel set up in Merton College. In the queen's rooms, Charles could almost believe that life was continuing much as it had always done before the war, as the ladies chattered about their latest conquests, sat for portraits by William Dobson, whose work sadly lacked the opulent glow and swagger of the now deceased Van Dyck's paintings, and encouraged the attentions of the court poets who composed endless odes to their beauty and grace. However, in the background, tensions simmered as the queen and her coterie of loyal supporters, which included her alleged lover, Harry Jermyn, did their best to encourage Charles to capitalise upon his current advantage, strike a decisive blow against Parliament and reclaim London as his capital. In the summer of 1643, this bold move may well have worked and perhaps even permanently turned the tide of the war but rather than heed his wife's advice, Charles instead decided to turn his attention towards Gloucester in the south west, which was under Parliamentarian command.

Left behind in Oxford, Henrietta Maria, veteran of eight pregnancies, may already have begun to suspect that her joyous reunion with her husband had had the unintentional and perhaps not altogether welcome side effect of resulting in the conception of another baby. A few years later she would declare this child a miracle, her *enfant de bénédiction*, sent by God as one last living souvenir of her beloved husband, but in late 1643, as reports arrived in Oxford of appalling Royalist losses in the south west as the siege of Gloucester ended in disaster and knowing full well that Parliament had placed a price on her head by declaring her a traitor who had 'levied war against the Parliament and Kingdom', Henrietta Maria had every reason to feel less than optimistic about the future and the wisdom of bringing another child into a world that was becoming increasingly unstable and dangerous.

Chapter Two

A Child of War

1644–1646

The buoyant mood that had prevailed through most of the previous year had mostly dissipated by the start of 1644 as a series of military defeats had effectively diminished the Royalist army and left them in a state of disarray. The news that a sizeable Scottish Covenanter army had invaded the north of England only served to increase the already uneasy atmosphere at Oxford, which worsened even more in April when missives from the north advised that the Covenanters had joined with the Parliamentarian forces led by Sir Thomas Fairfax and, calling themselves the 'Army of Both Kingdoms', were marching on York. At the same time, another Parliamentarian army led by the Earl of Essex, the son of Elizabeth I's executed favourite, and Sir William Waller was preparing to march on Oxford, which led to wholesale panic as the beleaguered Royalist forces were in no way equipped to be able to deal with this latest threat.

Terrified for his wife's safety, Charles insisted that she immediately leave the city before the Parliamentarian army encircled them and they found themselves under siege and unable to escape. Henrietta Maria was initially reluctant to leave her husband, arguing that her place was at his side and that they should face this new threat together. There was also the fact that she was now six months pregnant and suffering greatly from all manner of related aches and pains as well as anxiety attacks and what may well have been the first symptoms of tuberculosis. However, she was eventually forced to concede that it was in the best interests of both herself and the child that she carried if she left Oxford and travelled west, ostensibly to take the medicinal waters at Bath but in reality in the hopes of escaping Parliamentarian clutches. Henrietta Maria left Oxford for the last time on the 17 April, accompanied by her husband, two eldest sons and a small band of cavalry. This pitifully small entourage halted at Abingdon for the night, where husband and wife spent the night together in the congenial surroundings of Barton Court on the outskirts of the town before tearfully parting the next morning. As Charles sat on his horse and watched his wife and her small escort vanish out of sight, waving his feathered hat in goodbye as she hung out of the coach window in order to bravely smile and wave back at him, neither could possibly have imagined that this was to be the last time that they would ever set eyes upon each other and the final farewell of their nineteen year marriage.

After leaving Abingdon, Henrietta Maria continued west to Bath, passing through countryside that had been ravaged by war and its equally malignant companions, disease and famine. The fighting in the West Country had been particularly violent and the effects could be seen everywhere in the towns and villages that the queen's small cortege passed through, always careful to avoid the Parliamentarian troops that still patrolled the roads and dogged by the knowledge that the enemy army had turned away from Oxford and was now hot on their heels. After a short break in Bath, where a virulent outbreak of plague prematurely hastened their departure, the group continued further west towards the cathedral city of Exeter in Devon, having abandoned their original plan to continue on to the nearby port city of Bristol, which had been so triumphantly liberated from Parliamentarian hands by Prince Rupert the previous summer.

The intrepid little queen arrived in Exeter on 3 May and was escorted to Bedford House, a beautiful mansion, formerly a priory, belonging to the Earl of Bedford, who had recently returned to the Royalist fold after initially fighting on the Parliamentarian side. By Henrietta Maria's apparently inexact reckoning, her baby was due to be born within the next few weeks and she immediately began to prepare for the birth, which she was absolutely sure would be the death of her. Her ill health, anxiety and recent arduous journey from the Cotswolds had left her exhausted, listless and plagued by a hacking cough, terrible pains and attacks of numbness and pins and needles; she was convinced that she would not be able to survive the coming ordeal of childbirth. One of her first actions after settling into Bedford House was to write to Dr de Mayerne, who had overseen her previous confinements, begging him to come to her in Exeter – a perilous journey for a man of over seventy to be taking at that time. When de Mayerne quite naturally hesitated to leave his comfortable London residence and make the trip across war ravaged England, King Charles was forced to intervene with his famous plea of 'Mayerne, for the love of me, go to my wife' – an order veiled as a request which the venerable Swiss physician, who had been in royal service for decades, could not possibly ignore.

When de Mayerne eventually arrived in Exeter at the end of May, having managed to obtain permission for his journey from Parliament, he found the queen in a hysterical and overwrought state, almost out of her mind with worry about her husband and other children and still utterly convinced that she was about to die. When she informed him that she thought that she was on the verge of going completely mad, the wry old courtier, who was well used to Henrietta Maria's highly strung histrionics and had never been one of her greatest admirers, dryly responded with, 'Madame, you already are.' He was joined in Exeter by Madame Peronne, one of the most esteemed midwives of the day, who had delivered both Henrietta Maria's eldest son, Prince Charles, and also her nephew, Louis XIV of France. Alarmed by her sister-in-law's increasingly anxious letters from Oxford and Exeter, Anne of Austria, Dowager Queen of France, had immediately dispatched Peronne to Henrietta Maria's side, along with three manservants, a beautiful layette of baby clothes and bedding and a much-needed gift of cash. More importantly though, there was also an offer of asylum in France, should Henrietta Maria wish to escape England and return to the land of her birth. Since her flight from Oxford, the queen's determination to remain on English soil had suffered a reversal as she accepted that her presence was more of a hindrance than a help to her husband and his cause. If the offer of asylum had been presented to her just a few months earlier, then she would undoubtedly have reacted with angry disdain, mortified that anyone could even suggest that she should leave Charles' side, but she now found herself forced to give it serious consideration.

The baby, another daughter, was eventually born on 16 June and despite all of her gloomy predictions of death and disaster, both Henrietta Maria and the infant princess, who was named Henrietta for her mother, managed to survive the ordeal of labour, which was quite a feat for even the healthiest of women in the mid-seventeenth century. Although she had believed herself to be well overdue by the time she went into labour, the baby was so small and frail that it was thought more likely that the queen had miscalculated her dates and had instead given birth prematurely. Nonetheless, despite her small size and delicate appearance, the little princess was expected to thrive and even declared to be quite 'lovely' by the Marquis de Sabran, a French agent who visited the queen and her new baby just over a week after the birth. However, the new mother's physical and emotional condition still continued to cause much concern – it had been generally expected that her alarming symptoms had all been the consequence of late pregnancy and would naturally vanish once she had given birth but instead they only seemed to increase to the point that she remained completely bedridden, complaining of severe pains, breathlessness, partial blindness and even paralysis, complaining to her husband, who was utterly helpless to help her, that her pain was so intolerable that 'if it were not that we ought not to wish for death' then she would long to die and be done with it all. Nonetheless, she was still determined to take up her sister-in-law's offer of asylum in France and busily made plans for departure from her sickbed, much to the dismay of the Marquis de Sabran who was of the opinion that she would be better off remaining in the country and accepting the Earl of Essex's offer of safe conduct back to London.

Not unsurprisingly though, Henrietta Maria was not at all inclined to trust the word of the Earl of Essex, whom she knew was already marching on Exeter with the intention of laying siege to the town and seizing her person. She was also well aware that Parliament had declared her a traitor to the realm and were planning to put her on trial should she ever be unlucky enough to fall into their hands, with the possibility that she might well end up being executed, although it was far more likely that she would be used as a hostage during negotiations with her husband. She would have been even more determined to reject the offer had she known that, when Sabran initially approached Essex with a request for safe passage to Bath, the gruff Parliamentarian general had immediately rejected it and said that it would be better for the queen to be taken to London to face the consequences of her actions. No, London was to be avoided at all costs and so she ignored Sabran and continued to make her plans to leave the country and return, hopefully temporarily, to France. It would have been preferable, of course, to take her new born daughter with her but the secrecy of the venture, which would involve travelling swiftly at night through potentially hostile territory, as well as the relative frailty of the baby made it much more advisable to leave her behind in the care of trusted friends, who could be relied upon to keep her safe from harm in the absence of both her parents. She wrote to her husband two days before she set out on her adventure:

'I will show you by this last action that nothing that lies so near my heart as your safety and that my own life is of very little consequence compared with that. For in the present state of affairs your condition would be in great peril if you came to my relief, and I know that your affection would make you risk all for my sake. And so I prefer to risk this miserable life of mine, a thing worthless enough in itself, saving in as far as it is precious to you. My dear heart, farewell.'

Henrietta Maria left Exeter on the 30 June, heavily disguised and less than a fortnight after the birth of her daughter. She took with her a small band of companions, including her alleged lover, Harry Jermyn, and her dwarf, Jeffrey Hudson, who walked and rode alongside her litter as she slowly made her way towards Falmouth in Cornwall where she was to embark for France. Before leaving Cornwall, she sat down and wrote a last letter to her husband, informing him that if the winds were favourable then:

'I shall set off tomorrow … I am giving you the strongest proof of my love that I can give: I am hazarding my life, that I may not incommode your affairs. Adieu my dear heart. If I die, believe that you will lose a person who has never been other than entirely yours.'

Again, her gloomy presentiments were shared by those around her with even the previously dismissive de Mayerne being of the opinion that she would be fortunate to last another month, while a Cornishman who saw her leave for France later told his wife that Henrietta Maria, once the pampered, spoiled, pretty little French princess who had stolen hearts at court masques and balls, was now, 'the woefullest spectacle my eyes ever yet beheld … the most worn and pitiful creature in the world, the poor queen, shifting for one hour's life longer.' Nonetheless, once again she confounded all expectations, surviving a rough passage and a chase by Parliamentarian ships in order to safely land in France a few days later.

Meanwhile, back in Exeter, the baby Princess Henrietta was being cared for by her mother's dearest friend Anne, Countess of Dalkeith, a member of the powerful Villiers clan – the murdered Duke of Buckingham was her uncle while Barbara Villiers, later mistress of Charles II, was her niece – who was also the baby's godmother along with Lady Paulett of Hinton St George. Also at hand was Henrietta's godfather, the Governor of Exeter, Sir John Berkeley, who was devotedly loyal to the Royalist cause and swore to do all in his power to protect the infant princess from harm and keep her out of the clutches of the Earl of Essex, who was still marching on the city. The care of this latest scion of the Stuart royal house was of paramount importance to her guardians, who arranged that she should be christened on 21 July in Exeter Cathedral, with Dr Lawrence Burnell, Dean of Exeter, officiating and the three godparents in attendance. Relief came a few days later when King Charles arrived in the city, fresh from a resounding victory against Waller's forces at Cropredy Bridge, which had given the morale of the Royalist side a huge boost after two defeats at Nantwich and Cheriton earlier in the year. The king was naturally hugely disappointed to have missed his wife by just a few weeks but was consoled by his first meeting with his new daughter. The fourteen-year-old Charles, Prince of Wales, accompanied his father on this visit although it can hardly be expected that an adolescent boy would take much interest in a baby sister, no matter how delightful she might be. On this occasion, the king and his entourage were only able to remain in Exeter for one night but he returned two months later on 17 September and this time stayed for an entire week.

For all his many faults, both as a man and as a king, Charles was an affectionate and devoted father who lavished love and attention on all of his children, regardless of gender. The birth of another daughter would never have been a disappointment to him although he would naturally have shared Henrietta Maria's fears for the infant's future as he knew that he too would be leaving her behind all too soon to continue his military campaign. Before leaving Exeter for the last time, Charles appointed the Protestant writer and historian Thomas Fuller, who had accompanied him from Oxford, to be his daughter's chaplain – a relatively meaningless post as Henrietta was just over three months old but nonetheless beneficial for Fuller, who produced some of his best work while attached to her household in Exeter, including the book *Good Thoughts in Bad Times*, which he dedicated to Lady Dalkeith. Naturally, a very special copy, bound in fine blue leather and stamped with her official cypher, was presented to the infant Princess Henrietta but many years would pass before she would appreciate and be comforted by its collection of gentle meditations and prayers.

Although the fear of Parliamentarian besiegement had been temporarily eased by King Charles' victory over the Earl of Essex's forces at Lostwithiel in Cornwall in September 1644, it was not long before they mustered their troops and Exeter once again fell under threat. Meanwhile, life in Bedford House had at least some semblance of normality as the little princess grew up surrounded with every possible comfort, completely protected from the chaos that prevailed in the outside world and unaware of the desperate straits that her family had brought themselves to. There was even some romance in the air when Sir John fell head over heels in love with the very beautiful Lady Dalkeith. And although her father would never again be at liberty to visit her in Exeter, her brother Charles, who had recently been appointed Commander in Chief of the Royalist army in the West Country at the age of not quite fifteen, managed to return on 29 August 1645 for a month long stay before making his way to Launceston in Cornwall.

The long-threatened siege of Exeter began in December 1645, when Princess Henrietta was eighteen months old and continued until 9 April of the following year when the very real threat of starvation forced Sir John Berkeley to surrender the garrison into enemy hands, after hammering out terms with the Parliamentarian commander Sir Thomas Fairfax. One of these terms was that the Princess Henrietta, her household and all their valuable plate and belongings should be allowed to leave Exeter and be conducted without molestation to a royal residence of Lady Dalkeith's choosing. However, her initial request that they should be allowed to go to the old riverside palace of Richmond was turned down and she was instead offered Oatlands, near Weybridge in Surrey, which had been a favourite royal summer residence thanks to the excellent hunting opportunities that it offered. It had also been the location of Henry VIII's wedding to Catherine Howard a century earlier, but was now in a poor state of repair and rather shabbily equipped. At the same time, Lady Dalkeith was fending off entirely unwarranted criticism from Henrietta Maria, now safely ensconced in Paris, for not making more of an effort to get her small charge out of Exeter before the Parliamentarian forces managed to entirely encircle the city. Lady Dalkeith and Sir John had in fact considered several escape plans over the preceding months, no doubt taking the advice of Prince Charles during his visit the previous summer, but had eventually decided that it would be safer to remain in Bedford House and put their trust in the besieging Parliamentarian generals, Fairfax and Waller. This was not good enough for Henrietta Maria though and Sir Edward Hyde, another one of the royal governess' ardent admirers, was forced to intervene and write to Harry Jermyn in Lady Dalkeith's defence, informing him that:

'I think it will break her heart when she hears of the Queen's displeasure; which pardon me for saying, is with much severity conceived against her … the governess is as faultless in the business as you are, and has been as punctual as solicitous, and as impatient to obey the Queen's directions, as she could be to save her soul. She could not act her part without assistance; and what assistance could she have?'

The Parliamentarian side remained true to their word and not long after the agreement between Sir John and Fairfax was signed, Princess Henrietta's household was equipped with carriages and wagons and allowed to go on to Surrey. According to the treaty, financial provision would be forthcoming from Parliament to pay for Henrietta's upkeep at Oatlands but this inevitably failed to materialise and Lady Dalkeith was forced to pay the household expenses from her own pocket, which meant that they quickly fell into dire straits, royal households, even those of toddler princesses, being notoriously expensive to maintain. Undoubtedly mindful of more scoldings from the exiled royal court in Paris, which was becoming increasingly out of touch with the grim realities of the situation at home in England, Lady Dalkeith fired off a series of letters to the speakers of both Houses and Sir Thomas Fairfax, who had signed the original agreement, reminding them that they had promised to support the little princess' household, only for them to counter with a demand that Henrietta's household should be completely disbanded if it was too expensive to maintain and that she would instead be housed at St James's Palace in London with her elder siblings Princess Elizabeth and Prince Henry, Duke of Gloucester.

No doubt rightly divining that she too would be separated from her charge should Parliament get their way, Lady Dalkeith was seriously alarmed by this unlooked-for reaction to her letters, not least because she had faithfully promised both King Charles and Henrietta Maria that she would remain with their daughter no matter what happened. Clearly some sort of drastic action was required and the well-timed visit in June 1646 of King Charles' nephews, Prince Maurice and Prince Rupert, who had orchestrated some of the most daring and accomplished military manoeuvres of the war, gave Lady Dalkeith the perfect opportunity to lay plans for their escape. The princes were on their way to France via Dover when they stopped at Oatlands, having both been banished from English soil after finally surrendering Oxford into enemy hands, an action which marked the end of the first stage of the civil war. Although it might well have made sense for them to take Princess Henrietta with them when they departed, it was obviously decided that this would be far too risky and so plans were made for Lady Dalkeith, Sir John Berkeley, who had remained in the area to keep an eye on the Oatlands household, and two of the princess' servants, Thomas Lambert and Elinor Dyke, to make their own way to the coast on foot after the princes had gone.

The escape plan was put into operation on the night of the 24 July, when the small group slipped out of Oatlands and began the long, arduous walk to Dover, a journey of some ninety miles, which would take them well over thirty hours to accomplish on foot if they didn't stop and even longer if they rested along the way. The beautiful, willowy Lady Dalkeith disguised herself as a beggar woman for the adventure, even stuffing rags into the shoulder of her dress to give herself the appearance of a hunched back. However, it was Princess Henrietta who had the most dramatic transformation of all as she was unwillingly bundled into a suit of boy's clothes and, much to her displeasure, informed that for the duration of the journey she was to be known as 'Pierre'. Thus suitably attired, the little band slowly and steadily made their way towards the coast with Lady Dalkeith carrying the princess on her shoulders all the way. The little girl was already sufficiently aware of her rank to be embarrassingly indignant about the charade imposed upon her and had to be prevented from informing any strangers who engaged their group in conversation that she was not really called Pierre but was actually the Princess Henrietta.

Sir John had decided that it would be preferable for him to travel separately and watch over the escapees from a distance, always ready to swiftly intervene should they run into trouble along the way. Although the war was to all intents and purposes over, temporarily at least, the roads and towns were still riddled with roving patrols of armed cavalry hunting out renegade Royalists and pockets of resistance. It would have been deeply unwise to attract attention from them along the way and it is likely that the group made sure to cover as much ground as possible at night in order to evade any awkward questions. The journey must have been an exceedingly long, tiresome and uncomfortable one for all concerned as they plodded along seemingly endless roads towards their destination. The ever-present threat of possible capture must have only added to the desperate worry that Lady Dalkeith felt as she carried her precious burden towards safety.

Back at Oatlands, the departure of Princess Henrietta, her governess and various servants was not discovered until the following morning. Anticipating panic once they were found to have flown their gilded coop, Lady Dalkeith had the foresight to leave behind a letter explaining that she had found it necessary to remove her royal charge from the country. She would have been exceedingly gratified had she known that the servants at Oatlands waited three days before raising the alarm, buying the escapees some valuable time as they trekked across southern England so that by the time a message had been sent to alert Parliament to Princess Henrietta's departure, she was already safely on board a ship bound for France and freedom.

Chapter Three

The Exiled Court

1646–1649

As soon as they had disembarked at Calais, the thoroughly exhausted Lady Dalkeith sent a message to Paris to inform her royal mistress, Henrietta Maria that she had succeeded in smuggling her youngest daughter out of England. The letter reached the queen at the Château de Saint Germain just outside Paris, which had been granted to her as a summer residence and she immediately sent off a carriage and escort to bring the weary travellers to her. Henrietta Maria had been living in France for two years and although she might have wished that she had more money, she could not fault the kindness that her family, in particular her sister-in-law Queen Anne, showed towards her. Not only had she been presented with Saint Germain, a royal nursery château where she had spent many happy hours during her childhood, but she also had lovely apartments in the Louvre palace and a pension of 30,000 livres a month, which enabled her to keep a reasonably large household and live in some style. It was not exactly the life of luxury to which she had become accustomed as queen of England but she was comfortable enough and, if truth be told, rather relieved to be away from the stress, uncertainty and violence of her adopted country.

Now that the war had apparently ended with a victory for the Parliamentarian side, dozens of Royalists were scrambling across the sea to the Netherlands, where they were welcomed by Henrietta Maria's eldest daughter Mary, and France, where they joined what was rapidly becoming a small exiled court, presided over by Henrietta Maria, her eldest son Charles and her handsome Cavalier nephews, Princes Rupert and Maurice, who had all recently joined her in Paris. Most of these exiles were having a pretty miserable time, living in damp, tiny garrets in the less salubrious parts of the city and so poor due to being forced to leave most of their belongings and assets behind in England that they were constantly clamouring for handouts and favours from Henrietta Maria, who naturally felt obliged to do all she could to help them, even though she too was barely making ends meet. Her apartments at the Louvre had naturally become a focal point for these disaffected, unhappy exiles and her public chambers constantly teemed with people, most of whom were there because they wanted something from her, while others simply wanted to reminisce about the good old days before the war with like-minded company.

Although she could not help but be glad to be back in the city where she had grown up and indeed in the palace where she had been born, Henrietta Maria was naturally preoccupied with events on the other side of the Channel where her husband and four of her children still remained, the latter in the hands of her enemies. There was no reason to suppose that Parliament had any intention of mistreating any of the royal children but even so, this was a constant worry for their mother, who naturally imagined all sorts of neglect and abuse going on. There was also the additional problem of King Charles, who had escaped the besieged city of Oxford disguised as a servant in April 1646 but then, thanks to a series of various misfortunes and poor decisions, ended up in the not entirely friendly hands of the Scottish army, with whom he was still languishing in July of that year as they negotiated his fate with Parliament. Henrietta Maria was sick with worry about her husband and constantly expected to hear that he had been either handed over to Parliament or, worse, quietly murdered. The news that one of her children had been so dramatically smuggled out of the country and would soon be with her once again acted like a balm to the unfortunate queen's despondent soul and she lost no time in declaring that Henrietta's deliverance from the clutches of the wicked Parliamentarians was nothing less than a miracle and that the child herself must surely therefore be her *enfant de bénédiction*, her blessed child and gift from God.

As their carriage rattled towards Saint Germain, Lady Dalkeith did her best to prepare Henrietta for what would no doubt be an exceedingly emotional reunion with the mother that she had not set eyes upon for over two years. All trace of 'Pierre' had been thankfully left behind in Calais and the little princess of England was now attired in a manner that was more suited to her station and gender, ready for her first introduction to the famously image and precedence obsessed French court. It was very important that the little girl not put a foot out of line – despite her tender years she was expected to speak and act at all times like a princess. Her French cousins, particularly the young King Louis, had been carefully schooled since they were toddlers in how to behave appropriately and had exceptionally polished manners, graceful deportment and an enviable grasp of the intricacies of the intensely byzantine etiquette system that made life at the French court often so intolerable – it was therefore up to Lady Dalkeith as Princess Henrietta's governess to ensure that her young charge was up to scratch and would not show her mother up at this first crucial meeting.

When they eventually arrived at Saint Germain, Henrietta was taken to her mother, who burst into tears when she saw her daughter and clutched her to her bosom while lamenting the cruel fate that had necessitated their separation and kept them apart for two long years. The little princess, who had inherited the delicate features and red hair of her Stuart ancestors and the dark, dancing eyes of her mother's Medici forebears, was much admired, especially by her brother Charles who was delighted to be reunited with his youngest sister and finally get to know her properly. Even Prince Rupert, whose handsome face and aloofly romantic demeanour masked a gruff and rather choleric personality, fell for the little princess' charms. As for Lady Dalkeith, she was rightly hailed as a heroine by the exiled court, who flocked to pay their respects at her sick bed when she, not entirely unexpectedly, collapsed shortly after arrival, completely worn out by her heroic endeavours. Naturally, the celebratory mood was a little diminished by reports from England that Parliament's response to Henrietta's dramatic escape had been strikingly lacklustre, with most members agreeing that Lady Dalkeith had actually done them all a favour in removing yet another useless royal mouth from the country but overall everyone was thrilled by this small act of rebellion and it proved to be an enormous morale boost for the disappointed and rather demoralised Royalist side.

Shortly after her reunion with her mother, Henrietta was taken to the beautiful Palais Royal near the Louvre to make the acquaintance of her various French relatives, the most important of whom, naturally, was her first cousin Louis XIV, who had been King of France for just over three years, having succeeded to the throne at the age of four years old. Conceived when his parents, Louis XIII and the Spanish princess Anne of Austria, had been married for twenty-three years and had almost given up all hope of having a child, he was, like his cousin Henrietta, hailed as a miracle baby and a gift from God. Unlike Henrietta, however, Louis had been extremely spoilt from the very first by his adoring mother, who referred to him as her *Dieu Donné* and completely idolised him. Even the birth of her second son, Philippe, two years later failed to diminish Anne of Austria's passionate love for her firstborn and when Louis succeeded his father as king, it was she who instilled in him the total and unwavering belief in his divine right to rule that would be a defining feature of his reign. It is not known what Louis thought of Henrietta at this time but judging by his behaviour towards her not too many years later, we can probably assume that he was rather less than impressed by this delicate little English cousin – not that Louis objected to the presence of his Stuart relatives at his court, as evidenced by his ardent, hero worshipping admiration of Henrietta's older brother Charles, not to mention the dashing Princes Rupert and Maurice. To the pampered and somewhat sheltered Louis, the military exploits of these three princes made for thrilling listening and he was particularly envious of Charles, who was not that much older than himself but had still witnessed actual battles before having to flee the country – even if it horrified almost everyone else that such a young boy, especially one who was heir to a throne and really ought to have been enjoying a life of luxury and privilege in a palace not fleeing battlefields, should have been exposed to such danger and bloodshed before he had even reached his sixteenth birthday.

Louis' younger brother Philippe was not quite six years old and although closer to Henrietta's age was still old enough to consider his cousin just as tiresomely babyish and completely beneath his notice as his brother did. He was a strange little boy, quite different to the more self-assured Louis and prone to hysterical tantrums and sudden, terrible rages – his frustrations no doubt being exacerbated by the obvious preference that his mother showed towards his elder brother. The Bourbon kings had learned from the sad example of their Valois predecessors upon the French throne that younger brothers were usually untrustworthy and treacherous by nature and should be kept away from power at all costs, particularly when the heir to the throne was young and unable to fend for himself. The Bourbons were also very aware that in terms of the French monarchy, they were still a relatively new dynasty – Louis XIV was only the third Bourbon ruler and his extreme youth at the time of his succession made his mother all the more fearful that his authority might be usurped, although during his minority she was far more afraid of the pernicious influence of his uncle Gaston, Duc d'Orléans, heir to the throne after her sons, than Philippe. Nonetheless, assisted by her chief advisor, Cardinal Mazarin, Anne set out on a policy of ensuring that her younger son was dissuaded from taking any interest in politics and would instead be encouraged to focus on more frivolous matters, which would hopefully divert his attention from anything more serious.

Although the two boys were politely uninterested in their baby cousin, their mother, Anne of Austria, Queen Mother of France, was a very different matter and welcomed her new niece with open arms, showering her with gifts and attention. It may well have been the case that Anne, a rather gossipy and vain sort of woman, had always felt the lack of a daughter and so decided to treat the undeniably adorable Henrietta as if she were her own child. It almost certainly helped matters that Henrietta Maria now tactfully decided to bestow the middle name Anne upon her daughter in graceful tribute to her sister in law, so that from now on the child was known as Henrietta Anne. However, Anne's kindness towards Henrietta had the unfortunate side effect of annoying her other niece, nineteen–year–old Anne Marie Louise d'Orléans, who had rather enjoyed her position as the most lionised princess at the French court until the arrival of Henrietta, whose prestige was highly enhanced by her dramatic escape from Parliamentarian clutches. Undoubtedly encouraged by her notoriously mischievous father, Gaston, Anne Marie Louise, who was one of the wealthiest heiresses in all Europe, if not the entire world, thanks to inheriting her mother's vast fortune when that unfortunate lady died a few days after her birth, was also in the habit of looking down upon her beleaguered Stuart relations, whom she considered to be a drain upon French resources. The fact that her aunt Henrietta Maria made absolutely no secret of the fact that she would dearly love Anne Marie Louise to marry her son Charles only served to add to her contempt.

As a small girl, Henrietta would have had very little contact with the wider echelons of the French court at this time but the royal family was a close knit little circle and so she would have spent a great deal of time with her

Bourbon and Orléans cousins as she grew up. Although she was obviously far too young to really join in with the games of her older cousins, she got on better with her uncle Gaston's four younger daughters, the half-sisters of the intimidating Anne Marie Louise, who divided their time between Blois in the Loire Valley and the Palais du Luxembourg in Paris, which their father had inherited from his mother Maria de Medici. The eldest of these girls was Marguerite-Louise, who was almost exactly a year younger than Henrietta, while the second, Élisabeth Marguerite was born a few months after her arrival in Paris. Lively, amusing and pretty, the Orléans girls were most likely Henrietta's closest companions while she grew up, although their friendship was put on temporary hold when Gaston departed in disgrace to Blois after the failure of the Fronde rebellion, taking his younger daughters with him.

While King Louis was too young to rule for himself, the tedious business of statecraft and diplomacy was mostly handled by his mother and her chief advisor, Cardinal Mazarin, leaving Louis and the other royal children free to do as they pleased when they were not in lessons with their various tutors and governesses. Naturally, however, Louis was still required to make appearances on formal court occasions when the small boy, uncomfortably burdened with swathes of crimson velvet and opulent ermine would sit on his throne and politely nod to the ambassadors and grandees who queued to kiss his royal ring. As might be expected though, the atmosphere at court was relatively light hearted and the courtiers would frequently encounter the young king, his brother Philippe and their closest companions romping through the Palais Royal's stately painted galleries, sliding down the bannisters of the marble and polished wood staircases or playing at sword fighting in the grand gardens. However rough and tumble their play got though, it was noted that no one was ever allowed to forget that Louis, normally so reserved and quiet but who was capable of shoving and shouting and laughing as much as any of them, was still the king of France and the rest of his playmates were his subjects.

Even in the relatively enlightened environment of the French court, it was not considered necessary for royal princesses to receive the same level of education as their male peers and it was not entirely unusual for young women to leave their childhood barely able to read and write. The sixteenth century passion for educating royal young ladies as rigorously as their male counterparts was in the past and so Henrietta would have found her lessons far less taxing than, for instance, her great grandmother, Mary Queen of Scots, or aunt, Elizabeth, Queen of Bohemia had done in their youth. That's not to say that she was not relatively well educated though – both Henrietta Maria and Charles I had taken great pride in how elegant and refined their court was and wanted their daughters to be suitably decorative and accomplished ornaments at court occasions, capable of delighting everyone as much with their wit and intelligence as their dancing, singing and instrument playing. Although the glory days of Whitehall were in the past now and her personal circumstances were somewhat more straitened, Henrietta Maria was still determined to bring Henrietta up in just the same way as her elder sisters. It is possible that even at this early stage she was thinking ahead to her youngest daughter's future marriage prospects and perhaps thinking that she might be able to bring about a match with one of the two French princelings.

Although Henrietta Maria's allowance was undoubtedly generous, once she had paid her household expenses, paid allowances to various hangers on in Paris and sent money back to England to boost her husband's parlous financial situation, there was very little left and her formerly comfortable lifestyle began to look a little shabby and battered about the edges. However, her sister-in-law was in no position to help out, as her own financial situation was becoming increasingly precarious as she and Mazarin did their best to maintain the royal coffers which were being relentlessly emptied during the hugely expensive war that pitted most of the great Catholic and Protestant powers of Europe against each other between 1618 and 1648. However, their attempts to do so with the usual increases in taxation were blocked by the hostile Parlement de Paris, which led to a stalemate and eventually rebellion when Anne and Mazarin retaliated by having three of the most recalcitrant members arrested in August 1648 – only to be forced to release them a couple of days later amidst a storm of protests about this misuse of royal prerogative.

To Henrietta Maria, who was in the Louvre while this was going on, all of this must have seemed eerily reminiscent of the early stages of the rebellion that had toppled her husband from authority just a few years earlier and she watched in mounting horror as her sister-in-law and Mazarin failed to quell the burgeoning insurrection. King Charles had been a prisoner of Parliament since January 1647, when he was handed over by the Scottish Covenanters army, with whom he had sought refuge the previous year, once it became clear that he had no intention of accepting their Covenants, which supported the continuation of the reformist Presbyterian religion in Scotland and repudiated Charles' own plans for religious reform in his native country. Henrietta Maria never ceased to hope that her husband would either manage to escape or would, somehow, be released from his captivity and be allowed to go into exile and join her in France – a prospect that filled Queen Anne and Mazarin with dread as they knew that entertaining the exiled King Charles would prove to be both expensive and also deleterious to their ongoing relationship with the English Parliament, which was currently civil if not entirely cordial. The escape from St James' Palace of Henrietta Maria's second son, the fourteen-year-old James, Duke of York, in April 1648 only added to her hope that perhaps her husband might also somehow manage to break free of his confinement.

The queen's eighteen-year-old eldest son, Charles, Prince of Wales, was also very much on her mind at this time. He was still residing in Paris but the manifold attractions of court balls, drunken roistering with his many friends and delightful intrigues with charmingly witty and beautiful French ladies had long since palled and he was now restless, bored and keen to get back to England to rally the royalist troops once again and seize back his birth-right. He also had romantic notions of somehow rescuing his father from his captivity in Hampton Court Palace and was deeply annoyed and disappointed when his mother, alarmed by the prospect of him falling into enemy hands, absolutely refused to sanction any such enterprise. Although mother and son sincerely loved each other, there was a serious personality clash at play between them and they frequently got on each other's nerves and fell out, particularly when they were forced to live together in Paris – largely because they were both preoccupied with the fate of King Charles and the other royal children, Elizabeth and Henry, who were still stranded in Parliamentarian hands and too young to escape without assistance. It was Charles' belief that some sort of decisive action was required if his father and younger siblings were ever to be liberated but even though his mother desperately longed to be reunited with them again, she still refused to take the risk of losing her eldest son as well.

Frustrated by his mother's apparent apathy, Charles consoled himself by spending as much time as possible with his youngest sister Henrietta, who had turned four in June 1648 and was a delightful distraction for the discontented adolescent who was fond of children and happy to spend hours playing with her in the galleries and gardens of the Louvre palace. It is likely that it was at this time that his pet name for her, Minette, was born – a name that he would continue to use for her for the rest of her life. When Henrietta Maria finally changed her mind and agreed to let him travel to Holland to meet up with his brother James, who had taken refuge with their sister Mary, Princess of Orange in The Hague, Charles' only real regret was in leaving his little sister behind, as the pair had already developed the touching affection for each other that would later lead Charles to declare that his youngest sibling was the woman that he loved best in all the world. For her part, Henrietta almost certainly returned his adoration and considered her brother to be the epitome of all the manly virtues, even when he quite manifestly was not.

The already parlous situation in Paris only worsened after the Prince of Wales' departure for The Hague until finally, the tension in the city's streets tipped over into outright violence in late summer 1648 when rioting broke out and, in a foreshadowing of the terrible events of August 1792 when the Tuileries was breached, a large angry mob managed to enter the Palais Royal, where they roamed the corridors, loudly demanding to see their young king. Naturally, the terrified Queen Anne would dearly have loved to refuse this request but she was forced to unwillingly acquiesce and the crowd was led to Louis' bedchamber where the boy, shaking with mingled rage and fear, pretended to be asleep as the mob, reduced to awestruck, reverent hush by the sight of the apparently peacefully sleeping young king, filtered slowly past the foot of his canopied bed. Although the mood had swiftly turned from violent to benign, perhaps even sentimentally loyal, Queen Anne was taking absolutely no chances of such a thing ever happening again and immediately made arrangements to remove the royal family and their closest attendants from Paris to the Château of Saint Germain, leaving behind the city, which was now being held by rebellious forces known as the 'Fronde', so named for the makeshift slings that they had used to smash the windows of Cardinal Mazarin's Parisian mansion, and the disloyal Prince de Condé's army which now placed the capital under siege preventing all unauthorised movements around the capital. Naturally, her sister-in-law Henrietta Maria and niece Henrietta were invited to accompany them but the English queen had had quite enough of panic stricken escapes and moonlit flits between palaces and instead opted to remain behind in Paris, assuring Anne and her other friends that she did not believe that the mob would ever dare lay hands upon a daughter of the still fondly remembered Henri IV.

However, without the protection of Queen Anne, Henrietta Maria's already not entirely comfortable life became increasingly disagreeable as the Parisian merchants refused to extend her credit and she rapidly began to run out of basic commodities like food and firewood. The winter that year was bitterly cold and as the exiled Stuart court waited for news from the trial of King Charles, which had commenced at Westminster Hall on 20 January 1649, Henrietta Maria was also preoccupied with keeping body and soul together in her freezing cold rooms in the Louvre. When the Archbishop of Paris, an old friend and very popular figure in the capital thanks to his support of the rebellious Frondeurs, visited her that month, he was horrified to be led to the bedchamber of the little Princess Henrietta, who was still in bed even though it was the daytime while her mother shivered at her side beneath a mountain of blankets. When the Archbishop asked what on earth was going on, Henrietta Maria informed him that she had completely run out of fuel and that the palace was so cold that she had decided to make her daughter, whose health was always rather delicate, stay in bed where it was warm rather than get up and risk catching a cold. Appalled that a daughter and granddaughter of the great national hero Henri IV had been reduced to such straitened circumstances, the Archbishop hastened to alert the Paris Parlement to Henrietta Maria's plight, securing her a grant of forty thousand livres and, perhaps more valuable still, a passport that would enable her second son James, Duke of York to join her in Paris as she anxiously waited for news from London. 'Posterity will hardly believe that a queen of England and daughter of Henri Quatre and her daughter wanted firewood in this month of January in their house,' the Archbishop later indignantly noted.

Although the rest of the exiled court was not exactly optimistic about their king's chances of escaping execution, his wife desperately clung to the hope that he would somehow be exonerated and released, even though the charges against him were very grave and included the highly damning one of waging 'unnatural, cruel and bloody' war against his own subjects. To everyone else, King Charles' execution seemed inevitable and the trial a mere political formality designed to mollify his relatives in Spain, France and the Netherlands but Henrietta Maria was convinced that, when it actually came to it, the Parliamentarians, led by Oliver Cromwell, would balk at the very idea of spilling the blood of their own anointed king, no matter what their personal feelings might be about him and his actions. There was also the faint possibility that even if they did decide to go ahead with Charles' execution, the people would refuse to allow it and would rise up and release him. That the aloof, stammering and highly reserved Charles had never quite managed to properly endear himself to his populace was a fact that his unfortunate wife, who was not exactly wildly popular in England herself, wilfully ignored.

Desperate to help her husband in any way that she could, Henrietta Maria wrote letters to the two Parliament speakers, begging them to release him back to his family. Once upon a time they might well have jumped to at least consider her request even if they could not comply – now though, the letters were left unopened and completely ignored. Unaware of this, Henrietta Maria spent the next few days fretting as she waited for a response from London, eventually convincing herself that her messengers could not get through the blockade that surrounded Paris and that she would have to go to Saint Germain if she wanted to stay in the loop. However, an attempt to escape the city with her daughter came to an abrupt end when they were apprehended in the Tuileries gardens and forced to return to their apartments. As might be expected in the face of such a troubling silence about the king's fate, it didn't take long for the court rumour mill, always a potent source of lies, exaggeration and misinformation, to go into overdrive about what might have happened at the trial. Her closest companions did their best to prevent Henrietta Maria from hearing the rumours but were not able to stop her hearing that her husband had indeed been sentenced to death but that a furious crowd had rescued him from the scaffold. Naturally she was only too happy to believe this fantastical version of events and when her close friend Madame de Motteville visited her in the Louvre she found the queen in a hysterical state of mingled elation and distress, hardly knowing what to think and desperate for confirmation that her husband was still alive and perhaps even already on his way back to her.

On 8 February, unable to bear the terrible suspense for another day, Henrietta Maria tried again to send a messenger through the barricades to Saint Germain, where her nephew Louis and his court were still based. Previous attempts to contact her relatives outside Paris had ended in failure but this time the messenger had luck on his side and was able to pass unhindered through the Fronde troops at the city gates, then pick his way through Condé's besieging troops before going on to Saint Germain. When he did not reappear, the queen became extremely agitated, believing that this must mean that there was bad news – a suspicion that was confirmed when her Capuchin confessor, Father Cyprien de Gamache took the unusual step of remaining with her at the end of dinner that afternoon, having been discreetly warned that his services may be required. In the end, it was Henry Jermyn who took hold of Henrietta Maria's hands and gently broke the news that she had been dreading ever since her husband had been taken captive – that there had been no last minute reprieve and no loyal crowds waiting to deliver him from execution but that he had stepped out on to a wooden scaffold outside the splendid Banqueting House of Whitehall Palace on a freezing cold January morning over a week earlier, quietly placed his head upon the block and given the signal to the headsman that he was ready to leave the world forever.

Although she had been mentally bracing herself for the news of her husband's death for months, Henrietta Maria was nonetheless still struck dumb with shock and barely seemed to comprehend what few details Jermyn was able to tell her about Charles' final moments. It was at this point that Father Cyprien stepped in with his carefully rehearsed words of comfort, only for the queen to stare at him uncomprehendingly until finally he fell silent. It was only much later in the day that the spell that had seemingly fallen over Henrietta Maria and her companions was broken when her old friend, the Duchesse de Vendôme, came to see her with the little Princess Henrietta, who had been kept away from her mother during that difficult day. The Duchesse's sincere distress at seeing her friend in such a terrible state and the confused prattling of the little girl as she embraced her still and silent mother did what Jermyn's polished sympathy and Cyprien's prayers could not do and finally broke through the queen's terrifying catatonic state of shock so that at last she broke down and wept.

Chapter Four

The Widowed Queen

1649–1652

When Madame de Motteville returned to the Louvre a few days later to pay her condolences she found Henrietta Maria and her young daughter dressed in heavy mourning. The widowed queen was tearful but coherent and dignified and keen to talk at length about her dead husband, telling her friend that King Charles:

> 'whose death had made her the most afflicted woman on the wide earth, had been lost because none of those in whom he trusted had told him the truth; and that a people, when irritated, was like a ferocious beast, whose rage nothing can moderate.'

She then asked Madame de Motteville to convey a heartfelt message to Queen Anne, who was still sequestered in Saint Germain with her son and his court while the Prince de Condé continued to control the capital, counselling her to, 'hear the truth, and to labour to discover it; for … the greatest evil that could befall sovereigns was to rest in ignorance of the truth, which ignorance reverses thrones and destroys empires.' She then took her friend's hand and weeping, whispered:

> 'I have lost a king, a husband and a friend, whose loss I can never sufficiently mourn, and this separation must render the rest of my life an endless suffering.'

The atmosphere in Henrietta Maria's apartments was understandably deeply gloomy during those first painful months of her widowhood and it must have been some relief to her companions when she took herself off to the Carmelite Convent of the Incarnation in the Faubourg Saint-Jacques, where she had spent her last night in Paris before leaving to marry King Charles. There she sought comfort in the peace and quiet of the cloisters and attempted to grapple both with her loss and what she feared must be her own culpability in the downfall of her husband and their family. Meanwhile, back at the Louvre, the four-year-old Henrietta had been left in the care of Lady Dalkeith, who had become Countess of Morton when her father-in-law died the previous summer. Also on hand was her fifteen-year-old brother James, Duke of York who had arrived a few days after news of his father's death reached Paris. A quiet, sombre, unimaginative boy who did not share his elder brother's famous charisma and keen wit, he was nonetheless kind-hearted and his presence in the palace during those dark days was a great comfort to Henrietta, who was confused and upset both by the sudden plunge into mourning for a father that she had no recollection of ever meeting and the subsequent departure of her mother.

It was partially Princess Henrietta's distress that prompted her father's confessor, Father Cyprien to go to Henrietta Maria and gently implore her to return to the Louvre, admonishing her that her children needed her more than ever. He also reminded her that although she was no longer the wife of a king, she was still the mother of one and that her eldest son Charles, who had succeeded his father, needed her help and support more than ever. The victorious Parliamentarians and their supporters may be under the impression that the execution of Charles I had brought the tyranny of kings to an end in England but as far as everyone else was concerned, his eighteen-year-old son, who was currently living in exile with his sister Mary in The Hague palace, was now Charles II. He may well have had no country to govern, no throne or even crown to proclaim his sovereignty and, perhaps more worryingly at that point, very little money of his own, but as far as his many supporters, headed of course by his mother and siblings, were concerned, there was still everything to play for.

Father Cyprien's little pep talk apparently did the trick and when Henrietta Maria returned to the Louvre it was not as a defeated widow of a murdered husband but as the energetic and proactive mother of a reigning monarch. While her judgemental niece, Anne Marie Louise d'Orléans, professed herself to be quite shocked by the fact that Henrietta Maria was not entirely prostrated by grief and in fact quite scandalously cheerful, her older, more experienced relatives were relieved to see the widowed queen diverted from her grief by her son's cause and apparently tirelessly busy on his behalf, writing letters to anyone that she thought might be of use to him, gathering support, making plans for his next move and even finding the time to do a little matchmaking on his behalf with his cousin, the aforementioned Anne Marie Louise. Her niece was wrong though if she thought that Henrietta Maria had forgotten her husband – her grief was sharp and very real and she would continue to lament his passing and wear mourning for him for the rest of her life.

However, when the young king arrived in Paris in June, his mother was disappointed to find that he had no great wish to include her in his plans and was determined to do things his own way. The main problem was that Henrietta Maria still insisted upon regarding her husband as a righteous ruler betrayed by his people and could never quite accept that he had ultimately been the agent of his own destruction, due to flawed judgement and poor choices, while her son was only too aware that his father's mistakes had led him to the scaffold and privately felt that one of those mistakes had almost certainly been his reliance upon Henrietta Maria's advice and counsel. This was not a mistake that he intended to repeat and he informed his mother that although:

> 'he would always do his duty towards her with great affection and exactness, but that in his business he would obey his own reason and judgement and did as good as desire her not to trouble herself in his affairs.'

Harsh words perhaps but the young king and his mother were already at loggerheads over the fact that she was raising Princess Henrietta as a Roman Catholic, which was in direct contradiction of the marriage agreement signed at the time of her wedding in 1625, which stipulated that although her children were to be entirely under her care until the age of twelve, they were to be raised according to the rites of the Church of England. Her husband himself had reinforced this when he made arrangements for Princess Henrietta to be baptised in an Anglican service in Exeter Cathedral, then appointed the Protestant writer Thomas Fuller to be her chaplain.

Now though, Henrietta Maria flouted this agreement, much to the annoyance of her other children who saw, even if she didn't, that raising Henrietta as a Catholic would be regarded as an act of deliberate provocation by the Parliamentarians across the Channel and would hinder Charles' chances of gaining support from his Protestant subjects, who would now be fearful that he too was about to convert to Catholicism. He was particularly worried about his Scottish subjects, whom he regarded as his best chance of besting Parliament and regaining control of the entire country and who, he knew, would never countenance a Catholic monarch – after all it was his father's refusal to support the radical Protestant Covenant that had led to him being handed over to Parliament by the Scots. At first Charles toyed, although probably not very seriously, with the idea of having his sister removed from their mother's care and perhaps sent to The Hague to be raised by their elder sister, Princess Mary, who was as appalled as he was by their mother's plans for little Henrietta. He quickly discarded this impractical plan though and instead attempted to directly remonstrate with his mother, informing her in no uncertain terms just how much harm this policy would do to his chances of regaining his throne in a country where Catholics had been widely regarded with suspicion and hatred for several generations. When Henrietta Maria refused to listen and insisted that she had received the deceased King Charles' permission to raise her youngest daughter as a Catholic, he ended up storming out of the room and ordering his advisor, Edward Hyde, to deal with his mother as best he could. Hyde, who did not have the handsome face or charmingly flirtatious and polished manners that she liked to have about her, had never been one of Henrietta Maria's favourites though and his pleas also fell on deaf ears, although he was at least able to extract a promise that the Princess Henrietta was not destined for the convent, which was of some comfort to King Charles and Princess Mary.

Henrietta had in fact begun her instruction in the Catholic religion as soon as she arrived in Paris and had recently come under the spiritual care of her mother's gentle, softly spoken confessor, Father Cyprien, who delighted in his young pupil and became most sincerely attached to her. At Henrietta Maria's behest, he wrote and then published a manual for the religious instruction of the young Princess, which he entitled *Les Exercises d'une Ame Royale* (Exercises for a Royal Soul) and which comprised, as he later put it:

'the duties which every Christian owes to God, to the Saints, to his neighbour, and to himself, with the instructions and practices of the employments usual on working days and on holidays.'

It was, in short, a full guide to living a useful, peaceful and spiritually fulfilling Catholic life, underpinned by the basic Capuchin tenets of solitude, penance and simplicity. Naturally it would have been too much for Cyprien to expect his royal young pupil to fully embrace the austere redemption of worldly goods and even poverty that was the hallmark of the Capuchin existence but he could at least instil in her the fortitude to bear the many trials and sorrows that she faced throughout her life. It was no doubt the gentle teachings of Father Cyprien that helped the young Princess Henrietta endure the barbed comments and spiteful jokes of her cousin, Anne Marie Louise, and the other spoiled and pampered young ladies of the court when the dwindling fortunes of her family meant that she was forced to appear at court occasions in last year's dress and a simple pearl necklace.

Her beloved governess, Lady Morton, was still an invaluable and constant presence in Henrietta's life but as a staunch Protestant she could not sympathise with her pupil's enthusiasm for the Catholic faith and she was no doubt astute enough to perceive the damage that Henrietta's Catholicism could potentially do to her brother's cause. Henrietta Maria did not help matters much by encouraging her little daughter to attempt to convert her governess to Catholicism, with Father Cyprien later recalling an incident when Henrietta Maria said to her daughter, 'My dear child, as you are so devout yourself, why have you not tried to convert your governess?' To which the little girl sadly replied, 'Madame, I do my best, I embrace her, I clasp my arms around her neck, I say to her, "Do be converted, Lady Morton. Father Cyprien says you must be a Catholic to be saved. Do be a Catholic, my good lady and I will love you still more dearly.' Her charming wiles and pleas were all in vain however and Lady Morton remained stubbornly resistant to conversion, to the annoyance of Henrietta Maria and Father Cyprien, who resented the influence that she still maintained over the young Henrietta but naturally felt unable to oust her after the heroism she had shown in bringing the child to Paris. Lady Morton's position in the Louvre was often quite difficult but at least she had the full support of Charles, who even wrote to her husband, who was in Scotland, to thank him for the services that his wife had rendered to his little sister and express the hope that she would remain with her young charge for some time to come.

In the summer of 1649, Charles had a lot on his mind – as well as his sister's religious upbringing and the endless tiresome arguments with his mother, who still insisted upon treating him like a child and kept very close control over the purse strings, he was also preoccupied with making plans for another trip across the Channel either to Ireland or Scotland. The latter would be preferable of course but although the Scots had wasted very little time before having him proclaimed king at the Mercat Cross in Edinburgh, they were still refusing to let him set foot in the country unless he agreed to their demands which included, as always, a request that he accept the Protestant Covenant that his father refused to recognise. His mother was adamant that her son should do no such thing but Charles had probably already long since decided to ignore her, accept the Covenant and throw his lot in with the Scots, having worked out that this was probably his best chance of regaining his throne. Perhaps anticipating the fact that he was about to really let his mother down when he opened negotiations with the Scottish and accepted their terms, Charles attempted to mollify Henrietta Maria by acceding to her request that he pay court to his cousin, Anne Marie Louise, whose lack of physical allurements was more than amply compensated for by the enormous fortune that she had inherited from her mother. Although he was in desperate need of cash, Charles had never shown the slightest bit of enthusiasm for the match, mainly because he wasn't all that fond of his cousin and had no real desire to make her his wife. Luckily for him, Anne Marie Louise, was equally disdainful of the prospect, considering an impoverished, exiled king who couldn't even speak French properly (poor Charles had to use his cousin Rupert as translator when trying to flirt with Anne Marie Louise) completely beneath her – besides, she had her eyes firmly set on a much more splendid match with their cousin Louis.

When Charles left Paris in September 1649, he took his younger brother James with him. Both princes had had more than enough of their mother and were desperate to leave – that she loved them both and they returned her love is indisputable but she was also so possessive, self-pitying and highly strung that they both needed to get away. There had also been a few undignified squabbles about money as the pension paid to her by the French was barely enough to cover her own expenses let alone those of two adolescent boys with expensive tastes in clothes, wine and horseflesh and yet she was still expected to fund not just their daily expenses but their other activities as well. It was an arrangement that led to deep resentment on both sides as the Dowager Queen demanded to know every detail of her sons' lives and they in return sulked like schoolboys whenever they had to ask for a handout.

Yet again left behind in Paris, little Princess Henrietta missed her two elder brothers terribly. As her mother's acknowledged favourite child, she bore most of the weight of Henrietta Maria's possessive dependency upon her children, which admittedly probably did not feel as oppressive to an affectionate five-year-old as it did to her elder brothers but was nonetheless to become an ever increasing burden as the years went by. The presence of Charles and James, who were always so happy to put aside their own sadness and frustrations in order to amuse and entertain her for hours on end, was sorely missed though and she was certainly not the only one who felt that the Louvre was sadly quiet and much less fun without them. The delightfully pretty and amusing young society widow, Élisabeth-Angélique de Montmorency-Bouteville, Duchesse de Châtillon, but known to all her many friends simply as 'Bablon' was also particularly sad to see the young King Charles leave Paris.

Charles was not to return to Paris until the end of October 1651, during which time he had been defeated at the Battle of Dunbar, been held virtual prisoner by the Scots, evaded an attempt to marry him to the Duke of Argyll's daughter, been crowned king of Scotland at Scone and then led a failed invasion of England which ended in disaster and the final destruction of the Royalist cause at the Battle of Worcester on 3 September 1651. After his defeat at Worcester, Charles spent six weeks as a fugitive with a £1,000 reward on his head, hiding from Parliamentarian troops in priest holes, barns and even on one notable occasion, an apple tree at Boscobel House in Shropshire. Charles impressed everyone that he met during this difficult time with his courage, good nature and ingenuity but his escape from England, during which he suffered terrible privations and was forced to rely on the help of people who knew that they were risking their lives to assist him, was to have a profound and lasting effect on him for the rest of his life. He would always remain particularly touched by the Catholics who took him in at enormous risk to their own safety and would later ensure that everyone who assisted him was richly rewarded for their efforts. This time of largesse was still almost a decade away though and the Charles who stumbled unshaven, filthy and exhausted into the Louvre was in no fit state to reward anyone at all.

Things had changed at the Louvre as well during his absence – Lady Morton had departed for Scotland after her husband died but not before regretfully turning down a proposal from the still ardently besotted Sir John Berkeley. Henrietta Maria had been glad to see her go, as she had feared the Protestant governess' influence over her impressionable young charge and rather resented her position as heroine of the escape from Oatlands but Princess Henrietta was genuinely devastated by her loss. Another loss, albeit not one that was directly felt, was that of Henrietta Maria's middle daughter, Princess Elizabeth, who had died of consumption shortly after being moved from London to the rather less salubrious environs of Carisbrooke Castle on the Isle of Wight. The widowed queen had not set eyes upon Elizabeth for nine years as she had been kept in close but not cruel confinement by the Parliamentarians since the beginning of the war but she nonetheless felt her loss keenly and once again the small exiled court was plunged into mourning. The main change, however, as far as King Charles was concerned was in his sister Henrietta, who was now seven years old and more delightfully pretty and engaging than ever.

The young king put on a great show of bravado about his exploits and seemed to like nothing better than spend hours on end regaling the ladies of the French court with his tales of Scotland, battles and, most thrillingly of all, his daring escape after the Battle of Worcester. To his closest associates however, including the family and friends who had known him since childhood, he had returned from England a changed man, one who was prone to long periods of brooding silence and brief bouts of depression during which he would shut himself away from the inane chatter that filled his mother's apartments. The only person who could cheer him up when he was feeling morose was his little sister Henrietta, whose uncritical adoration of her eldest brother never faltered and did much to assuage the shame and guilt he felt about throwing his lot in with the Covenanter Scots, failing to reclaim his birth-right and then being unceremoniously chased out of his own country, perhaps never to return. Charles II was just twenty-one years old when he returned to France in late 1651 and had spent almost half his life fighting first for his father's cause and now for his own – his spirit had not been vanquished by recent events and he was just as determined and courageous as ever but he was tired of war and bloodshed and content, for a while at least, to lick his wounds, regroup and plan his next move.

One unexpected benefit of Charles' time away from France was that the young king had finally grown into his previously lanky, rather awkward physique, cut off his long dark hair, grown a beard and acquired a certain brooding, Heathcliff-like, swarthy skinned glamour during his time on the run, much to the pleased surprise of Anne Marie Louise, who now intimated that she might well welcome his overtures should he care to repeat them and to the amusement of the entire court even got up early and put her blonde hair in fashionable ringlets on the morning that he was due to arrive back in Paris. This time, the unfortunate Prince Rupert's translation skills were not required, no doubt much to his relief, as Charles had been working on his French while he was away and was now able to flirt with absolute fluency. Even though his mother was inordinately delighted by this sudden about face and did everything that she could to encourage this budding romance, it was clear right from the start that it was never going to end in wedding bells as Anne Marie Louise was not so desperate to become a queen that she was prepared to take on the penniless Stuarts and all the boring endless expense of financing their military campaigns against Parliament while for his part, Charles had no great wish to spend the rest of his life being bossed around by his snobbish, over bearing, self-righteous cousin.

Although her mother was disappointed when romance failed to flourish between Charles and Anne Marie Louise, Princess Henrietta was undoubtedly pleased not to have to welcome Anne Marie Louise as a sister-in-law. Her much older cousin had never made a secret of the disdain that she felt for her Stuart relatives and was particularly unkind to the little princess, probably because she had never quite got over her sense of pique at having her position as Queen Anne's favourite niece so resoundingly usurped when she first arrived in France. She was also painfully aware that, like all the rest of the Stuarts, impoverished and unlucky though they may well have been, Henrietta had an abundance of just the sort of beguiling charm that she herself quite conspicuously lacked and would have given anything to acquire. The fact that Henrietta had acquired a certain amount of glamour from her thrilling escape from the clutches of the Parliamentarians just served to infuriate Anne Marie Louise, who fancied herself as something of a dramatic heroine, even further.

Although the final months of 1651 were fairly bleak on the whole as violent insurrection continued to rage around Paris and the exiled Stuart court, often trapped inside the Louvre by the fighting on the streets outside, came to terms with the shattering defeat at Worcester and total destruction of the Royalist cause in England, Princess Henrietta at least had reason to feel cheerful. Thanks to generous donations from Queen Anne and other aristocratic patrons, her mother had recently acquired land on the Chaillot hill overlooking Paris in order to found a convent for twelve nuns from the Sisters of the Visitation, a relatively new religious order founded in 1610 which appealed to aristocratic ladies thanks to its relatively gentle lifestyle and lack of the more off-putting austerities such as lengthy fasting and perpetual abstinence that were the hallmarks of more rigorous and established orders like the Poor Clares. It was particularly appealing to widows like Henrietta Maria, whose worldly responsibilities towards their families meant that they were unable to commit to a fully reclusive convent existence. Once the convent was established, Henrietta Maria and her daughter would spend weeks on end living with the nuns on their hill with its grand, sweeping views across Paris, enjoying a simple, wholesome life of prayer, tranquillity and calm meditation far away from the gossip, intrigue and dazzling splendour of the Louvre. Although she would never be as highly strung as her often extremely difficult and occasionally even hysterical mother, Henrietta was still an extremely sensitive child who felt things deeply and shared the family tendency, inherited from her great grandmother, Mary Queen of Scots, of being physically prostrated and having to take to her bed with mysterious pains when under stress. The simple life at the Chaillot convent, surrounded by the gentle, unassuming nuns and enjoying plain good food and plenty of fresh air suited her very well.

The Abbess at Chaillot was the aristocratic Louise de la Fayette, a former maid of honour to Queen Anne, who had had the dubious honour of catching the eye of Anne's husband, Louis XIII. However, unlike most young ladies who found themselves in the same much sought after position at the French court, Louise valued her virtue and had absolutely no desire to succumb to the king's pleas that she become his mistress, although she did agree to become his platonic companion and confidante and was even responsible for reconciling him with his previously estranged wife. Eventually, however, the still virginal Mademoiselle de la Fayette decided that she had had enough of the empty glitter and intrigue of court life and retired to the Sisters of the Visitation, publicly taking her leave of King Louis before she went. The utterly bereft king continued to visit her in the convent though and it is said that it was thanks to Louise's advice and encouragement that Louis and Anne eventually managed to conceive the child that would in time succeed as Louis XIV. Certainly, Queen Anne always regarded Louise, now called Mère Angélique, with great favour and was very generous with her grants to the Chaillot convent. Princess Henrietta got to know the Abbess, who was still as beautiful as ever, very well during these years and the two became extremely fond of each other. Mère Angelique was particularly impressed by Henrietta's sincere humility, particularly when she served the nuns at dinner, which was so very different from the arrogant pride of her cousin Anne Marie Louise.

After a period of relative peacefulness, the Frondeurs began to regroup once again in the faubourgs of Paris, their usual subversive activities of beating up known supporters of Cardinal Mazarin, molesting anyone who looked even remotely wealthy, looting shops and smashing windows eventually rendering the city so unstable and dangerous that once again Henrietta Maria, her family and entourage found themselves trapped inside the Louvre palace, unable to go out and certainly not able to make the journey out to Chaillot. The widowed queen, courageous as ever, did not fear death on her own account, although she admitted to her sister Christine, Duchess of Savoy, that she was terrified of being violently killed by the mob. Instead, most of her fears were for her children – in particular Prince James, who was thoroughly bored and restless thanks to his cooped up, restricted life in Paris and was longing to go off and join the French army under the command of the legendary Marshal of France, Turenne, much to his anxious mother's disapproval. King Charles, who was naturally sympathetic to James' feelings as he was just as frustrated and fed up himself, was of the opinion that his brother should be allowed to go and make a name for himself in the army but he was yet again overruled by his mother and her advisors and so both brothers were reduced to sulkily kicking around the Louvre in a state of impotent limbo while outside, insurrection raged through the Parisian streets.

Matters reached a head, as they generally do, in the sticky heat of a Parisian high summer when the rebellion tipped over into violent clashes between the Frondeurs and Royalists, resulting in several casualties and the mobilisation of Condé's troops against the royal army led by Prince James' hero, Turenne. The Prince de Condé, himself a celebrated war hero, was of the opinion that King Louis, who had turned thirteen, the age of majority, in September 1651, was still unfit to rule thanks to his dependence upon the malign foreign influence of his Spanish mother and her alleged lover, the hated Italian Cardinal Mazarin and was determined to do everything in his power to prevent the young king from taking sole charge of the government. To this end, he had joined forces with the rebellious Parlement de Paris and taken effective control of the capital city. Now, however, Turenne's superior forces were within a few leagues of the city and Condé had no choice but to venture out with his own men and face them, even though they were massively outnumbered. Things did no go well for Condé's army, who quickly found themselves trapped against the city walls and under heavy bombardment from Turenne's cannons and things quickly went from bad to worse when they attempted to retreat back into the city only to find that the Parlement had panicked and locked the St Denis gate against them.

It was at this desperate point that Henrietta's cousin, Anne Marie Louise d'Orléans saw her opportunity to become the heroine that she always felt that she was destined to be and in an impulsive act of rather splendid recklessness and bravado, seized the initiative and ordered Parlement to open the city gates to Condé's troops before climbing to the top of the Bastille and ordering that the infamous fortress' cannons should be fired at Turenne's royal army as they pursued the rebel forces. It would later be rumoured that Anne Marie Louise herself lit the fuses and as she did nothing to contradict this tale and in fact rather gloried in it, she effectively destroyed any slim remaining chance that she would ever realise her long cherished ambition to marry

Louis and become Queen of France. Her young cousin had witnessed the whole sorry incident from his vantage point on the Charonne heights along with other members of the royal court and was exceedingly unimpressed when reports of Anne Marie Louise's involvement were brought to him. 'She has killed her husband,' Mazarin murmured as word spread through the royal party that the king's own cousin was responsible for this dramatic reversal in Condé's fortunes. Just as Louis would never in all his long life forget just how terrified he had been when the Parisian mob broke into the Louvre and entered his bedchamber, he would never forgive Anne Marie Louise for her actions at the Bastille.

As Condé's soldiers, many of them Spanish and German mercenaries with no particular feeling of loyalty to Paris and its populace, swept through the city's cobbled streets, the Stuart court huddled together in their splendid Louvre apartments and waited for calm to be restored to the capital. Henrietta Maria was thoroughly disgusted by her niece's actions at the Bastille but was no doubt also exultant about the fact that Anne Marie Louise had so decisively kissed goodbye to any chance of ever marrying King Louis, which could only increase her chances of making a match between him and her own little Henrietta. It had always been her sister-in-law Queen Anne's fondest wish that her son would eventually marry the Infanta of Spain, the eldest daughter of her brother Philip IV and the French princess Élisabeth, which made her first cousin twice over to Louis XIV. The ongoing hostilities between the French and Spanish had, however, forced Anne to put this ambition on the back burner and encouraged Henrietta Maria to foster her own private hopes that perhaps Louis might be persuaded to look a little closer to home for his bride. In the summer of 1652 though her only thoughts were of surviving the upheaval in Paris and getting her family and their entourage to safety – her fears reaching a head when a vast mob of furious Parisians and Condé's soldiers attacked the beautiful old Renaissance Hôtel de Ville on the Place de Grève, killing and wounding around thirty deputies who were known to be supporters of Cardinal Mazarin, while an estimated hundred and fifty ordinary Parisians also perished in the fighting before the building was burned to the ground.

When Henrietta Maria heard that the mob were considering turning their attention to the Louvre, she decided that she had had enough and seized the first possible opportunity to leave the capital, accompanied by her children. Charles took on the unenviable task of ensuring that his mother and sister safely made it to Saint Germain, where they were welcomed by Queen Anne and King Louis, both of them still in a state of high indignation about Anne Marie Louise's treachery. The royal court remained at Saint Germain until Turenne finally took control of Paris and was able to ensure the safety of the king and his family. Louis XIV returned to his capital on the evening of the 21 October 1652, riding at the head of a magnificent torchlit procession that included his mother, brother and the Stuart royals. However, things would never be the same again for Henrietta Maria and her daughter, for the newly returned king decided that he would require the entirety of the Louvre, including the apartments of his aunt and her children, for his new grander, more regal household and so proposed that they should instead move into the nearby Palais Royal.

Chapter Five

The Palais Royal

1652–1656

Although the Palais Royal was a much more elegant residence than the Louvre with all its cold and draughty state rooms and damp corners, it was also significantly smaller which meant that Henrietta Maria was forced to slightly reduce her household. On the whole though she was pleased with the move – the Palais Royal would be cheaper to staff and maintain and had the added bonus of only having a Catholic chapel, unlike the Louvre which had a small Anglican one put aside for the use of Henrietta Maria's Protestant courtiers. The widowed queen had recently been doing her best to rid her immediate household of Protestants by insisting that they convert to Catholicism and also discouraging them from worshipping under her roof, so she was very pleased to find that they would not be able to do so at the Palais Royal.

With the royal court established at the Louvre once again, things got much more interesting for the younger members of Henrietta Maria's household. Princess Henrietta was far too young at this point to participate much in the many court balls and galas that took place that winter as King Louis and his courtiers settled back into the traditional Parisian residence of the French monarchy and life continued just as it had done for generations with all the usual court etiquette and ceremonial. Charles and James were much more fortunate than their sister though and were able to enjoy all the pleasures that court life offered – at least until the latter was granted his greatest wish and allowed to enlist as an officer in Turenne's army, where he distinguished himself so much that the great General felt compelled to comment that 'if any man in the world was born without fear, it is this man, James, Duke of York'. High praise indeed and no doubt a compliment that James treasured for the rest of his life.

Although James' loss was keenly felt in the Palais Royal, it was not long before a new playmate arrived for Henrietta in the form of her twelve-year-old brother, Henry, Duke of Gloucester, who had been recently released from his confinement by order of Oliver Cromwell, who gave him £500 before he left, and allowed him to go to his eldest sister Mary, the now recently widowed Princess of Orange in The Hague Palace. Handsome, intelligent, good natured Prince Henry was considered by many Royalists to be the best of his generation and there were quite a few people who would have preferred to have him as king rather than Charles – certainly his Protestant faith was without doubt, ironically in part because of the decade he had spent under the care of the Parliamentarians, and he was so cheerful that those who did not know him better thought that he might be malleable and easier to control than his elder brother. Certainly, some Parliamentarians had also been of that opinion and had even considered placing Henry on the throne as a powerless puppet king after his father's execution. Henry and his sister Elizabeth had been permitted to go to their father the night before his death in order to say farewell and the experience, particularly Charles' urgent warning to his son that he must resist all attempts to make him king instead of either of his brothers or else also lose his head, remained with him always.

Although Henry was happy to remain at The Hague indefinitely and his sister Mary was keen to keep him with her, it was not long before Henrietta Maria began to insist that her son come to her in Paris. Like Charles, Mary had been distinctly unimpressed by the fact that Henrietta was being raised as a Roman Catholic and was afraid that her mother would make a concerted attempt to convert Henry as well, should he go to the Palais Royal. With Charles' connivance she contrived to keep her youngest brother with her for as long as possible but in the end was forced to let him go and in late spring, the young prince made the journey to Paris, where he was reunited with his mother for the first time in over a decade.

It was particularly delightful for Princess Henrietta to have such a charming new companion join her in the often intensely stressful atmosphere of the Palais Royal. Henry was just four years older and his long period of estrangement from his family and the tragedy of losing first his father and then the sister who had shared his captivity had apparently done little to dampen the inherent cheerfulness of his disposition. He had in fact been treated very well by his Parliamentarian captors and even Oliver Cromwell himself had deigned to take an interest in his welfare and visit him from time to time – a fact that must have fascinated his mother and siblings, none of whom had ever personally encountered the new Lord Protector and so had no idea what this fearsome personage was actually like in the flesh. The young prince was also exceedingly popular at the French court where he was known as the 'Petit Cavalier' and much fêted by everyone on account of his good looks and that famous Stuart charm. Henrietta Maria had every reason to be proud of her youngest son but as Mary and Charles had feared, Henry's manifold charms and virtues were not enough to save him from a concerted effort on the part of his mother to convert him to her faith. In this she was enthusiastically assisted by her chaplain and chief almoner, Walter Montague, Abbot of Pontoise – a son of the Earl of Manchester, who had become a Roman Catholic in his mid-thirties and still retained all the intensely passionate zeal of the newly converted.

Montague was not much liked at the Stuart court and was particularly unpopular with Charles and James, both of whom regarded him as their mother's evil genius and resented the ever increasing amount of influence that he held over the widowed queen. Henrietta Maria, lonely and starved of male attention since the death of her husband and loss of her crown and youthful good looks, absolutely depended upon him though and appreciated his absolute loyalty. Now that Charles was beginning to come into his own as a monarch and making it clear that he no longer required his mother's assistance, Montague played up to the Dowager Queen's fear of becoming isolated and ignored and encouraged her to feel hard done by and taken for granted by her offspring. It was at Montague's instigation that Henrietta Maria had decided to aggressively attempt to convert Prince Henry, who was the most avowedly Protestant of her children, to Catholicism – her determination to succeed only increasing as Henry strongly resisted both her tears and entreaties and also Montague's threats of eternal damnation. It is not known what part Princess Henrietta played in the attempt to convert her brother, to whom she was most sincerely attached, but if her behaviour towards her old governess Lady Morton is anything to go by, it is likely that she too was an enthusiastic participant in the group effort to bring Prince Henry to the true faith.

It is probable that Montague and Henrietta Maria believed that the good natured and eager-to-please Henry would be a pushover but to their surprise and deep displeasure, the young prince turned out to be highly resistant to all of their efforts to convert him. Unlike his siblings, Henry had not grown up against the background of his mother's Catholic faith and therefore felt very little sympathy for what he considered to be the superfluous fuss and antiquated ceremony of Mass. He was also, unlike Henrietta Maria, all too well aware of public feeling against Catholics in England and knew that it was of paramount importance for his brother Charles to remain untainted by any suggestions of Papistry within his immediate family (with the obvious exception of his mother) and household. Like Henrietta, Prince Henry hero-worshipped his eldest brother and would do anything within his power to serve him and further his cause – it was therefore entirely unthinkable to him that he would endanger Charles' reputation in England by converting to Catholicism.

Matters reached a head in the spring of 1654 when Cardinal Mazarin decided that King Charles had overstayed his welcome in Paris as his presence there was becoming something of a hindrance to keeping relations between France and England relatively amicable. The Cardinal had never been overly keen on the Stuart exiles anyway and would quite cheerfully have sent all of them off to Princess Mary at The Hague if he could get away with it but he knew that he was at least stuck with Henrietta Maria and the little princess as his patroness Queen Anne was so unaccountably fond of them both. The king and princes were a different matter however and when Cromwell intimated that the signing of the Treaty of Alliance between France and England depended upon King Charles leaving French soil, Mazarin cheerfully seized this opportunity to get rid of at least one dependent Stuart. Although his mother was humiliated and distressed to see her son effectively banished by his own cousin, Louis XIV, at the behest of the hated Cromwell, Charles was actually quite pleased to be on the move again. His transient experiences during the war had left him with itchy feet and since the final defeat at Worcester he had found himself becoming increasingly restless and demoralised. Unlike James, there was no way that he would be permitted to join the army and put his life at risk as a glorified mercenary and there was absolutely no chance that he could take to a career in gentlemanly piracy like his cousins Rupert and Maurice. Instead his life was a narrow and rather boring one spent lounging around the Palais Royal and Louvre with occasional forays into the less salubrious areas of Paris.

Before Charles left for Cologne, where he was to meet up with his sister Mary, he made one last attempt to persuade his mother to stop trying to convert Prince Henry to Catholicism, only for Henrietta Maria to evade the issue and refuse to make any promises either way. To add insult to injury, she then handed Charles a fully itemised bill for all the money that she had spent supporting him in her household, even including all of his meals as well as other small expenses that had been incurred along the way. In fairness to Henrietta Maria, she had been expected to maintain her son's household out of her own allowance but even so, it cannot have been very pleasant for Charles and probably added to his sense of relief that he would no longer be dwelling under his difficult mother's roof. He was, however, sincerely sorry to be leaving behind his youngest brother and sister and no doubt wished that he could have taken both with him. Although Henrietta Maria's utterly devoted love for her children could not be doubted, the atmosphere at the Palais Royal was not exactly salubrious and Charles had no great love for the people that she now chose to surround herself with. Still, there was nothing that could be done about it and he was forced to leave Henry and Henrietta behind even though he expected that the former at least would soon be at mercy of Walter Montague once again.

As he feared, Henrietta Maria and Montague stepped up their campaign to force Prince Henry to convert almost as soon as his elder brother had left Paris for good. When Henry remained adamant that he had no desire to abandon his Protestant faith, they dismissed his beloved tutor, Richard Lovell, who had been with him for several years, then effectively kidnapped the young prince and took him off to Montague's abbey in Pontoise, where the plan was to keep him there for as long as it took to intimidate him into accepting the Catholic faith. The thoroughly frightened Henry fired off a desperate letter to his eldest brother, who was by now in Cologne, informing him that things had taken a serious turn and begging him for any help that he felt able to give. Charles had clearly seen enough of his mother and Montague in action to recognise a lost cause when he saw one and, perhaps realising that his only hope of avoiding disaster was to frighten his brother into standing firm, replied with unusual firmness to Henry's pleas for salvation, reminding him that:

'I do not doubt that you remember very well, the commands that I left with you at my going away concerning that point. I am confident that you will observe them; yet your letters that come from Paris, say, that is the Queen's purpose to do all she can to change your religion, in which, if you hearken to her, or to anybody else in that matter, you must never think to see England or me again; and whatsoever mischief shall fall on me or my affairs from this time, I must lay all upon you as being the cause of it. Therefore, consider well what it is to be, not only the cause of ruining a brother who loved you so well, but also your king and country. Do not let them persuade you either by force or fair promises; the first they never dare nor will use, and for the second, as soon as they have perverted you, they will have their end, and they will care not more for you.'

As if this was not all bad enough, he ended with a final reminder that Henry should:

'remember the last words of your dead father, which were, to be constant in your religion, and never to be shaken in it; which if you do not observe this shall be the last time you hear from, dear brother, your most affectionate brother.'

This letter was entrusted to the Marquess of Ormond, one of Charles' most reliable and trusted advisors, who was sent back to Paris with the delicate mission of persuading Henrietta Maria to see reason and, if necessary, extricate the young Prince Henry from whatever situation he had found himself in and take him to his brother and sister in Germany. When Ormond arrived at the Palais Royal, he found the Dowager Queen more intractable, difficult and stubbornly defiant than ever and the hated Montague apparently in full command of the whole situation and even talking about sending Prince Henry off to the Jesuit college in Clermont for proper indoctrination into the Catholic church. In vain did Ormond attempt to make Henrietta Maria see reason; she remained annoyingly obstinate and even informed him that she didn't know what all the fuss was about. When Ormond reminded her that King Charles had asked her to promise not to attempt to convert Prince Henry in his absence, she replied that she had made no such promise but then conceded that she had however vowed never to use any actual physical or verbal violence in the attempt. When Ormond remained unmoved by this, she changed tactic and tried to shame him by reminding him that as the prince's mother, it was her moral duty to oversee his spiritual welfare and what sort of mother would she be if she did not at least attempt to save her youngest boy, who had furthermore fallen under the pernicious influence of Cromwell and the other Puritan Parliamentarians during his time in England, from eternal damnation? When Ormond then asked what had become of Henry's tutor, Mr Lovell, who was still in Paris and complaining far and wide about his sudden dismissal and subsequent poor treatment by Henrietta Maria and her entourage, the Dowager Queen insisted that Lovell had left of his own free will and that anything that anyone might say to the contrary was nothing but a pack of lies.

When Ormond suggested that it might be a good idea for him to talk to Henry himself, Henrietta Maria fell into a panic and tried her best to dissuade the Marquess from making the trip out to Pontoise, only just stopping short of outright forbidding him from seeing her son. Undaunted, Ormond nevertheless went off to the abbey the very next day and was horrified to find the young prince in such a miserable state of depression and apprehension that he ended up bringing him straight back to Paris, where he lent him his full support in the face of a barrage of threats, manipulation and sulking from Henrietta Maria, Montague and Queen Anne, who tried to convince him that he was putting his immortal soul in the most grievous peril by refusing to go to the Jesuits. To the great relief of Ormond and Charles, the young prince remained absolutely unmoved by any attempts to coerce him into changing his religion, even if he was privately drawing close to breaking point in the face of his mother's increasing hostility towards him. In the end, matters reached a head at the end of November when, in one last interview at the Palais Royal, Henrietta Maria informed her youngest son that she would have nothing more to do with him if he did not agree to become a Catholic then fell into a hysterical rage when the boy remained absolutely adamant that he would not give up his faith even if it meant being banished by his own mother. Before a crowd of appalled onlookers, she screamed at Prince Henry to get out of her house and never return then silently swept straight past him without even looking in his direction when the weeping boy knelt down at her feet and begged her to give him her blessing before he left. They were never to see each other again.

Henry was to receive a much more affectionate farewell from his little sister Henrietta, who was deeply distressed to be losing yet another brother. She was now ten years old, an extremely sensitive, affectionate and intelligent child whose fragile health and delicate appearance made the adults around her feel more than usually protective. Already very perceptive, she had no doubt already worked out that the common factor in all the distressing departures from the Palais Royal was her mother and that her position as most favourite child would probably offer very little protection should she ever somehow manage to displease Henrietta Maria and end up in her bad books as well. Although Henrietta sincerely loved her mother, it was always her brothers that she absolutely adored and their absence from the Palais Royal hurt her a great deal – her cousins across the way in the Louvre were not exactly great substitutes either, as Louis was too aloof and grand to pay much attention to a small female cousin while Philippe thought she was a boring little goody two shoes. Even so, Henrietta Maria still hoped that she might one day contrive a match between her youngest daughter and one of her French cousins. Normally, Henrietta's position as a virtually penniless and entirely dependent exile would have very much counted against her but while the Franco-Spanish War rendered a match with the Infanta of Spain impossible, Queen Anne found herself wondering if a marriage closer to home might not be a better option – the fact that Princess Henrietta was extremely good natured and obviously malleable enough not to usurp Anne's authority at court could also only be in her favour as the Queen Mother had not the slightest desire to see her place behind Louis' throne usurped by another woman.

Although Henrietta had participated in family events, most notably the coronation of Louis in June 1654, ever since her arrival in France, it was not until after her tenth birthday that she was considered mature enough to take part in the richly costumed and ornate pageants and galas that were a weekly occurrence at the French court. Like her mother, Henrietta adored getting dressed up and performing in front of an audience and she threw herself with great enthusiasm into the round of learning lines and practicing dance steps. Her début appearance was in a masque held by Cardinal Mazarin to celebrate the marriage of his niece, Anne Marie Martinozzi, to the Prince de Conti, where she was given the relatively prestigious role of Erato, the Goddess of love poetry. Tiny, pretty Henrietta must have looked thoroughly charming as she tripped out to the front of the stage in her toga with a floral wreath on her auburn hair and nervously clutching a small lute. However if her mother and aunt were hoping that this prominent role would help her catch the eye of her cousin Louis, they were doomed to disappointment for he continued to be entirely engrossed with Cardinal Mazarin's bevy of glamorous, seductive nieces, whom he had shipped over from Italy in order to look decorative in his palace, acquire some all-important Parisian gloss and, hopefully, make a few advantageous marriages within the French aristocracy. Collectively known as the Mazarinettes, this group of young women dominated court life at this time and were particularly popular with King Louis, who fell madly in love with each in turn before eventually settling on Marie Mancini, who was actually considered to be one of the least pretty of the seven.

Undaunted, Henrietta Maria and Anne did their best to endear Henrietta to Louis but all of their efforts were to be in vain and the young king continued to be entirely indifferent to his youngest cousin, haughtily informing his mother that he 'did not like to dance with little girls' when she insisted that he open a court ball with Henrietta rather than Mazarin's much more comely Italian niece, the Duchesse de Mercoeur. Highly offended by this remark, Henrietta then folded her arms and announced that she had no great desire to dance with Louis either and there then ensued a lengthy impasse between the two mutinous cousins, both of whom had inherited a healthy dose of Bourbon stubborn pride. As the ball could not start until the king opened the dancing, the two were eventually convinced by their harassed and anxious mothers to reconcile and, no doubt extremely sulkily, step out on to the dance floor together but the damage was done and from that point on, there was very little chance that Louis would ever agree to marry his cousin. Henrietta's feelings on the matter, if she was even aware of her mother's machinations on her behalf, are rather more obscure. In light of later romantic developments between the two cousins it is of course tempting to assume that on Henrietta's side at least there was possibly some sort of childish infatuation but it is more likely that she regarded Louis' crushing remark as just yet another in the long line of humiliating put downs that she and the rest of her family were forced to endure at the French court and that she was not exactly enamoured with him either. There was also her brother Charles' rather ignominious recent departure from Paris to consider. Although Mazarin was clearly the chief instigator behind this, it cannot be denied that King Louis did nothing to support his cousin or attempt to keep him in France and this must surely have rankled with Henrietta.

The Stuart star had fallen exceptionally low in the mid-1650s and even by the standards of this always most dramatic and tragedy prone of royal dynasties, it has to be said that things were looking exceedingly bleak for Henrietta Maria and her surviving offspring, who were now scattered across Europe yet again. The widowed queen may have longed to have all of her children with her, if only to present a united front against their enemies, but her own difficult and demanding personality had effectively driven them all away so that the only one left was Henrietta, her *enfant de bénédiction* and most favourite child and even there, as the little girl pined for her brothers and perhaps quietly resented her mother for their departure, she must have found herself wondering just how long she would be able to keep her with her before she too flew away. The disdainful attitude of most of their French relatives only added insult to injury and often made life at court unbearable for Henrietta and her mother, who tolerated a seemingly never ending string of slights and indignities during this time, most particularly from Anne Marie Louise, who never lost an opportunity to sneer at the Stuart ladies' threadbare dresses, outmoded accessories and general lack of the trappings of wealth and privilege to which she had such plentiful access. Although Louis and Philippe were on the whole rather kinder towards their dependent relatives, they too had their moments – especially Philippe, who had a catty, malicious nature and a sharp tongue. The younger of the two Bourbon boys turned fifteen in September 1655 and was already rumoured to be homosexual thanks to the coterie of effeminate, flamboyantly dressed handsome young men with which he surrounded himself. If he noticed Henrietta at all, it was only in order to make jokes at her expense.

The regular retreats to Chaillot were a definite boon at this time as it meant time away from the spiteful, pushy atmosphere at court as well as making a virtue of what had become a fairly frugal lifestyle. It was at Chaillot that Henrietta first met Marie Madeleine Pioche de la Vergne, who had recently married the brother of the Mother Superior, Louise de la Fayette. The new Madame de la Fayette was a former maid of honour of Anne of Austria and had close connections both to the royal family and many aristocratic families as well as being heavily involved in the celebrated and highly elitist Parisian intellectual groups that met in the beautifully decorated salons of various aristocratic women of letters in order to discuss books, music, philosophy and the affairs of the day with likeminded individuals. The most celebrated *salonnière* was the Marquise de Rambouillet, who was the centre of a particularly erudite and elegant circle popularly known as the Précieuses, who prided themselves on their witty conversation, exquisite turn of phrase and literary aspirations. Marie Madeleine, who had ambitions of becoming a writer, was a popular member of the Précieuses and was responsible for inspiring Princess Henrietta to emulate their lyrical, cultured and rather affected manner of speaking. The young princess, who had turned eleven in the summer of 1655, proved to be an apt pupil – like most of her siblings, she was already naturally blessed with a quick wit, excellent sense of humour and that famous sparkling Stuart charm.

A stream of tutors took care of Henrietta's other educational requirements, ensuring that she would eventually become one of the most accomplished women at court. Like her mother, she was a gifted musician, skilled with the guitar and harpsichord, a graceful dancer, enthusiastic actress and also blessed with a lovely, melodious singing voice. From her father, whose extraordinary art collection still forms the backbone of the current royal collection, she inherited a keen appreciation for art, particularly painting. She was also a bit of a bookworm, who delighted in the well-stocked libraries of the Louvre and Palais Royal and had a particular fondness for poetry, which she absolutely loved. Outdoor pursuits were not ignored either – like all Stuarts, she enjoyed vigorous exercise and was an exceptional equestrienne. She even learned how to swim, probably from one of her elder brothers, and would go for lengthy daily swims during the warm summer months. Gardening was also a favourite pastime during the summer, particularly at Chaillot where she was expected to assist the nuns with their daily duties, which included tending the vegetable patches, feeding chickens and gathering flowers – her later gardening exploits at Saint Cloud and the Palais Royal would be on a much grander scale but there was an intrinsic simplicity to Henrietta's personality that suggests that her more modest endeavours at the convent were perhaps rather more to her taste.

This quiet life was interrupted in February 1656 when Henrietta's eldest and only surviving sister Mary, Princess of Orange arrived in Paris for a rare visit – ostensibly to see her mother and little sister but in reality to petition for more French support for the Stuart cause, mend bridges between her mother and brothers and, it was rumoured at the French court, attempt to flirt a little with King Louis, who was now eighteen years old and still unmarried. Mary hadn't set eyes on her mother since she left Holland thirteen years earlier in 1643 and she had never even met Henrietta, who had been born two years after she left England to be married. Mary was now twenty-four years old and just as pretty, vivacious and lively as ever, her recent widowhood having done little to dampen her high spirits, even though she had been sincerely fond of her husband. Like Henrietta, she was entirely devoted to her brother Charles' cause and had even left her son's court at The Hague in order to preside over Charles' makeshift court in exile at Cologne in Germany. Blessed with more than her fair share of charm, Mary was popular everywhere and even managed to gain the grudging approval of her judgemental cousin, Anne Marie Louise, who enjoyed Mary's company and sincerely admired her splendid collection of pearls and precious jewellery. Thanks to her advantageous marriage to the wealthy Prince of Orange, Mary was considerably better off than anyone else in her family and therefore able to dazzle everyone at the French court with her splendid gowns and modish appearance. Luckily for Henrietta, she also loved to give presents and ensured that her sister's rather scanty and sadly threadbare wardrobe was generously replenished and brought more up to date.

The only fly in the ointment, as always, was their mother. Although the reunion between mother and daughter had been utterly delightful at first, relations between them quickly soured when Mary, always the most outspoken of the royal children, began to take her mother to task over her poor treatment of Charles, James, Henry and even little Henrietta, whom she suspected of being secretly destined for a convent. Henrietta Maria's ham-fisted attempts to convert Mary to Catholicism only served to make the already uncomfortable atmosphere at the Palais Royal even worse. As Mary had never made any secret of her disapproval of her mother's high-handed endeavours to control the spiritual beliefs of her children, it seems incredible that Henrietta Maria should have made even the most desultory attempt to steer her eldest daughter on to the path to what she considered to be the one true faith, but as with Prince Henry, one senses the hand of her evil genius, Walter Montague, a man wholeheartedly despised by all of the widowed queen's children, in her efforts.

Nonetheless, it must have been pleasant for Henrietta to have her sister in Paris with her for so many months – Mary was sociable, amusing and fun-loving and the perfect antidote to the often dour atmosphere that prevailed in the Palais Royal. She had been Charles I's favourite child and had naturally been deeply distressed by his violent death – however, unlike her mother, Mary was not inclined to dwell on the sorrows that fate had dealt to her and instead preferred to live in the present and enjoy life as much as possible. She had very little patience with Henrietta Maria's melodramatics and before her departure did her best to demonstrate to her little sister that the best way to deal with their mother's hysterical outbursts and petulance was simply to ignore it. Towards the end of her visit in the autumn of 1656 she was honoured with a grand fête thrown by her cousin Philippe, which the entire court and royal family attended. When it was suggested that as guest of honour, Mary should open the ball by dancing with King Louis, she gracefully demurred and instead the honour went to her sister Henrietta, who was much admired as, blushing with pride and wearing a pretty new dress, she stepped out with her small hand on Louis' arm. This time the cousins were apparently content to partner each other and their respective mothers must have heaved a collective sigh of relief as the dance passed without another embarrassing incident.

Chapter Six

Colombes

1657–1660

In the summer of 1657, Henrietta Maria made good use of a recent increase of her pension and acquired the pretty Château de Colombes from Basile Fouquet, eldest brother of King Louis' genius Superintendent of Finances, Nicolas Fouquet. Although called a 'château', Colombes was more of a large manor house or country villa than a grand castle, which suited Henrietta Maria and her daughter very well as it meant that they had no need of a large entourage during their visits and, as at Chaillot, could make a virtue out of their need to live a relatively frugal existence. Although Colombes had a distinctly rustic atmosphere, it was only six miles away from the centre of Paris, which meant that the Stuart ladies could go there without too much fuss whenever they liked. It was especially pleasant for Henrietta Maria to finally have somewhere of her very own – her other residences in France were effectively on loan from King Louis, whereas Colombes had been bought with her own money and belonged entirely to her. Little wonder therefore that both Henrietta Maria and her daughter considered it to be their home and lavished so much attention on its refurbishment over the next few years, paying particular attention to the gardens, which were especially lovely.

This quiet and uneventful existence was thrown into uproar at the end of December when Henrietta Maria's niece, Princess Louise Hollandine of the Palatinate, the daughter of Charles I's sister Elizabeth, Queen of Bohemia and a younger sister of Prince Rupert, suddenly arrived in Paris and announced that she intended to convert to Catholicism and enter a convent. Princess Louise bore more than a passing resemblance to her handsome elder brother, not just in looks but also in manner and personality, and had long chafed at the restrictions placed upon her by virtue of her sex and position. Although no one knew precisely why she had decided to run away from her family's apartments in the Hague palace in the middle of the night and take a ship for France, it was later suggested that it was provoked by the execution in 1650 of the dashingly handsome Marquess of Montrose, with whom she had been in love and who had even, it was rumoured, asked her family for permission to ask her to marry him before his betrayal by her cousin Charles II led to his downfall. If this was the case, then it is hardly surprising that Louise resolved to leave The Hague, with all its sad associations with her doomed love affair, behind and retreat completely from the world.

However, Louise, with her tempestuous, artistic and boisterous personality, was not exactly stereotypical convent material and poor Henrietta Maria must have wondered what on earth she was going to do with her eccentric niece when she arrived at the Palais Royal and informed everyone that she intended to become a nun. On the plus side, she very much enjoyed writing to her sister-in-law Elizabeth, who had been a constant thorn in her side over the years and had most recently annoyed her by siding with her eldest children over the failed conversion of Prince Henry. Informing Elizabeth that her daughter had decided to become a Catholic was no doubt sweet revenge, although one wonders if the subsequent estrangement between the two women was worth this brief, vengeful moment of satisfaction. Princess Henrietta must have been absolutely delighted by this new and very exciting cousin though, not least because she bore such a vivid resemblance to her old friend Prince Rupert but also because she came from just the sort of large, eccentric and affectionate family – Louise was one of thirteen children born to Elizabeth Stuart, nine of whom survived childhood – that she herself longed to belong to. However, Princess Louise's most surprising conquest turned out to be King Louis, who took a great liking to this most unusual of princesses and later facilitated her appointment as Abbess of the prestigious Cistercian convent at Maubuisson after she had completed her noviciate at Chaillot.

Henrietta turned fourteen in June 1658 and we catch a delightful glimpse of her at this age in a description of her appearance and character by one of her mother's friends, Madame de Brégis, who was also one of the most respected of the Précieuses who met in the salon of the Marquise de Rambouillet:

'I must tell you that this young princess is still growing, and that she will soon attain a perfect stature. Her air is as noble as her birth, her hair is of a bright chestnut hue, and her complexion rivals that of the gayest flowers. The snowy whiteness of her skin betrays the lilies from which she sprang. Her eyes are blue and brilliant, her lips ruddy, her throat beautiful, her arms and hands well made. Her charms show that she was born on a throne, and is destined to return there. Her wit is lively and agreeable. She is admired in her serious moments, and beloved in her most ordinary ones; she is gentle and obliging, and her kindness of heart will not allow her to laugh at others as cleverly as she could if she chose. She spends most of her time in learning all that can make a princess perfect, and she devotes her spare moments to the most varied accomplishments. She dances with incomparable grace, she sings like an angel, and the spinet is never so well played as by her fair hands. All this makes the young Cleopatra the most admirable princess in the world, and if fortune will untie the fold that wraps her eyes, to gaze upon her, she will not refuse to give her the greatest of earthly glories, for she deserves them well.'

With so much fulsome praise on offer, it is hardly surprising that many assumed that this paragon of royal virtue was destined to marry her cousin King Louis. Certainly, the allusion to 'the young Cleopatra' strongly suggests that Henrietta was now popularly regarded as the most likely mate for the young Caesar himself and had the approval of the influential Parisian *salonnières*.

However, if Henrietta harboured any secret ambitions to one day become queen of France, she was doomed to suffer disappointment, for behind the scenes her aunt, Queen Anne, was already secretly negotiating with her brother, King Philip IV of Spain. It had always been Anne's greatest wish that her son would one day marry his cousin, the Infanta María Theresa and now that the war between Spain and France seemed to be coming to an end, she was determined to seize the opportunity to make it happen. Publicly however, Anne pretended to be enthusiastic about a different proposed match with yet another first cousin, Princess Margherita of Savoy, the daughter of Henrietta Maria's eldest sister and favourite correspondent,

Christine. Henrietta Maria flew into a terrible rage when she heard that her sister, who was well aware of her own ambitions that way, had been secretly plotting to marry her own daughter to Louis and the two did not speak for quite some time, which must have added to the tense atmosphere at the Palais Royal and Colombes. It is not hard to imagine the effect that this must have had on Henrietta – the children of toxic parents with a tendency to fall out with everyone around them often seem to become extremely passive and will generally do anything to avoid confrontation. They also tend to be inordinately sensitive to the humours of others, with a habit of taking the bad moods of those close to them personally, becoming overwrought at the slightest sign of altercation and desperately trying to make sure that everyone around them is as happy as possible, which, of course, is one sure fire way of ensuring quite the opposite. Certainly, Henrietta spent a great deal of time trying to keep the peace between her mother and other siblings, which must have been an exhausting and often thankless task.

Their relationship with their French relatives also hit an all-time low at this point, no doubt exacerbated by the fact that Henrietta was no longer being even vaguely considered as a prospective bride for her cousin. There was an unfortunate incident at a fête thrown by the Chancellor of France, Pierre Seguier, when her cousin Anne-Marie swept past her as they all went in to supper, breaking the all-important etiquette rule that stipulated that Henrietta, as daughter and sister of a reigning monarch, had precedence over the daughters of her uncle, the Duc d'Orléans. When Queen Anne chided her unrepentant niece for this *faux pas*, her son Philippe, who was generally accepted to be the reigning authority on court etiquette, defended her by saying, loudly enough for Henrietta and her mother to be able to hear, that she was perfectly right to go first because 'things have come to a pretty pass if we are to allow people who depend upon us for their bread to pass before us into supper'. Queen Anne did her very best to smooth things over but the damage was done and Henrietta Maria and her daughter were left feeling utterly humiliated. It was perhaps worse for the widowed Queen of England however as, unlike her daughter, she could still remember a time when she had had all the money that she could wish for and had presided over her own magnificent court and it was bitter indeed to now be referred to as a charity case by the very relatives that she depended upon for support.

Henrietta, however, had never known anything different and so was more able to cheerfully accept the frugality of their life and the barbed comments of their more fortunate relatives.

In early September 1658, however, news arrived from England that could well change everything for Henrietta Maria and her family – Oliver Cromwell, who had adopted the role of Lord Protector after the execution of King Charles and was regarded by the exiled Stuarts as their arch enemy, was dead. To Henrietta Maria's great annoyance, Cromwell had not died in battle or, better still, by the hand of an assassin, but instead had passed away quietly in what had once been her husband's great bed in Whitehall Palace before being ceremoniously laid to rest, in a magnificent and indisputably royal ceremony that echoed the funeral of her father-in-law James I, in Westminster Abbey. That the hated usurper Cromwell had died surrounded by all of the pomp that had been denied to King Charles, who had in contrast been rather unceremoniously buried in the chapel at Windsor Castle, was a bitter blow indeed to Henrietta Maria but she was at least in part mollified by the seemingly endless stream of courtiers who now arrived at the Palais Royal to congratulate her upon her enemy's demise. Naturally it was widely hoped that Cromwell's death would lead to King Charles' restoration to the throne but it quickly became clear that matters were not going to be quite so straightforward as Cromwell's son, Richard, inherited the title of Lord Protector and Parliament, ostensibly at least, showed no inclination to change the current status quo and invite the Stuarts back again. In some ways, the situation must have seemed more hopeless than ever – Henrietta Maria had fixated upon Cromwell as being the instrument of her family's current predicament yet even after his death it appeared that nothing had really changed and the Stuarts were just as unwelcome in England as they had been a year earlier while Charles' chances of ever claiming back his throne looked more distant and unlikely than ever.

The departure of the French royal family and much of the court shortly afterwards to inspect Henrietta Maria's niece, Princess Margherita of Savoy, at Lyons was another great blow to morale at the Palais Royal. The Stuart ladies declined to accompany their relatives on the trip, not just because they simply couldn't afford it but also because it would have been just too galling to witness Louis paying court to Christina's daughter. Not that the young king was all that pleased by the prospect either – he had recently fallen madly in love with Mazarin's niece, Marie Mancini, and was even said to be considering marrying her, much to his mother's dismay. The witty, highly intelligent and extremely amusing Mademoiselle Mancini accompanied the court to Lyons and the infatuated pair spent barely a moment apart during the journey, much to the amusement of the courtiers and horror of Queen Anne and Mazarin, who had no great desire to see all of the hard work he had put into boosting France's important diplomatic relationships with Savoy and Spain effectively destroyed by his own niece. Their remonstrations were in vain though – Louis was by now so entirely besotted with Marie that he was naturally inclined to be critical of Margherita's charms and although he conceded that she was perfectly comely in appearance, if a bit sunburned due to not wearing a protective mask while out riding with the other ladies, it was clear from the outset that the match was not going to happen and the trip to Lyons had just been an excuse for a pleasant road trip through the French countryside with his girlfriend.

Nonetheless, as Mazarin had hoped, the Lyons trip had the effect of galvanising the hitherto complacent King Philip of Spain into action, suddenly panic stricken that Louis, the most eligible match in France and the only one really suitable for his eldest daughter, might not be on the marriage market forever. The fact that France and Spain were still at odds with each other was, of course, a hindrance but both countries had long since lost their appetite for continuing the conflict and what better way to bring it to an honourable end than with a new marriage alliance between the two. Negotiations therefore began in earnest between Mazarin and King Philip and at long last it really looked as though Queen Anne was going to get her own way after all and see another Spanish Queen upon the throne of France. Her son was, naturally, much less thrilled by the prospect, not least because the Infanta Maria Theresa of Spain was said to be even less pretty and much more dull-witted and shy than Margherita of Savoy, but with the optimism of youth he was hopeful that perhaps it might all still go awry and Mazarin might be persuaded to let him marry the far more alluring Marie instead. He was inevitably doomed to disappointment however and the marriage contract, known as the Treaty of the Pyrenees, was signed in November 1659 after he had been forced to end his relationship with Mademoiselle Mancini, presenting her with a parting gift of a pair of magnificent pearl earrings, hastily purchased from his aunt Henrietta Maria, who was in desperate need of money yet again.

Although Henrietta Maria was undoubtedly extremely disappointed that her Henrietta had lost out to the Spanish Infanta, the Stuart exiles were preoccupied with their own affairs in the second half of 1659, when news arrived from England that Richard Cromwell's Protectorate had quickly floundered then fallen completely apart less than a year after his father's death. At first, he was replaced by a temporary government and it seemed as though the Royalist cause was as dead in the water as it had always been but King Charles, still in exile and obviously feeling like he had nothing left to lose, secretly opened a channel of communication with the influential Parliamentarian statesman and commander General Monck, who seemed relatively sympathetic to his cause and was becoming increasingly powerful since the undignified departure of Richard Cromwell. Weary of life in exile and always naturally inclined to be far more conciliatory than his father had been, Charles was more than ready to negotiate and appear entirely amenable to whatever demands were made of him. In short, he was prepared to do whatever it took to enable him to return home to England and just as his grandfather Henri IV of France had cynically declared Paris to be 'worth a Mass' when he was forced to convert to Catholicism in order to claim his throne, so too was Charles ready to promise absolutely anything to bring the current impasse between monarchy and state to an end.

His attempts to supplement his dwindling resources with a rich marriage also continued in 1659 when, having long since given up on his first cousin Anne Marie Louise, he instead turned his attention to Hortense Mancini, Marie's elder sister and Mazarin's favourite niece, who was set to inherit a significant amount of his enormous fortune as well as coming with a very generous dowry. However, no one, least of all Charles himself, was in the least surprised when his advances were turned down with icy politeness by the Cardinal, who made it clear that he thought he could do rather better for Hortense than a penniless, exiled king with very little prospect of ever regaining his throne.

Taking advantage of the absence of Mazarin and King Louis, who had travelled to Fuenterrabia in Spain to meet with the Spanish court and sign the Treaty of the Pyrenees, Charles paid a secret visit to his mother and sister at Colombes in November of that year. They had not set eyes on each other for over six years and there was a potentially awkward incident when Charles initially mistook one of his mother's maids of honour for his sister Henrietta and embraced her instead before someone pointed out his error. Thanks to her letters, we know enough about Henrietta's impish sense of humour to be able to assume that she found this highly amusing rather than insulting, which was lucky for Charles. She was now fifteen years old with the delicate, kittenish prettiness of her mother in her youth and a winsome, engaging manner that was all her own. The only criticism that her brother could possibly have had as he kissed her cheeks and fondly looked her over was that she was far too thin and looked almost painfully delicate beside the more sturdy young ladies of their mother's entourage. There was nothing invalid-like about Henrietta though and if Charles was initially worried by her physical fragility, his concerns would have been quickly allayed by the animation of her manner and her vigorous enjoyment of dancing and riding.

When he wasn't enjoying getting reacquainted with his youngest sister, Charles was spending hours closeted with his mother, discussing his secret correspondence with Monck and the current situation in London. At this delicate point, it could still go either way for the Stuart cause and more than ever before, he needed his family to display a united front against their remaining enemies on the other side of the Channel. It was especially imperative that his mother do absolutely nothing that might prejudice his chances of regaining his throne and so he asked her to consider building bridges with the close family members, particularly her sons James and Henry, that she had fallen out with over the past few years. The two younger Stuart princes had been fighting for the Spanish army under the command of the rebel Prince de Condé and had impressed everyone with their courage and military ability. James, Duke of York, had been deeply upset to be removed from his command under his hero Turenne after he was expelled from France in his brother's wake and never quite reconciled himself to fighting against his former comrades-in-arms on the French side. Prince Henry, however, was a very different matter – he relished the unprecedented freedom that army life gave him and formed a close, almost filial bond with his commander, the Prince de Condé, who shared his deep distaste for Catholicism. When the war ended and he was free to return to France, Henry made no attempt to reconcile with his mother and instead accompanied Condé to his magnificent château at Chantilly, where he was encouraged to pay court to the Prince's niece, Charlotte Louise d'Orléans, the eldest daughter of the Duchesse de Longueville. The match ultimately came to nothing but may well have gone a long way towards improving relations between Henry and his mother as Charlotte Louise was a Roman Catholic.

Charles was only able to stay at Colombes for a few days before Mazarin got wind of his presence and sent word that he was to leave France immediately. It was a humiliating and depressing reminder of just how low the young king's standing was in Europe and his mother felt especially despondent about the future as they said their goodbyes and he took to the road yet again. There was a silver lining to this enforced absence though as it was at this point that the often astonishingly frank and warmly affectionate correspondence between Charles and his youngest sister began and would continue until her death just over a decade later. Henrietta's first known letter to her brother was written at Colombes shortly after his departure in November 1659 and is redolent of the deep and completely heartfelt admiration that she had always felt for her eldest brother:

> 'I would not let My Lord Inchquin leave, without assuring Your Majesty of my respect, and thanking you for the honour that you do me, in writing to me so often. I fear that this may give you too much trouble, and I should be sorry if your Majesty should take so much trouble for a little sister, who does not deserve it, but who can at least acknowledge and rejoice in the honour you do her. I hope the peace will give you all the happiness you desire, and then I shall be happy, because of the love and respect that I bear Your Majesty. It is a cause of great joy to me, since it gives me the hope of seeing you, which is most passionately desired by your very humble servant.'

In a later letter, sent from Brussels in early February 1660, Charles would beg his sister to 'not treat me with so much ceremony, or address me with so many Your Majesties, for between you and me there should be nothing but affection'. Possibly, he also felt a little embarrassed by what was at that time an empty and vainglorious title but within just a few days of Charles writing this letter, events had taken a dramatic turn in London and at last, after all his years of wandering Europe as a penniless exile, it began to look like fate might at last be about to smile on the young king. His secret correspondent Monck effectively took control of the capital and Parliament and having cannily gauged that the overwhelming majority were weary of the seemingly endless chaos and confusion that had prevailed since the death of Oliver Cromwell and were in favour of restoring Charles to the throne, decided that it was time to openly throw his lot in with the Royalist cause and open serious negotiations with the exiled king.

In Paris, Henrietta and her mother waited with baited breath for news from The Hague, where Charles was staying with Princess Mary while he negotiated with Monck and his commissioners. Everything now depended on the young king's ability to convince the Parliamentarians that not only would he not repeat his father's mistakes but, more crucially, there would be no revenge taken against those implicated in Charles I's trial and execution. This last point was naturally of great concern to those who had signed the late king's death warrant in 1649 as they rightly assumed that Henrietta Maria would waste no time before urging her son to wreak bloody vengeance on any surviving regicides. Luckily, Charles managed to persuade them that his inclinations were far more merciful than those of his mother and on the first day of May, the Declaration of Breda, in which he publicly offered a 'free and general pardon' to his father's old enemies as well as other valuable concessions such as religious tolerance and the payment of any wages still owed to the army, was distributed to members of both houses of Parliament, who then unanimously voted for his return. However, although it may have appeared as though Charles was keen to put the past behind him, a closer reading of the Declaration, in which his 'free and general pardon' actually excluded 'such persons as shall hereafter be excepted by parliament', might have alerted some members to the fact that perhaps he wasn't feeling quite so merciful after all.

Events moved gratifyingly quickly after this and on the 25 May 1660 Charles II, accompanied by his brothers James and Henry, landed at Dover. Almost nine years had passed since the bedraggled, exhausted and desperately demoralised young king had fled England in the wake of the Battle of Worcester, pursued by his enemies and with a price on his head. If he had been caught before reaching the coast then he would almost certainly have been tried and executed, along with everyone who assisted him during his weeks on the run. Now though he was greeted by Monck and a large welcoming committee of statesmen, local grandees and ordinary people – all of whom had turned out to get a good look at the king as he walked down the gangplank and with a huge smile took possession of his country. The royal entourage did not linger in Dover but instead hurried on towards London, which Charles planned to enter at the head of a grand procession on his thirtieth birthday, a few days later. Although he was naturally preoccupied with state affairs and the often tiresome logistics of his return, he still found time to pen a quick letter to his sister Henrietta, to whom he had asked their sister Mary to send the gift of a magnificent green velvet covered side saddle trimmed with rich embroidery and gold lace.

'I was so tormented with business at The Hague, that I could not write to you before my departure, but I left orders with my sister to send you a small present from me, which I hope you will soon receive. I arrived yesterday at Dover where I found Monk (sic) with a great number of nobility, who almost overwhelmed me with kindness and joy for my return. My head is so dreadfully stunned with the acclamation of the people, and the vast amount of business, that I know not whether I am writing sense or nonsense. Therefore pardon me if I say no more than that I am entirely yours.'

Chapter Seven

Restoration

1660

While King Charles was receiving the homage and acclamations of the enormous cheering crowds that had gathered to witness his triumphant return to London, his mother and sister were gladly accepting the congratulations of the French nobility, who hastened to the Palais Royal in order to ingratiate themselves with the Stuart royal ladies. Even people who had previously snubbed them now hurried across the road from the Louvre to pay their respects, headed of course by Anne Marie Louise, who was now beginning to rather regret spurning Charles' admittedly half-hearted attempts to woo her. She too had been massively disappointed by Louis' betrothal to the Infanta Maria Theresa and at thirty-three (she shared the same birthday, 29 May, as her first cousin Charles) was naturally beginning to wonder if perhaps she was destined to remain unmarried forever. Snobby and self-righteous though she may have been, however, Anne Marie Louise was at least gracious in defeat and her behaviour towards her aunt and cousin Henrietta became markedly better from this point on.

Once the poor relations, living on the fringes of the French court and at one dark point even unable to heat their home, Henrietta and her mother now found themselves with more money than they quite knew what to do with and barely a spare moment to themselves as they entertained a constant stream of well-wishers. Henrietta Maria wrote to her son to assure him that:

'if you are torn to pieces in England with kindness I have my share of it also in France … I am going this instant to Chaillot to hear the Te Deum sung, and from thence to Paris, to have bonfires lighted.'

Most gratifying of all, of course, were the sincere congratulations of their French royal relatives, particularly King Louis, who was fond of his aunt Henrietta Maria and genuinely pleased for his cousin Charles. Even Mazarin paid a visit to Henrietta Maria at the Palais Royal, although his pleasure in their good fortune was probably more due to the fact that they would now no longer be a drain upon the French treasury rather than any especial fondness for the Stuart clan, whom he had always collectively viewed as an embarrassing nuisance. Like Anne Marie Louise he also now regretted snubbing Charles' clumsy attempts to secure himself a rich wife and discreetly let it be known that his niece Hortense and her enormous dowry were still available should the newly restored king care to cast his eyes in her direction once again. Sadly for the scheming Cardinal, however, Charles had by now realised that he could do rather better for himself than one of the Mazarinettes, no matter how undeniably pulchritudinous they were, and was already looking further afield to Portugal for a bride who could bring him not just money but also the all-important trade and dynastic links that he needed to properly secure his throne. If he had felt rather more secure, then perhaps he might have considered Mazarin's offer but as the newly returned king of a very recently unstable kingdom, he was taking absolutely no chances whatsoever when it came to selecting a bride and knew that an actual bona fide princess with royal blood would naturally inspire more confidence in the continued longevity of the newly restored Stuart dynasty than one of the Mancini girls, whose father was, furthermore, well known to have been a necromancer.

The period immediately after her brother's restoration to the throne was a magical time for Henrietta. As she had had the misfortune to be born after the start of the war, she had never known anything other than exile, poverty, turmoil and privation and although her mother was fond of telling long winded stories about the long ago days when she had presided as queen over the glittering Stuart court at Whitehall, she had no direct experience herself of what it truly meant to be a princess of England. She was beginning to have some inkling now however as she was fitted for dozens of pretty new dresses, had her hair fashionably curled every day and was flattered and courted by courtiers who had not so very long ago completely ignored her. A less sweet natured girl might have resented this blatant, two faced hypocrisy, so typical of the sycophantic nature of court life, but Henrietta sunnily accepted it for what it was and appeared only too happy to put all past slights behind her as she embarked on her exciting new life. She had always had a gift for making friends and inspiring affection (even the formidable Mazarin could find nothing bad to say about her) and this turned out to be an invaluable quality as she began to be seen more at court in the spring of 1660. And naturally, as Henrietta turned sixteen in June of that year and her confidence began to truly blossom thanks to all the flattering new attention that she was receiving, her mother's thoughts began to turn once again to her inevitable marriage.

As the penniless youngest sister of a dispossessed king, Henrietta's marital prospects had previously been extremely poor. There had always been a small chance, of course, that her biddable good nature and natural sense of gratitude towards her French relatives might override her lack of dowry and status and endear her to Queen Anne as a prospective bride for King Louis but that had ultimately come to nothing and without a sizeable fortune there was little prospect of anyone else offering for her hand. The fact that any potential husband would naturally be expected to finance and support her brother's cause was also highly off-putting to the Catholic princelings of Europe. There was also the fact that the English Parliament, who still occasionally felt compelled to scold her mother for raising the youngest Stuart princess as a Roman Catholic in direct contravention of the terms agreed in her marriage contract, would doubtless make a huge fuss should she end up betrothed to a Catholic. In short, until 1660, Henrietta was in an impossible position and her sister Mary's fears that the girl might well end up in a convent were beginning to look less and less melodramatic. With the restoration of her brother, however, everything changed and suddenly Henrietta became one of the most eligible and sought after young women in all Europe. Naturally her fortune could never match that of Anne Marie Louise and unlike Hortense Mancini she had no great inheritance to look forward to either but her royal lineage was impeccable and she had, furthermore, been extremely well brought up within the constraints imposed by her mother's limited resources.

Of course, King Louis was not Henrietta's only cousin and there had been some talk of her marrying Charles Emmanuel, Duke of Savoy, the

eldest son of her aunt Christine or even Cosimo de' Medici, the heir of her
mother's cousin, the Grand Duke of Tuscany. However, perhaps luckily
for Henrietta as neither young man turned out to be stellar husbands to
their future wives, these schemes were rejected out of hand thanks to her
lack of dowry and they would eventually both go on to marry her pretty
Orléans cousins, Françoise Madeleine and Marguerite Louise, the younger
daughters of her disreputable uncle Gaston. All was not lost however for
now a far more superior match presented itself much closer to home when
Philippe, the younger brother of King Louis, who had recently inherited
the title of Duc d'Orléans after his uncle Gaston died in February 1660,
surprised everyone by expressing his interest in marrying Henrietta.
Unlike his elder brother, Philippe had never shown much sexual interest in
the ladies of the court, although he had never been averse to gossiping with
them about their love affairs with other men, so eyebrows were definitely
raised when he suddenly started mooning after his pretty little cousin. It
wasn't even as though he had ever really paid Henrietta much attention
before either, other than to sneer at her outmoded clothes and bashful
manner, but now he was apparently head over heels in love and begging his
mother to let him marry her.

Relieved that her younger son had finally shown a romantic interest in a
member of the opposite sex and perhaps feeling a trifle guilty that she had
ultimately looked elsewhere for Louis' bride, Queen Anne did all she could
to encourage this blossoming romance between the two cousins. Very little is
known about Henrietta's feelings for Philippe at this time but she was almost
certainly flattered by the attention that he was paying her and perhaps even a
little in love too – after all, Philippe was handsome, well mannered, amusing
and always beautifully dressed so why wouldn't she be? That he was more
than a little effeminate and was well known to be an enthusiastic cross-
dresser in the privacy of his own apartments in the Louvre may well have
rung alarm bells for an older, more sophisticated woman but to Henrietta,
who was just sixteen and whose life had hitherto been extremely sheltered,
his flamboyant sense of style, bitchy sense of humour and slightly mincing
manner marked him out as nothing more unusual than any other fashionable
young man about the court. Her friend Madame de Lafayette's description
of him at this time is rather discouraging though:

'He was by inclination as much disposed to the pursuits of women as the King was averse to them. He was well made and handsome, but with a stature and type of beauty more fitting to a princess than to a prince and he had taken more pains to have his beauty admired by all the world than to enjoy it for the conquest of women despite the fact that he was continuously amongst them. His vanity, it seemed, made him incapable of affection save of himself.'

None of which boded well for his match with Henrietta, who was in contrast described as warm hearted, affectionate and eager to please.

Henrietta Maria was naturally thrilled by this unlooked for development, which would make her daughter the official third lady at the French court after Queen Anne and Louis' new bride and would, more importantly, ensure that Henrietta would be able to remain close to her in France rather than being sent overseas to marry a total stranger, which was the more usual fate of princesses during this period. She had also always been extremely fond of Philippe, who was just the sort of gossipy, amusing, fashionable, rather theatrical young man that she had always liked to surround herself with – if she had any suspicions about his sexual predilections then she kept them to herself and certainly did not share them with her daughter. On the 24 August, Queen Anne ended months of speculation about the blossoming romance by visiting Henrietta Maria at the Palais Royal and formally requesting Henrietta's hand on the behalf of her son. The widowed queen was only too delighted to give her approval but ultimately it was up to King Charles to give permission for the marriage to go ahead and although Henrietta Maria was confident that her son would gladly do so, there was always a chance that the often annoyingly mercurial Charles, who had never had much time for Philippe, might not oblige. Nonetheless, Henrietta Maria immediately fired off a letter to her eldest son, assuring him that Henrietta was 'not at all displeased' about the match and that Philippe was 'violently in love and quite impatient for your reply'.

Two days after Queen Anne's visit, all of Paris turned out for the official entry into the capital of King Louis and his new wife, the Infanta Maria Theresa. The couple had been married in June then made their way back by slow stages via Fontainebleau and Vincennes, where Henrietta and her mother were formally introduced to the new queen, who was the daughter of Henrietta Maria's sister Elisabeth. Unlike Henrietta, Maria Theresa had been raised in the stiflingly staid atmosphere of the Spanish court and had never been encouraged to think independently, develop any creative talents or even have much of a personality – with the result that she came across as rather stupid and unimaginative although not entirely without a sense of humour. Her dumpy little person made a sad contrast to the vivacious ladies of the French court, although it was generally agreed that her blonde hair and fair complexion were unusually lovely even if the rest of her appearance, exacerbated by the unwieldy Spanish fashions that she insisted upon clinging to, was considered highly inelegant. It was not in Henrietta's nature to be unkind to another woman though and she warmly welcomed her cousin and tried to befriend her, even if it was doubtless something of a challenge to find any common ground other than the Catholic faith that both girls were devoted to.

Henrietta and her mother watched Maria Theresa's official entry from one of the balconies of the Hôtel de Beauvais on the Rue François-Miron, the home of Catherine Bellier, one of Queen Anne's ladies in waiting who was popularly believed to have relieved the much younger King Louis of his virginity. While everyone else was eager to catch a glimpse of the new Queen, Henrietta had eyes only for Philippe as he rode past – like his elder brother, he was a splendid horseman and looked extremely dashing and handsome on horseback. It was fondly noted by those close at hand that Philippe was obviously equally pleased to see his pretty little cousin and that he gazed lovingly up at her as he went by. As Philippe was undeniably homosexual we can only speculate about why he was apparently so powerfully attracted to Henrietta before their marriage - unlike her more strident cousin, Anne Marie Louise, there was nothing remotely Amazonian about her, although like Philippe she looked wonderful when mounted on a horse. It's impossible to say though what exactly he found so attractive but perhaps it was actually Henrietta's innate purity and goodness that appealed to him as well as her delicate prettiness, which made such a perfect foil to his own rather feminine good looks. Whatever the reasons, there can be no doubt at all that Philippe believed himself to be entirely in love with his cousin during this period and was full of impatience to have their betrothal approved by Charles. The news that Charles was also considering proposals from the Holy Roman Emperor Leopold I and King Alfonso VI of Portugal only served to fuel Philippe's ardour and confirm Henrietta's standing as one of the most eligible princesses in Europe.

King Louis was rather bemused by his brother's rather unexpected passion for their cousin and was heard to joke that as no one else had wanted to marry her because she was so thin that she resembled the 'bones of the holy innocents', it had fallen to Philippe to step in and save her from spinsterhood. This was quite untrue, of course, but it must still have rankled when the malicious court gossips made sure that Henrietta heard all about it. In principle, though, he approved of the match as it would strengthen the ties between France and England as well as making several close family members extremely happy. The only person who might have been a little disappointed by this new development was, of course, Anne Marie Louise who, having failed to secure Louis as a husband, had been thinking that she might accept his younger brother as a consolation prize. She had never been particularly happy about allowing Henrietta, as the sister of a reigning monarch, to have precedence over her and was even more annoyed now about the prospect not only of seeing her once impoverished little cousin becoming the third lady in the land and enjoying such prestige at court that she would henceforth be known by the honorific title of 'Madame' but, worse still, bearing the title of Duchesse d'Orléans, which had once belonged to her own mother. As usual, Anne Marie Louise vented her frustrations via the medium of circumventing and flouting court etiquette whenever she could but it all backfired on her when an attempt to barge past Henrietta at a ball resulted in a public scolding from Queen Anne, who informed her in no uncertain terms that she was behaving like 'a mad woman' and ought to be thoroughly ashamed of herself.

Encouraged by his brother and Cardinal Mazarin, about eighteen months earlier in October 1658, Philippe had acquired the Château of Saint Cloud, which was built on a hill overlooking the Seine just outside Paris. He had been too busy gutting and refurbishing it to really entertain much but nonetheless decided to honour Henrietta with a fête there on 12 August, where she appeared dressed in shimmering white silk and looking, it was generally agreed, extremely beautiful as Philippe led her out to start the dancing. The young couple appeared again a few weeks later at another ball, this time held by Cardinal Mazarin, where once more Henrietta dazzled everyone in pure white silk and it was noted that her devoted partner Philippe, who had opted to arrive with her rather than with his own family, had eyes for no one but her. After years of being virtually ignored on the sidelines of the French court, she seemed set to become if not its queen then at least its brightest star. All that remained now was for her brother Charles to give his permission for the marriage to go ahead and with this objective in mind, Henrietta Maria decided that it was about time that she returned to England for a visit, taking her youngest daughter with her. It was over fourteen years since Henrietta had last set foot in the country of her birth and although she was doubtless reluctant to be leaving France, albeit temporarily, just as things were getting exciting, she was also looking forward to being reunited with her family and seeing with her own eyes the royal palaces of England, which she had only ever experienced second hand via the doubtless often exaggerated stories of her mother.

Although the primary purpose of the visit was to be reunited with her children and support her eldest son as he settled back into Whitehall and the other palaces, Henrietta Maria had another motive for her trip across the Channel. Her second son, James, Duke of York, had fallen in love with one of his sister Mary's ladies in waiting, Anne Hyde, during her visit to Paris in 1656 and, after pulling the old trick of promising to marry her one day, had made her his mistress. When Anne became pregnant in the summer of 1660, James honoured his promise and announced their betrothal to his brother – who, in fairness, was rather pleased as he'd come to appreciate the firm control that the domineering and opinionated Anne exercised over his annoyingly irresolute and weak-willed brother. The fact that Anne was the eldest daughter of Charles' Lord Chancellor and most trusted advisor, Edward Hyde, Earl of Clarendon, only served to complicate matters, although contrary to court gossip, Hyde in no way favoured the match and even informed his defiant daughter that she would be dead to him if she went ahead and married the Duke, which she duly did at the start of September. Naturally, when Henrietta Maria, who couldn't abide the Hyde family, heard about all of this, she immediately decided to intervene and somehow extricate her son from his predicament, whether he wanted her to or not. It was some consolation to her, however, that Charles, whose love affairs had been a constant source of disappointment to her, was at least fully prepared to do his duty when it came to arranging his own marriage and she was looking forward to helping him select a suitably eligible, Catholic bride with which to continue the Stuart line. As she wrote to her sister Christina, happily reinstated in her good books now that Henrietta was on the verge of a glittering marriage, it was Henrietta Maria's intention while in England to 'marry off the King my son, and to try and unmarry the other.'

Although the two had resumed a relatively cordial correspondence, Henrietta Maria had not yet managed to fully reconcile with her third son, Henry, Duke of Gloucester, who had accompanied Charles to England earlier that year. The Queen had always, quite rightly, felt rather remorseful about the way that they had parted all those years before and was looking forward to seeing him again and mending their tattered relationship. Henrietta, too, was eager to be reunited with her youngest brother as they had become extremely close during his residence at the Palais Royal. Universally popular and a great favourite within his family, Prince Henry was thought by many to be the best of Henrietta Maria's three surviving sons and it was generally agreed that, should Charles die without a son, it would be better if he were to succeed rather than the much less well liked James, who was strongly suspected to have Catholic sympathies and was furthermore just a little too like his father in personality to inspire much confidence in his abilities as a monarch. Disaster struck however in September when Henry fell ill with smallpox, the most feared and cruellest disease of the age and was forced to take to his bed. The overall prognosis was good though and it was believed that he would make a full recovery once the disease had run its course. Smallpox was as unpredictable as it was deadly though and on 13 September, just as it was beginning to look as though he was over the worst of it, he had a sudden relapse and died. He was just twenty years old.

The entire Stuart family was understandably devastated by Henry's loss, particularly his mother who would now never have the opportunity to properly reconcile with him and would always be haunted by remorse for the terrible way in which they had parted. Henrietta was also deeply distressed by the death of her brother, which must have seemed particularly cruel as it came at a time when the family finally seemed to be putting their troubles behind them and looking forward to a peaceful, happy and united future. Poor Henrietta could not even bring herself to sit down and write a letter of condolence to Charles until 10 October, almost a month later:

'Since I last wrote to you so cruel a misfortune has occurred that until this hour I could not make up my mind to speak of it to you, not finding any fit terms in which to do so. The sorrow which it has caused you is so just that one can but take one's part in it, and I have the honour to share it equally with you. Besides, I think it best to be silent, which I shall be when I have told you that the thing that I desire most on earth is to have the happiness of seeing you, which I hope will be soon; and then I shall be able to show you how much I am your very humble servant, which all kinds of people may tell you, but assuredly there are few who are so as truly as I.'

Although Henry's premature death had undoubtedly cast a huge damper on proceedings, not least because the court now went into mourning for the next six weeks, plans still went ahead for Henrietta's visit to London and on 29 October she and her mother were given a splendidly royal send off from Paris as they set out on their journey. Philippe was particularly distressed by her departure and even begged Henrietta's mother to promise that she would be returned to him – the reports that King Charles was considering another match had evidently left him feeling unusually insecure and he was now in a panic lest his prize should be snatched away from him. The Stuart royal ladies, accompanied by a large entourage, stopped at Beauvais for the night before carrying on to Calais where James, who had just been created Lord High Admiral, was proudly waiting for them with a splendid fleet of English ships, which fired their guns in tribute to Henrietta and her mother, creating 'a noise most marvellously loud and delightful' according to Father Cyprien, who was accompanying his pupil to London. Thanks to clement weather conditions which left the sea unhelpfully still and calm, the crossing took rather longer than usual, delaying their arrival into the port at Dover, where King Charles, Princess Mary and the rest of the court, all of whom were still dressed in mourning for Prince Henry, were impatiently waiting for them. Henrietta had not seen her eldest brother since he hastily left Paris, ejected by order of Cardinal Mazarin, a year earlier and much had changed since then – Charles was now firmly ensconced on the English throne and Henrietta was the pampered, fêted and adored darling of the French court. Their lives had been transformed beyond anything that they could possibly have ever hoped for even in their wildest dreams and as they embraced and wept for mingled joy and sorrow on the shore at Dover, both no doubt gave heartfelt and humble thanks to God for the merciful bounty that he had chosen to bestow upon them both after all their long years of strife and adversity. It was time for a new beginning and both Charles and Henrietta were determined to enjoy it to the full.

Chapter Eight

Whitehall

1660–1661

The royal party made their way up to Dover Castle, the gloomy old fortress overlooking the Channel where Henrietta Maria had spent her first night in England when she arrived to marry Charles I in May 1625. The intervening thirty-five years had not been kind to the vivacious little French princess that she had once been, in fact that they had been downright cruel, but as she looked around the table during their banquet that night, she must surely have felt a great amount of satisfaction to see her four remaining children all together for the first time at long last. To her son Charles' great exasperation though, it seemed at first as though his mother had learned nothing from the tribulations of the last two decades as she did nothing to prevent Father Cyprien from standing up and saying grace straight after the king's Protestant chaplain had blessed the table and performed a Catholic blessing, much to the horror of the assembled courtiers. It was precisely the sort of high-handedness that had led to the civil war in the first place and it seemed incredible to everyone that Henrietta Maria was still up to the same old tricks with apparently no thought for the ongoing security of her children, particularly King Charles, who relied upon the support of his Protestant and Puritan members of Parliament and subjects to keep him on his throne.

The rest of the dinner passed without incident however and they enjoyed a very merry gathering, albeit one tinged with sadness as they all remembered the passing of Prince Henry, who would otherwise have been the life and soul of the party as always. Amongst Henrietta Maria's large entourage was Prince Edward of the Palatinate, a younger son of her sister-in-law, Queen Elizabeth of Bohemia, who had married a Franco-Italian noblewoman, Anne Gonzaga, daughter of the Duke of Mantua, in 1645 and subsequently converted to Catholicism, thus earning himself the disapproval of his avowedly Protestant mother. He was as lively, handsome and highly intelligent as the rest of his ramshackle family (with the exception of his eldest brother Karl, who was very dull indeed and had, furthermore, incurred the enmity of his whole family when he threw his lot in with the Parliamentarians before his uncle Charles I's execution) and as he was a great favourite with both Henrietta and her mother, it would fall to him to lighten the atmosphere when it became gloomy. His elder brother Rupert, who never strayed far from the side of his cousin King Charles, was also present at the family gathering in Dover Castle – as darkly handsome and charismatic as ever, he was known within the family as 'Robert the Devil' thanks to his choleric temper and love of explosive scientific experiments. Rupert was an old friend of Henrietta's and although he had not seen her for many years and she was no longer the tiny scrap of a girl that he had known so long ago, he apparently still felt extremely protective of her and it was even rumoured, although there is little actual evidence for this, that he approached Charles with an offer to marry her, probably in order to provide a means to permanently keep her in England at her brother's side.

Henrietta caught her first ever glimpse of London two days later when the royal party travelled by boat from Lambeth to Whitehall. As Samuel Pepys noted in his diary, the return of Henrietta Maria 'do please but very few' so her arrival was marked with very little in the way of public pageantry, although many Londoners hired boats in order to go out on to the Thames and attempt to catch a glimpse of their former queen. Nineteen long and eventful years had passed since she last set foot in Whitehall Palace and she was deeply moved to find herself back there once again. Her youngest daughter, however, felt only excitement as their boat made its way slowly up the Thames, past the venerable old buildings of Westminster, including the great hall where her father had been tried and condemned to death and outside which the heads of a group of regicides who had been hanged, drawn and quartered a week earlier had been placed on spikes, their blank eyes turned towards the spot outside Whitehall Palace where Charles I had been executed. Having become accustomed to Paris, then the largest and grandest capital city in Europe, with its red brick mansions and extravagant Baroque churches, she would have been astonished by London's ramshackle old buildings and winding streets which teemed with activity and noise from dawn until dusk. It was a boisterous, rowdy, vibrant city that confused, bewildered but still somehow enchanted foreign visitors even if they found its proud inhabitants, with their baffling sense of humour and frank enjoyment of life's pleasures (then as now, visitors were bemused and not a little appalled by the English appetite for alcohol), completely incomprehensible if not downright unfriendly towards outsiders. Henrietta was not an outsider though and she arrived in London determined to please and be pleased by everyone she encountered. Perhaps she even knew that her upbringing as a Catholic in France had made a bad impression on the English, who wondered if she was a bigoted and inveterate troublemaker like her mother.

Bonfires blazed in the city that night, although Pepys noted that there were not as many as might have been expected. Still, it must have made a splendid spectacle as their boats landed at Whitehall steps and the royal party, wrapped up against the November chill, hurried inside. The years had not been kind to the old royal palace either. Although the magnificent painted ceilings and actual structure of the rooms remained intact, it was looking distinctly shabby due to lack of care while many of the precious art works collected by Charles I and his predecessors were missing from its walls, having been sold for a pittance by Cromwell. Henrietta Maria was ensconced back in her old rooms overlooking the Thames, while her daughter was lodged close by with her sister Princess Mary. The first month back in London was perhaps one of the happiest times of Henrietta's short life as she reacquainted herself with her surviving siblings and explored the vast and echoing rooms of Whitehall Palace, where she would have grown up as a princess of England if the war had not turned everything upside down for her parents. There were poignant moments too amongst all of the revelry – she would almost certainly have visited the spot where her father was executed, just outside the great Inigo Jones designed banqueting house of the palace and there would still have been plenty of other reminders, hidden away during the Protectorate but now returned to their original locations, of the deceased king around the palace.

Just like any other sixteen-year-old girl, Henrietta loved to have fun and her brother and his courtiers were only too happy to oblige her with a seemingly never ending round of balls, parties, concerts, plays and banquets. On 5

November, she enjoyed the traditional bonfires and fireworks that marked the failure of Guy Fawkes' doomed plot to assassinate her grandfather, James I, and make her aunt Elizabeth a Catholic puppet queen in his place. However, as this annual celebration was usually viewed by the Londoners as an excuse to express anti-Papist sentiments, her mother almost certainly boycotted the event. Henrietta was in her element though and quickly became genuinely beloved both at court and beyond thanks to her prettiness, warmth and natural vivacity, which drew men and women alike towards her. There were even some hints of a budding romance when it became obvious that one of her brother's more rakish courtiers, George Villiers, Duke of Buckingham, had fallen desperately in love with her. As George was the son of the Duke of Buckingham who had caused so much trouble for her in the early years of her marriage to Charles I and had himself eventually thrown his lot in with the Parliamentarian, Lord Fairfax, Henrietta Maria was hardly likely to look upon his ardour for her daughter with much favour. That he had actually married Fairfax's daughter and heiress, Mary, a few years earlier was just the icing on the cake as far as Henrietta Maria was concerned, although on the plus side he could hardly make any serious overtures towards Henrietta if he was married already.

On 16 November, King Charles paid an informal visit to his sister's apartments in Whitehall, bringing with him the French Ambassador, the Comte de Soissons, whose wife Olympe, was the elder sister of Marie Mancini and yet another one of Mazarin's nieces, and Soissons' secretary, Monsieur Bartet. The visitors were delighted to find their hostess casually dressed in a brightly coloured Indian cotton robe with a mob cap atop her auburn ringlets and playing Ombre, a card game for three players, with her siblings James and Mary. Monsieur Bartet was particularly struck by Henrietta's appearance and wrote to let Mazarin know that 'you can tell Monsieur that I never saw her more beautiful in full dress than she appeared to me at that moment.' As Philippe had been hearing all sorts of rumours about the attentions that the Duke of Buckingham, whose father's well known flirtation with Queen Anne in her youth had almost caused a scandal, was paying towards Henrietta, we cannot be sure that this description of his beloved's glowing good looks and casual apparel when entertaining unrelated male guests was really going to put his jealous mind at rest. He would, however, be much relieved to learn that Soissons returned to pay a far more ceremonial visit to King Charles four days later in order to officially request Henrietta's hand in marriage for the lovelorn French prince and that Charles had finally given his permission for the betrothal to go ahead – a little court pantomime that had no doubt been rehearsed by Soissons and Charles during the more casual visit a few days earlier.

Henrietta was far more properly attired when she entertained a formal deputation from the House of Commons, headed by the Vice-Treasurer Arthur Annesley, who officially welcomed her to England and presented her with the very generous gift of £10,000, which would be appropriated by Charles. Henrietta, whose command of the English language would never be impressive, then proceeded to charm this sombre group of stuffy middle aged men with her broken attempt to thank them in their own language with one of them later reporting that 'the Princess with great affection acknowledged the kindness of the House, excusing herself that she could not do it so well in the English tongue, which she desired to supply, with an English heart.' Like her eldest brother, Henrietta was clearly imbued with the Stuart gift, which had so signally eluded their brother James, of always knowing the right thing to say and being able to win any audience to her side with an apparently effortless winning combination of charm and disarming affability.

As reports of Princess Henrietta's delightful prettiness and charm spread through the capital, people became increasingly impatient to catch even the briefest glimpse of her either at Whitehall or when she ventured out, perhaps to watch a play at the Cockpit on Drury Lane, where her crown of golden roses was much admired, and she soon found herself besieged by huge crowds of gawping admirers wherever she went. Even Samuel Pepys recorded the 'very joyful condition' of his French Huguenot wife when he was able to inform her on 20 November, the same day that King Charles gave his official permission for Henrietta's marriage to Philippe, that he was taking her to Whitehall to see the princess for herself a few days later, although in the event this noted connoisseur of female beauty was left rather cold by Henrietta's girlish charms, describing her as:

'very pretty, but much below my expectation; and her dressing of herself with her hair frizzed short up to her ears, did make her seem to much the less to me. But my wife standing near her with two or three black patches on, and well dressed, did seem to me much handsomer than she.'

Henrietta and her mother were originally only intending to remain in England until the end of November but to her great happiness, the visit was extended for a few more months, which would enable her to spend more time with her siblings and also see a little more of England than just Whitehall and its immediate environs. Most of her time was still spent in London though, where she spent almost every hour with her brothers and sister. It was a halcyon time for all of Henrietta Maria's surviving children but as they began to prepare for the Christmas festivities, the first to be held in Whitehall Palace for well over a decade, disaster struck once again when Princess Mary was taken suddenly ill with a particularly virulent case of smallpox.

Having already lost one child in the past few months to this cruel disease, Henrietta Maria quite understandably fell into a great panic and immediately had Henrietta and her household moved from Whitehall to nearby St James' Palace, where it was hoped that she would escape any contagion. There, Henrietta waited for news about her beloved sister, consoled her mother who had been banned from the sick room due to fears that she might attempt to convert Mary to Catholicism when she was too weak and ailing to be able to resist and prayed for her recovery in the Queen's Chapel, which had been built for Henrietta Maria when she first arrived in England and was still consecrated to the Roman Catholic faith. Charles spent most of his time at Mary's bedside but still found time to pen a quick note to his youngest sister, reminding her that:

'the kindness I have for you will not permit me to lose this occasion to conjure to you to continue in your kindness to a brother that loves you more than he can express, which truth I hope that you are so well persuaded of, as I may expect those returns which I shall strive to deserve. Deare sister, be kind to me, and be confident that I am entirely yours.'

Sadly, Henrietta's desperate prayers were destined to remain unanswered for, after four days of terrible suffering, Mary passed away on Christmas Eve with Charles at her side and was buried alongside her brother Henry in the Stuart vault at Westminster Abbey five days later. The eldest princess' death plunged the entire court back into mourning again for yet another six weeks and cast a definite pall over the royal Christmas that year, which passed very quietly indeed in comparison to the great, extravagant revelries that had been planned by Charles to celebrate the much longed for reunion of his family. This latest shocking disaster had a most unexpected but not entirely unwelcome effect on Henrietta Maria however – having lost two children in just a few months, she determined to make more effort with the three remaining to her and in a dramatic about face agreed to officially sanction the marriage of her son James to his mistress Anne Hyde, who had given birth to his son two months earlier. She even received Anne in her apartments on New Year's Day and according to Pepys, appeared to treat her new daughter-in-law, whose existence had been an absolute anathema to her just a week earlier, with 'much respect and love'. That this volte-face owed as much to Mazarin's icy reminders that she was no longer a pensioner of the French court and from now on would be relying on Anne's father, who was her son's Lord Chancellor and therefore held the purse strings, to pay her promised jointure of £30,000 a year as her desire to make amends to her remaining children, was politely ignored by everyone.

When news of Mary's death arrived in Paris, Philippe, always prone to melodramatics particularly when they involved matters of health as he was a noted hypochondriac, became quite demented with worry about Henrietta. One of the cruellest aspects of smallpox was that even if a sufferer was fortunate enough to recover from the disease, there was a very high chance that they would be left permanently scarred, perhaps even horribly disfigured, and it is not entirely unfair to speculate that Philippe, so preoccupied with matters of appearance, might well have been more afraid that Henrietta would be left physically impaired than dead, should she be so unlucky as to catch her sister's illness. In the event, he need not have worried as she was perfectly safe at St James' Palace, where the air was considered to be much more healthy, but that didn't stop him firing off several anguished letters to her mother and brother Charles, demanding that she be returned to France immediately. Although Henrietta would no doubt have been happy to stay and comfort her elder brothers, her mother had had enough of England and plans were duly made for their return to Paris. A Venetian resident in London reported to the Doge that Henrietta Maria had:

'decided to leave for France, overcoming the severity of the weather and caring nothing that the roads have been rendered impassable by the quantity of rain that has fallen these last days. Her start is fixed for next Wednesday evening, and she is counting the moments and only longing for the time to set out. She declares roundly that if she stays in England she will soon end her days; so neither the king nor anyone else tries to detain her.'

King Charles accompanied his mother and sister out of London at the start of January, breaking up their journey with a brief, bittersweet visit to Hampton Court Palace, the beautiful old Tudor mansion beside the Thames where Charles I and Henrietta Maria had spent their honeymoon in 1625 and where the former had been held prisoner before his trial. Hampton Court had been conceived as a pleasure palace and in its more informal surroundings, Henrietta was able to enjoy a few last hours with her beloved eldest brother either beside the great roaring fires in the royal apartments, most of which are now sadly lost forever thanks to the rebuilding project of Henrietta's niece and nephew, Mary II and William III, or going for walks in the wintry splendour of the privy gardens. The visit to Hampton Court was all too brief but Charles continued with them to the coast and was there to wave them off in the man-of-war, the *London*, which was commanded by Pepys' cousin and patron, the Earl of Sandwich, who was another great admirer of Princess Henrietta and paid her a great deal of attention. To Henrietta Maria's great annoyance, the Duke of Buckingham, who was also still completely infatuated with her daughter, had somehow managed to obtain permission from Charles to accompany them to Paris. Henrietta was delighted to have his company though, but the flirtation was entirely innocent on her side, not least because Buckingham was twice her age and had rendered himself completely ineligible by his unfortunate *mésalliance* with the daughter of a notorious Roundhead commander. She enjoyed playing cards and games of chance with him however – now that she had seemingly limitless amounts of money at her disposal for the first time in her life, she discovered a taste for spending it and Buckingham, that inveterate rake and man about town, was only too happy to help her lose it at the gaming table.

Their fun was destined to be short lived though as their ship ran aground in a storm and when they finally managed to set sail again, Henrietta fell ill with a rash and terrible fever and they were forced to return to port for a second time. Naturally it was feared that she too had fallen prey to smallpox but it turned out to be measles – although this was of small comfort to her anxious mother as measles could also be a killer in the seventeenth century. Back in London, all sorts of rumours began to fly about that perhaps this trio of illnesses were not due to natural causes, with Pepys noting in his diary that the worrying news from Portsmouth:

> 'do make people think something indeed, that three of the Royal Family should fall sick of the same disease one after another. This morning likewise, we had order to see guards set in all the King's yards.'

While in Paris, Mazarin was forced to imprison several pamphleteers after they spread a rumour that he had offered King Charles a dowry of several million pounds to marry his niece, Hortense, and threatened to bring about the end of Philippe and Henrietta's betrothal if the English king did not comply with his demands.

Meanwhile on board the *London*, there was tension between Henrietta's two admirers Buckingham and Sandwich who were both in their thirties and really should have known better than to almost come to blows over the amount of attention that each was paying to the sickly princess, who was slowly beginning to recover, thanks to the ministrations of two of her brother's finest doctors. We can only imagine how diverted she was when she heard that Buckingham had had to be forcibly dissuaded from challenging Sandwich to a duel when her illness was at its height. Henrietta was ill for quite some time and the party remained in Portsmouth until 25 January, when she was finally judged well enough to be able to cope with the choppy waters of the English Channel. Their return voyage took five days and they landed at Le Havre at the very end of January. Desperate to be rid of the troublesome and embarrassingly lovesick Buckingham, Henrietta Maria took the opportunity to send him on ahead to Paris to let Philippe, who had been so stricken by news of Henrietta's illness that he had lost his appetite and had to take to his bed, know that they were back on French soil but would be returning by easy stages as Henrietta was still weakened by her recent illness. It was while they were staying at Abbé Montague's abbey near Pontoise that they finally heard the much-anticipated fanfare announcing the arrival of the French royal party who had travelled from Paris in order to meet them.

Naturally Philippe was at the very forefront of the new arrivals, apparently desperate to see Henrietta again after just over three months apart. He was accompanied by Queen Anne as well as Louis and the new little Spanish Queen – a signal mark of respect for both Henrietta and her mother. While the rest of the party discreetly admired Abbé Montague's vast collection of treasures, both secular and religious, Philippe and Henrietta retreated to a quiet spot in order to talk about her adventures in England and their forthcoming marriage. It was much remarked upon by the cynical courtiers that had accompanied the royal group to Pontoise that Philippe could hardly bear to drag his eyes away from Henrietta's animated face and listened to her speak as though her words were made of purest gold. All in all, they made a very pretty little pair, which was doubtless a significant part of Henrietta's appeal for her always image-conscious cousin – after all, he had to marry someone, so why not pick a girl who complimented his delicate good looks and made the other courtiers comment about how good they looked together? Later on Henrietta would sadly recall that Philippe would only be in love with her for their engagement and then the first two weeks of their marriage and certainly that would seem to be a fairly accurate if rather bleak view of the situation. Although later events may well suggest otherwise, there is no reason to think that Philippe did not genuinely think himself totally in love with Henrietta at this time and there was certainly no reason for anyone who saw them together to think that they would be anything other than blissfully happy. Besides, if there were any lingering doubts in anyone's mind about the strength of Philippe's feelings towards his betrothed, his clear and obviously jealous loathing of Buckingham should have been enough to dispel them. He had been deeply displeased to find the handsome Duke apparently so firmly ensconced in Henrietta's good graces and, to the obvious satisfaction and approval of Henrietta Maria, would waste no time at all in having him icily dismissed and packed off back to England with his tail between his legs. He was not much missed.

The rest of the party continued on to Paris with Monsieur accompanying Henrietta and her mother most of the way alone before they were joined by the others at Saint Denis for a grand procession through the streets of Paris. This was the first time that Henrietta had participated in such an event and her first real taste of what it would mean to be married to the king's brother. Previously she had always been an observer, watching from the sidelines as her French cousins took the centre stage but now she was being welcomed into the centre of their world - an intoxicating and exciting sensation for any young girl. Although both parties were keen for the wedding to take place as soon as possible, their relationship as first cousins meant that a Papal dispensation, that bane of royal lives, was required to sanction a match between them and that could take quite some time to arrive. In the meantime, Philippe enjoyed squiring Henrietta, who was still in mourning for her sister, to quiet parties and concerts and gave every sign of being entirely besotted with his betrothed. Always very pretty, Henrietta really began to blossom at this time – she now had more than enough money to be able to dress exactly as she chose (and like the rest of her family, whatever other faults they might have had, she had exquisite taste and a keen eye for style) while her new status and the attention that it garnered did much to boost her confidence and erase much of the shame that she had sometimes felt about her previously dependent position. Perhaps fearing the effect that all this admiration and worldly frivolity was having upon her impressionable young daughter, Henrietta Maria swiftly put an end to it and whisked Henrietta off to Chaillot for a period of quiet contemplation and prayer.

The much anticipated Papal dispensation arrived from Pope Alexander VII in Rome on 9 March, which turned out to be an extremely inauspicious day, for while Henrietta was giving thanks to God that her wedding could now go ahead, Cardinal Mazarin was breathing his last on the other side of Paris in the Château de Vincennes. The portents from the heavens were not promising either as a huge comet (now identified as Comet Ikeya-Zhang) had blazed across the Parisian sky the night before, leading the always ironic

Mazarin to comment dryly on his deathbed that 'the comet does me too much honour'. Not that Henrietta and Philippe, with the optimism of youth, cared much about such omens – in fact the latter was mostly preoccupied at this time with the fact that the Cardinal's, to his mind, ill timed and extremely inconvenient, death had delayed their wedding even more as now the entire court would have to go into mourning for a fortnight. The ceremony was already likely to be a very quiet one anyway as it would be taking place during Lent and Henrietta had yet to come out of mourning for her sister Mary. In the end, the date was set for the 30 March and Henrietta could finally throw herself with gusto into preparations for her wedding, which was to be held in her mother's private chapel in the Palais Royal.

As a special concession to the importance of this match, King Louis decreed that court mourning for Cardinal Mazarin could be put aside for two days so that the wedding guests could wear their most magnificent clothes and jewels rather than plain black, which would have given the ceremony a rather funereal atmosphere. Henrietta would have been especially pleased about this as she had been provided with beautiful pearl and jewel encrusted gowns for both the wedding and the official betrothal ceremony, which took place the night before in the great salon of the Palais Royal and was attended by the entire royal family and most important courtiers. She also had a plethora of spectacular new jewels to wear to the ceremonies, which had been sent over from London as a wedding present from her brother Charles. Her spiritual preparations were not forgotten either in all the fuss – as well as the retreat at Chaillot, Henrietta took Holy Communion in the splendid old church of Saint Eustache in nearby Les Halles on the morning before her wedding.

The wedding itself passed without incident although there was an argument beforehand between Henrietta Maria's meddlesome favourite Abbé Montagu and Philippe's Grand Almoner, Daniel de Cosnac, Bishop of Valence about which of them would have the honour of officiating at the ceremony. Although Henrietta Maria naturally supported Montagu's claim, Cosnac eventually won the day and the ceremony duly went ahead as planned, attended by the immediate royal family and the most important members of the nobility. To Henrietta's delight her new husband presented her with yet more magnificent jewels to add to her growing collection, while he was no doubt very well pleased with the dowry of £60,000 in cash, jewels and plate that she brought with her. In addition to all of this, Henrietta was to have her own income of 40,000 livres a year from the French royal treasury as well as the lovely old Château de Montargis near Orléans to enjoy as her own private residence, although there is no evidence that she ever actually went there, preferring to spend her time at the magnificent Château de Saint Cloud instead. After the religious solemnities had been completed and the guests had enjoyed an informal supper hosted by Henrietta Maria, it was time for Henrietta to leave her home with her new husband and go with him to his apartments in the Tuileries palace, which would be their Parisian residence for the foreseeable future. However, when the moment came for Henrietta to say goodbye to her mother, from whom she had not been separated since her arrival in France as a toddler fourteen years earlier, her poise entirely deserted her and she broke down in tears, which naturally set her mother and a few of the guests off crying as well.

Although the letter that we know Henrietta wrote to her brother after her wedding, informing him that her period started on her wedding night and that Philippe turned in a very poor performance when he eventually managed to consummate the marriage, has sadly been lost, we still have the brief note written by her new brother-in-law King Louis the next morning. He confirms that the wedding so desired by everyone has finally taken place and assures King Charles that:

'having always considered the marriage with my brother with your sister, the Princess of England, as a new tie which would draw still closer the bonds of our friendship, I feel more joy than I can express, that it was yesterday happily accomplished; and as I doubt not that this news will inspire you with the sentiment as myself, I was unwilling to delay a moment in sharing my joy with you, nor would I lose the opportunity of this mutual congratulation, to confirm to you by these lines that I am, my brother, very sincerely your good brother Louis.'

Chapter Nine

Madame

1661–1662

As the Abbé de Choisy wrote in his splendid *Mémoires*:

'Never has France had a Princess as attractive as Henriette d'Angleterre when she became the wife of Monsieur … So fascinating, so ready to please all who approached her. Her whole person seemed full of charm. You felt interested in her, you loved her without being able to help yourself. When you met her for the first time, her eyes sought your own, as if she had no other desire in the world but to please you. When she spoke, she appeared absorbed in the wish to oblige you.'

While the king and rest of the court departed for Fontainebleau, Henrietta and Philippe remained in their apartments in the Tuileries with their own households for a month. In the absence of Louis and Maria Theresa they were the undisputed king and queen of Paris and enjoyed a halcyon honeymoon period as the centre of a seemingly endless round of frivolity. Henrietta was much admired by the Parisians as she took her daily drives along the Seine with her bevy of pretty young maids of honour and was agreed by everyone to be the very epitome of how a princess should be and the antithesis of the dull and rather unattractive Maria Theresa, who had failed to make herself very popular at court since her arrival in France. Even the normally extremely fussy Philippe, who always loved to find fault in the appearance and behaviour of others, could find nothing to criticise about his new wife and in fact gave every appearance of being extremely proud of her as she gracefully took on the daunting rôle of third lady at court after her aunt and sister-in-law. From now on she would be known by the honorific title of 'Madame', which underlined her very special status.

At the start of May, Henrietta and Philippe paid a brief visit to her mother at Colombes before travelling on to Saint Cloud, which would be her principal residence outside Paris from this point onwards. It was a magnificent château, almost palatial in its dimensions and style now that it had been extensively remodelled and refurbished by her husband. Philippe was just twenty years old at this point but already had excellent taste and the changes he had made to Saint Cloud were generally agreed to be very much for the better. No expense had been spared and he had employed the finest architects for the project, while the extensive and famously beautiful gardens were the preserve of the celebrated up and coming landscape gardener Le Nôtre and architect Mansart, both of whom would later work together with glorious results on his brother Louis' great project at Versailles. Henrietta would become passionately fond of Saint Cloud and would take particular pleasure in the lovely gardens, which had grand sweeping terraces overlooking Paris, splendid fountains and charming fairy like arbours where she could hide away from the world with a good book or her closest friends, which at the time included Madame de la Fayette, the Princesse de Monaco, the Duchesse de Châtillon (the same Babet who had so enchanted her brother Charles during one of his visits to Paris) and Françoise de Mortemart, who would later be better known as Madame de Montespan. The interior was also very much to her taste as the usually flamboyant Philippe turned out to have an elegant lightness of touch when it came to interior design so that all of the rooms were harmoniously decorated and filled with exquisite furniture and objects. Henrietta's rooms in the left wing of the château were particularly lovely and decorated by the great painter Jean Nocret with scenes from Greek mythology, although his great masterpiece depicting the family of Louis XIV as deities, with Henrietta as a very lovely Flora, would not be commissioned for her rooms until 1670. However, in the meantime there was a delightful painting in the bedchamber of Henrietta as Venus welcoming Mars, who naturally looked exactly like Philippe, back from war.

The couple lingered at Saint Cloud for several days before going to Fontainebleau, where they were to join the rest of the court who were to remain there for the entire summer. It was extremely hot that year and Fontainebleau with its extensive park and expanse of forest was considered to be the very best place to endure the discomfort of a heatwave. Just before

Henrietta set off from Saint Cloud she received a very affectionate note from her new brother-in-law Louis in which he assured her that:

'if I wish myself at Saint Cloud it is not because of its grottoes or the freshness of its foliage. Here we have gardens fair enough to console us, but the company which is there now, is so good that I find myself furiously tempted to go there, and if I did not expect to see you here tomorrow, I do not know what I should do, and could not help making a journey to see you. Remember me to all of your ladies, and do not forget the affection that I have promised you, which is, I can assure you, all you could possibly desire, if indeed you wish me to love you very much.'

This was indeed a great change from his previous dismissive and rather contemptuous attitude towards Henrietta and certainly, even allowing for the extremely flowery literary conventions of the time, suggests that his feelings about her had become much warmer and more complicated, probably since her triumphant return from England. During her time away she had completely shed her previous sad persona of the impoverished little exile and instead become entirely comfortable with her new status as the honoured sister of a reigning monarch, developing a certain kittenish charm that was considered extremely becoming and was, most crucially for the daughter of the now austerely censorious Henrietta Maria, just short of outright flirtatiousness while still having a hypnotic effect on those lucky enough to have the full force of her attention turned upon them. At the same time, her massively inflated income, which allowed her to greatly improve her appearance, and the flattery that her enhanced position inspired both conspired to give her a newly minted confident glow that apparently made Louis regret his earlier rather bullying behaviour towards her, when he even noticed her at all, which was probably very rarely.

Her mother's great friend Madame de Motteville left behind a very compelling verbal portrait of Henrietta at this time, which unusually for the period is not entirely flattering when it comes to her physical appearance although she takes some pains to emphasise that Henrietta's physical imperfections in no way diminished her overall charm or the great attractiveness of her person:

'The Princess of England was above middle height; she was very graceful, and her figure which was not faultless, did not appear as imperfect as it really was. Her beauty was not of the most perfect kind, but her charming manners made her very attractive. She had an extremely delicate and very white skin, with a bright, natural colour, a complexion so to speak, of roses and jasmine. Her eyes were small but soft and very sparkling, her nose not bad, her lips were rosy, and her teeth as white and regular as you could wish, but her face was too long, and her great thinness seemed to threaten her beauty with early decay. She dressed her hair and whole person in a most becoming manner, and she was so loveable in herself, that she could not fail to please. She had not been able to become Queen, and to make up for this disappointment, she wished to reign in the hearts of worthy people, and to find glory in the world by her charms, and by the beauty of her mind. Already much sense and discernment might be traced in her mind, and in spite of her youth which had hitherto hidden her from the public, it was easy to judge, that when she appeared upon the great theatre of the court of France, she would play upon it one of the principal parts.'

The first public clue that everything was changing between the two cousins, Louis and Henrietta, was the fact that although he managed to restrain himself from visiting her at Saint Cloud, he still felt compelled to ride out from Fontainebleau in order to meet them half way. It may be that he also wished to do his younger brother honour as a new husband but it was Henrietta, who always looked her very best on horseback, who rode at his side when they returned to Fontainebleau. And she was to remain almost constantly at his side for the next few months, giving rise to all manner of gossip around the court and causing her husband to suffer terrible jealousy, although at this distance it is impossible to tell which one of Henrietta and Louis, he was most annoyed with as their flirtation developed over that long hot summer. Henrietta had obviously been to Fontainebleau before but never as the wife of the king's brother and her apartments were consequently much grander than the ones that she had previously shared with her mother. Life at the grand old Renaissance palace was much more carefree than that endured by the court in Paris although certain formalities like the King and Queen's ceremonial *lever* in the morning and *coucher* last thing at night were still practised and there were all the usual grand galas and balls both in the palace's beautiful ballroom and, mercifully on the most swelteringly hot days, outside in the vast gardens. For the most part though, the vibe at Fontainebleau was very restful and laid back and the courtiers were encouraged to have fun and enjoy themselves.

At this time, Louis and Maria Theresa were just twenty-two years old (both would turn twenty three in September 1661) and the court that surrounded them was also distinctly youthful in ambience and behaviour. The old guard remained, of course, in the persons of the men and women who had known his father Louis XIII in his youth but they were being gradually replaced by a new generation of bright young things with their own fashions, codes of behaviour and ideas. Louis completely understood the value of the more venerable old courtiers and liked to keep them around him as advisors, especially now that he had personally taken on the reins of government in the wake of Mazarin's death. However, he naturally preferred the company of young people of his own age, especially in his limited free time and it therefore should be no surprise that his brother Philippe, of whom he was extremely fond, and the lovely Henrietta, who just seemed to get prettier and more delightful with each passing day, should be his most favourite companions at this time. Although Henrietta would always be physically rather delicate, she enjoyed being outside and really came into her own during the summer months when she could indulge her passion for long walks, riding and swimming. Usually rather pale, the fresh air added a most comely colour to her cheeks although like all fashionable ladies of this time, she wore a black velvet mask when out riding in order to protect her complexion from the sun's harsh rays. Bored with his dumpy wife, who hated going outside and preferred to spend her days lying on a sofa, and feeling overwhelmed by the great task that he had just taken on of single-handedly governing France, Louis was desperate for diversion and in Henrietta, who rode like an Amazonian, looked like an angel and roared with laughter without the slightest trace of self-consciousness when someone told her a joke, he believed that he had found his ideal woman. It was just a pity that he had not come to that realisation before he found himself strong armed by his mother into marrying Maria Theresa.

Nonetheless, however little his wife appealed to him, Louis had still managed to do his duty and in May 1661 she was pregnant with their first child. Always inclined to be rather lazy anyway, Maria Theresa was more indolent than ever that summer, which gave Louis the perfect excuse to spend more time with Henrietta, who took on the social duties that his wife would otherwise have had to perform. Philippe may well have simmered with jealous anger at the sight of his wife dancing with his brother but there was nothing that he or anyone else could do about it when at face value, she was simply doing her duty and stepping in for the incapacitated little Queen. The budding romance between Henrietta and Louis certainly added an extra sparkle to that season's stay at Fontainebleau and the courtiers fortunate enough to be present agreed that they could not remember a season quite like it as every day and night was packed with delightful pastimes and revelries, notably the one held for Henrietta's seventeenth birthday in June. During the day, Henrietta and her ladies enjoyed simple, bucolic pleasures and would go for walks in the gardens, their delicate complexions protected by brightly coloured silk parasols, or venture into the woods dressed in simple cotton frocks, in search of streams to bathe in. They changed into their most lovely silk dresses in the evenings though and after a concert, ball or perhaps a play, would go for long walks through the moonlit gardens, squired by their favourite gentlemen. Naturally, Henrietta would find herself walking alongside Louis and the two would wander off alone deep into the woods, their soft laughter floating behind them on the breeze. Sometimes they even arranged for the boats on the canal to be manned by sailors late into the night and spent hours drifting on the water while the king's personal orchestra, his so-called *Petits Violons* played on the shoreline and servants scurried between the trees ensuring that the coloured lanterns that lined the lake remained alight. Nothing could have been more romantic or more designed to appeal to both Henrietta's sensibilities and Louis' desperate wish to find some modicum of personal happiness in his life and so it is hardly surprising that the pair fell gently rather than passionately in love and became completely inseparable. When Queen Anne attempted to separate them by whisking Philippe and Henrietta off for an extended visit to her old friend Madame de Chevreuse at lovely Dampierre, Louis could hardly conceal his sulking and bad temper while she made her great joy to be reunited with him upon their return plainly obvious for all to see.

Whether or not their relationship ever became sexual is highly doubtful however. Naturally, it is difficult for some modern writers to accept that a handsome, healthy, mutually attracted young couple like Louis and Henrietta should have kept their obvious infatuation with each other entirely platonic but that is to view them through the filter of twenty-first century sensibilities and does a great disservice to them both. Like Henrietta, Louis had been brought up to have a very strict moral code (although in his case it was obviously rather more flexible) and to have an absolute respect for the reputation of both their family and the institution of monarchy itself. Henrietta had been trained since birth to become the wife of a great prince and was fully aware of the responsibilities that this would entail – to be decorative and bring absolutely no scandal to his house while at the same time turning a blind eye to whatever peccadilloes he chose to indulge in. Above all, however, it was her job to ensure the continuation of his name by providing a male heir and it would have been unthinkable to her to do anything at all that would jeopardise her reputation and the legitimacy of any potential children that she might one day have. There was also the fact that both Louis and Henrietta had been raised by devoutly pious mothers to be devoted children of the church and were both very well aware that according to the rules of the Catholic faith, it was considered sinful and incestuous for them to even marry should one of them become widowed let alone indulge in a clandestine relationship. That their flirtation was intense and that there were very deep feelings on both sides cannot be doubted but it is still highly unlikely that matters went as far as modern writers would have us believe.

As both Louis and Henrietta were passionately fond of ballets, the more sophisticated modern version of the court masques that their respective mothers had so delighted in, these were a regular occurrence at Fontainebleau that summer with the enjoyment coming as much from the hours of practising, learning lines and trying on costumes as from the performance itself. Maria Theresa was not at all fond of dancing or play acting and so naturally it fell once again to Henrietta, who adored both, to take the leading roles opposite Louis, who also loved nothing better than dressing up and dancing before his court. In July, the couple danced together in Benserade's elaborate *Ballet des Saisons* with Henrietta taking the part of the goddess Diana and Louis, in an unusual comic turn, performing first as the goddess Ceres and then as the personification of eternal Spring. Everyone agreed that Henrietta made a delightful Diana in her silvery robes and with a crescent moon resting on her auburn ringlets but for a few members of the audience, the main attraction was not the lovely Madame but instead one of her more lowly maids of honour, Mademoiselle de la Vallière who was not even important enough to have a starring role but instead appeared simply as an anonymous nymph at her mistress' side. It was gleefully noted by some of the more observant courtiers that although Louis' attention was still primarily fixed on Henrietta, he was also sneaking the occasional glance at the pretty fair haired Louise de la Vallière, who blushed most becomingly every time the royal eye rolled in her direction.

Initially this new romance was intended as yet another piece of play acting – a ruse that appealed to both Louis and Henrietta thanks to their shared love of dramatics. As the summer went on it became increasingly difficult to hide their obvious infatuation from the always watchful eyes of the court and rumours of their romance eventually reached the ears of both Queen Anne and Henrietta Maria, who naturally reacted very badly to any suggestion of possible wrong doing on the part of their precious favourite children. As might have been expected, Queen Anne decided to lay most of the blame squarely at Henrietta's door and took her aside to remonstrate strongly about her neglect of poor jealous Philippe, her inappropriately flirtatious manner with Louis and the injurious effect that all those delightful night time walks were having on her already delicate health at a time when everyone was naturally hoping that she would soon become pregnant. When Henrietta paid little attention to her mother-in-law's scolding, it was decided to deploy the big guns and Henrietta Maria was persuaded to leave Colombes, where she was enjoying a peaceful retirement from the stress of court life, in order to pay a visit to Fontainebleau where she too tried to make her daughter see reason but with very little success. Irritated and amused by this maternal interference, Louis and Henrietta decided to play a little game with their interfering mothers and hit upon a scheme whereby he would pretend to pay attention to one of her maids of honour instead. Naturally Louis chanced his arm by suggesting two of Henrietta's most attractive and coquettish ladies, Bonne de Pons and Françoise de Chimerault but she was understandably unenthusiastic about this plan and instead suggested Louise de la Vallière, one of the newest arrivals at court and a girl whose profound innocence and naivety would, she hoped, preclude any actual romantic shenanigans occurring.

However, what Henrietta did not know was that Louise, who was herself the daughter of a minor nobleman, had grown up with the youngest daughters of Louis' uncle Gaston, Duc d'Orléans at Blois and had conceived a girlish passion for Louis during one of his rare visits there. Far from being the model of virginal restraint, she was in fact ripe for the picking where the handsome young king was concerned and could hardly believe her luck when he picked her out from amongst Henrietta's attractive bevy of maids of honour, many of whom, like the gorgeous redhead Mademoiselle de Pons, had much more right to claim his attention. Louis was initially amused rather than aroused by Louise's slavishly uncritical devotion but as the weeks passed he found himself first intrigued and then attracted – she was, after all, extremely pretty with huge blue eyes and masses of ash blonde hair and like Henrietta, she was an excellent sportswoman and an exceedingly graceful dancer. That she was rather stupid and not the slightest bit amusing or witty did not seem to matter all that much when he could still go to Henrietta for the stimulating, sparkling conversation that he craved. Naturally, as soon as Queen Anne and Philippe heard that Louis was paying marked attentions to Mademoiselle de la Vallière they did everything that they could to promote this new romance by placing her as close to him as possible at supper and concerts, which of course Henrietta could hardly complain about without making herself appear completely ridiculous.

By the time the three main players took part in the *Ballet des Saisons* at the end of July 1661, Mademoiselle de la Vallière had capitulated and, with a lot of crying and melodramatics, lost her virginity to her royal lover, who was beginning to fall quite deeply in love with her. As she smilingly danced opposite her brother-in-law, who still politely made a great show of being as attentive towards her as ever, Henrietta knew that their relationship, platonic or otherwise, was at an end and she was well on her way to being entirely replaced. A less well brought up young woman might well have made an enormous fuss about being superseded by her own maid of honour, and especially one as comparatively humble as Louise de la Vallière, but Henrietta had been well schooled by her mother and so she resolved to give way gracefully, earning herself Louis' eternal gratitude and ongoing affection as a result. Dealing with the rest of the court would be tricky however – they had made no secret of their feelings for each other and with Louis' attentions towards his new mistress becoming ever more marked and obvious, it was only a matter of time before Henrietta began to feel herself completely humiliated as news spread that she had been replaced. There was nothing to do, however, but endure the stares and whispers of the courtiers and wait for it all to blow over.

In the meantime, she had other matters on her mind when a prolonged bout of exhaustion and headaches was revealed to be caused not by all those late nights spent walking through the Fontainebleau forest arm in arm with her handsome brother-in-law but by pregnancy, the baby having been conceived around the middle of July at about the time when Louis had switched his affections to Mademoiselle de la Vallière and Henrietta had no doubt thought it politic to pay a bit more attention to her husband. Although she was well aware that this was all part of the dutiful life that she had been raised for, Henrietta reacted just like any other fun-loving seventeen-year-old girl to the news that she was going to be a mother and was not exactly best pleased by the prospect, although her husband, who was fond of children and keen to become a father, was naturally over the moon. Sadly for Henrietta, however, she was not one of those fortunate women who blossom and glow during pregnancy but instead became more thin and sickly than ever, developed a hacking, rather alarming cough and had to spend large amounts of time in bed, often dosed with opium, which she found exceedingly boring even if her friends did their best to liven things up by paying her long visits with all the latest gossip, books and music on hand to entertain her. When Louis' suspiciously fabulously wealthy Superintendent of Finances, Nicolas Fouquet, invited the entire court over to his newly refurbished and very beautiful château at Vaux le Vicomte on 17 August, Henrietta was still determined to attend and a litter was provided so that she could be carried around the gardens and not miss any of the illuminations and entertainments that had been laid on, ostensibly in her honour but really so that Fouquet could flatter and impress his master, King Louis.

The fête at Vaux le Vicomte has rightly gone down in history as one of the most famous parties of all time, not least because its outrageous magnificence only served to confirm Louis' suspicions that Fouquet was cheating him and using royal funds to feather his own opulent nest. Although he did his best to smile and compliment the unfortunate Fouquet, who would be arrested a few weeks later, the king could hardly conceal his chagrin and jealousy as he sat through a specially commissioned performance of Molière's new comedy *Les Facheux* (The Bores), which was followed by an elaborate firework display and then a magnificent supper, accompanied by apparently endless amounts of the finest wines, that went on for several hours. It may have been of some consolation to him that Henrietta, in whose honour the fête was being held, was having a terrible time as well – she was bored to tears in her litter which she felt cut her off from all the fun that everyone else was having and also deeply fed up with her pregnancy, the jealous rages of her husband and the growing ascendancy of Mademoiselle de la Vallière, who was becoming increasingly influential at court. Her only small consolation was the rather unexpected and increasingly pointed attentions of the handsome Comte de Guiche, who was her husband's closest friend and, in fact, generally rumoured to be his lover until he transferred his affections to Henrietta in that fateful summer of 1661.

Guy Armand de Gramont, Comte de Guiche was twenty-three years old and the eldest son of Antoine, Duc de Gramont and his wife, Françoise-Marguerite du Plessis de Chivré, who was a niece of Cardinal Richelieu. His younger sister, Catherine, was one of Henrietta's closest friends and had recently married the Duc de Valentinois, who was the eldest son and heir of the Prince of Monaco. Guiche was extremely handsome but rather aloof, which naturally led other less favoured courtiers to accuse him of being vain and exceedingly haughty if not outright unfriendly. He had been at court since boyhood and had therefore known Philippe for many years, eventually becoming part of the tight little circle of bitchy, handsome young men that surrounded the young Duc d'Orléans. Guiche was rather different from Philippe's other friends though as he was not at all effeminate in appearance or nature and was not much given to sycophancy either; Monsieur's cousin

Anne Marie Louise would later recount a story about Guiche gleefully kicking Philippe on the backside at a court ball. It was still nonetheless something of a surprise to everyone when his loyalty gradually began to shift from Philippe to Henrietta during that long, hot summer at Fontainebleau. As he was so exceedingly handsome, she was of course extremely flattered by his attentions but did very little to encourage them, probably because she was still preoccupied by Louis and also conscious of the fact that Guiche was very much Philippe's man and therefore probably not to be trusted. The fact that he had been married since January 1658 to Marguerite Louise Suzanne de Béthune, daughter of the Duc de Sully, probably put Henrietta off as well, although the marriage was, even by the low standards and expectations of time, unhappy and the couple saw very little of each other.

His attentions towards her became more marked as they rehearsed together for the *Ballet des Saisons*, in which he had a small part alongside her husband but when Henrietta gave him a polite brush off via his sister, he decided to teach her a lesson and instead pretended to pay court to her nemesis, Louise de la Vallière, which naturally backfired when Louis found out and made it clear that he was either to leave her alone or be sent away from court. As her romance with Louis faltered and then died, Henrietta became only too happy to look rather more favourably upon Guiche and was actively involved in a flirtation with him by the end of autumn, when the court returned to Paris after the birth of Louis and Maria Theresa's son on 1 November. Henrietta's health was still causing concern and the royal physicians insisted that she remain in bed until her own baby arrived. The horrible labour endured by Maria Theresa, which had lasted for twelve hours during which she was serenaded by traditional Spanish music played beneath her windows, had made everyone feel rather afraid for Henrietta, who was far more physically delicate than Louis' dumpy little wife. Typically, it was the fact that Maria Theresa had somehow managed to produce an enormous, almost obscenely healthy baby boy that Henrietta, who doubtless had rather too much time on her hands thanks to her enforced bedrest, fixated upon and she announced that she too would do the same.

When it came to her brother Charles' ears that she was still entertaining her friends at her bedside and staying up until all hours chatting and listening to music, he felt compelled to gently remonstrate with her that 'for God's sake, my dearest sister, have a care of yourself and I believe that I am more concerned in your health than I am in my own.' There was talk at the time of a meeting between Louis and Charles at Dunkirk and Henrietta wrote to say how ardently she hoped for this come about so that she would be able to see her brother again – a feeling that he obviously shared, assuring her that 'I shall be very impatient until I have the happiness to see ma chère Minette again'. Sadly, this much longed for meeting failed to transpire but their loss is history's gain for their correspondence flourished during this period and provides a uniquely fresh and candid view of court life in England and France at this time. The letters that Henrietta wrote to her brother during the dramatic spring, summer and autumn of 1661 have sadly been lost, doubtless destroyed by Charles' orders as they contained juicy details of her flirtation with their cousin Louis, so the first we have from her in a while dates from January 1662 when she was back in Paris and enduring bedrest while awaiting the birth of her first child. The letter itself was given to Charles by one of her mother's ladies, Mrs Stewart who left Paris at the end of 1661 with her very beautiful pair of daughters, the eldest of whom, Frances, was to become maid of honour to Charles' new wife Catherine of Braganza.

Frances Stewart, destined to become one of the most celebrated beauties of her age, was just fourteen years old when she first arrived in London and had spent her entire life in Paris on the edges of Henrietta Maria's motley court of disaffected exiles. As she was three years younger than Henrietta and their mothers were close friends it is not at all far-fetched to assume that the two girls had more or less grown up together and knew each other very well before Frances departed for England; certainly Henrietta speaks about her in extremely glowing terms in the letter she entrusted to Mrs Stewart's care:

> 'I would not lose this opportunity of writing to you by Mrs Stuart, who is taking over her daughter to become one of the Queen your wife's future maids. If this were not the reason for her departure, I should be very unwilling to let her go, for she is the prettiest girl in the world, and one of the best fitted of any I know to adorn your court.'

As Henrietta predicted, Frances was indeed destined to become an adornment to her brother's court but to Charles' extreme disappointment she was as virtuous as she was lovely and refused to become his mistress, preferring instead to make an honourable marriage with a duke.

By the start of 1662, Henrietta was completely caught up in her romance with the handsome Comte de Guiche, who was in constant attendance at her side during this time. As it was customary for fashionable ladies to entertain both men and women in their bedchamber, his presence did not raise eyebrows, although his extreme attentiveness certainly raised suspicions that he was more than just a friend to the little Duchesse. When Henrietta's health began to improve at the start of her third trimester, she was permitted to leave her bed and instead recline upon a sofa in her drawing room, where she was entertained by plays and ballets written and performed by her friends and family, with even Philippe taking part. Louis continued to be a regular visitor to her apartments in the Tuileries too, although everyone knew that he was really there to moon over Mademoiselle de la Vallière, who was still a member of Henrietta's household, much to her annoyance – she did not dare dismiss the girl as she knew that Louise's presence at court depended on her position in her household and that Louis would be furious with her if she jeopardised this in any way. The fact that Maria Theresa had recently been sent a spiteful anonymous letter, mercifully intercepted by one of her ladies before it reached her hands, informing her of her husband's adultery with Louise de la Vallière simply complicated matters further as it made Louis' mistress's position all the more precarious now that his wife was being extorted by a secret correspondent, who was almost certainly Olympe Mancini, Comtesse de Soissons assisted by her lover, the Marquis de Vardes, to consider if she could 'tolerate the thought of the King in the arms of another, or if you will put an end to a situation so humiliating to your dignity.'

Louise was not the only former denizen of the old Duc d'Orléans' household to find her way to the Tuileries – her former best friend, Anne-Constance de Montalais, whom she had known since childhood, was also one of Henrietta's maids of honour and had managed to make herself so indispensable and worm herself so far into the Duchesse's good books that it was to her that Henrietta and Guiche entrusted the delicate task of delivering their love letters to each other. This was a big mistake on their part as Montalais, apparently so faithful and loyal, was in fact a scheming, two faced, indiscreet liar who really should not have been trusted with their secrets and was cheerfully blabbing to all and sundry about Henrietta's affairs behind her back. The lovers were impressed with her diligence and ingenuity though – she displayed impressive sleight of hand while delivering their love notes and on one occasion even smuggled Guiche, disguised as a fortune teller, into Henrietta's apartments at a time when she was not receiving guests so that they could be totally alone together. Naturally this precarious state of affairs could not continue for long in an atmosphere as bitchy and spiteful as the French court and when Montalais unwisely let drop to Louise de la Vallière that their mistress had been entertaining Guiche alone in her rooms and Louise in turn went to Louis and told him all about it, all hell broke loose at the Tuileries.

Incensed by Louise's hypocrisy, Henrietta threw caution to the wind and insisted that she leave her service immediately, which Louise, whose stupidity belied an excellent turn for melodrama, duly did – by immediately running away to a convent and making sure that Louis knew all about it and where to find her. In the meantime, word of the drama quickly reached Philippe's ears and he lost no time in denouncing his former best friend and demanding that Louis have Guiche banished from court, preferably forever. Louis, who had decided to blame Henrietta for the whole miserable affair, readily agreed to this before hurrying away to rescue Louise from the convent, where he pleased her very much by falling to his knees and begging her to return to court. As he knew that neither his mother nor his wife would, quite understandably, accept Louise in their households, this meant that he would have to swallow his annoyance with Henrietta and lean on her to take his mistress back as a maid of honour, which she duly but unwillingly did, when he promised to rescind his order to have Guiche banished from court in exchange for her word that she would never again entertain him in private.

Henrietta's first child, a daughter, was born slightly prematurely at three in the morning of 27 March 1662. When she heard that she had failed to outdo her sister-in-law Maria Theresa by producing a son, Henrietta immediately ordered that the child be thrown out of the window. This lack of maternal feeling was thankfully short lived as she was thereafter a most devoted and affectionate mother to her little girl, who was christened Marie Louise in the chapel of the Palais Royal on 21 May. Unlike a lot of men, Philippe was in no way annoyed that his first child was not the son that his wife had most ardently longed for but was instead rather delighted to have a daughter to dress up and show off around court – that the little girl was from the very first as delightfully pretty and clever as both of her parents and as good natured as her mother only added to his pride in her and she would in fact remain by far his most favourite child for the rest of his life.

Chapter Ten

Vardes

1662–1664

On 21 May 1662, the same day that Marie Louise d'Orléans was being christened in the Palais Royal chapel, her uncle King Charles of England married the Portuguese Infanta, Catherine of Braganza in Portsmouth. As Henrietta was unable to attend the wedding, her brother made time to write to her two days later, letting her know that he was now a married man, assuring her that 'I think myself very happy' and no doubt hoping to make her laugh by letting her know that as had happened on her own wedding night, Catherine's ill-timed period had prevented any attempt to consummate the marriage but that he hoped that he was 'not as furious as Monsieur was … yet I hope that I shall entertain her at least better the first night than he did you.' In the event, although Charles was almost certainly much better at sexually pleasing his wife than Philippe, he would prove himself to be just as terrible a husband to the poor Infanta, who had to tolerate his many affairs without even having the joy of giving birth to a living child who would perhaps have consoled her for the lonely life that she led in England.

Henrietta's husband may have been jealous, spiteful and vindictive but at least she had her daughter and a large circle of friends and family on hand to support her when he tried to make her life difficult. She was also singularly fortunate in being able to remain in France when so many other princesses, poor Catherine of Braganza included, were forced to travel hundreds of miles away from home in order to marry and would almost certainly never see their families again. To Henrietta, not having to leave the places and people that had been familiar to her since early childhood almost certainly more than made up for the occasional indignities that she suffered at the hands of Philippe and his friends in the wake of her flirtation with Guiche becoming public knowledge. Although they still on occasion managed to get along reasonably well and even contrived to conceive more children, her relationship with Philippe would be increasingly shaky from this point on as he struggled with his feelings of intense jealousy that she might be more popular with his brother and the court than he. Henrietta longed for the close, trusting and affectionate relationship that her own parents had enjoyed and which she knew that she would never have with Philippe. Their romance was well and truly over and Henrietta, who was not even out of her teens, could only foresee years of increasing unhappiness ahead of her – especially when it seemed as though even the great consolation of having her mother close at hand was to be denied to her when Henrietta Maria announced that she was planning to return to England at the end of July, ostensibly to meet Charles' new Portuguese bride but really with the intention of taking up permanent residence and seeing out her days there. The loss of her mother was a terrible blow to Henrietta. The two maintained a lively, and now sadly lost, correspondence while Henrietta Maria was in England, but it was not at all the same as having her mother living either across the road in the Palais Royal, which now became the Parisian residence of Henrietta and Philippe, or a few miles away at Colombes and although Henrietta Maria had reasoned that Henrietta now had absolutely no need of her, in actuality her daughter needed her more than ever as her marriage became increasingly unsatisfying and her personal affairs seemed to become ever more complicated.

Although she had promised never again to entertain Guiche in her rooms, Henrietta felt so miserable after the birth of her daughter that it was not long before the clandestine letters and visits gradually started again. This time, the couple relied upon Olympe Mancini, Comtesse de Soissons and her lover, François-René Crespin du Bec, Marquis de Vardes and a Gentleman of the Bedchamber to act as go-betweens along with the apparently still faithful Montalais. Olympe had never been particularly friendly with Henrietta but they became very close at this time, while Vardes made a great show of befriending and winning the trust of Guy Armand. The fact that this scheming pair had been jointly responsible for the so called anonymous *Letter Espagnole* which would have revealed Louis' affair with Mademoiselle de la Vallière to Maria Theresa had one of her Spanish duennas not intercepted it, does not seem to have troubled Henrietta all that much when perhaps it ought to have alerted her to the fact that Olympe and Vardes were not to be trusted with her secrets. However, she was not yet eighteen years old and although she had grown up on the fringes of the French court, her sheltered upbringing meant that she lacked the intrinsic sophistication of the Mancini girls or her good friend Françoise de Mortemart, who had recently changed her name to the much more glamorous Athénaïs. Henrietta was intelligent and a fast learner and over the course of the next twelve months would finally acquire the worldliness that she had hitherto lacked.

Lulled into a false sense of security by Vardes' relationship with Olympe Mancini, Henrietta had no idea that this incorrigible womaniser had decided to seduce her and was already subtly doing his best to sow dissension between herself and Guiche, while pretending to be their friend. When his attempts to cause issues between them failed to result in a permanent break, he went to Philippe and, in the guise of a concerned friend, informed him that Henrietta had broken her promise and was once again enjoying secret meetings with Guy Armand. Aware that Guiche had managed to evade exile last time, he also paid a visit to the Comte's elderly father, the Duc de Gramont and again, pretending to be worried about Guy Armand's wellbeing, advised him to have his son sent away from court before he found himself being accused of having improper relations with Henrietta and sent to the Bastille. Suitably alarmed by this, Gramont, who was a Marshal of France, pulled some strings and with the connivance of Louis and Philippe, who also wanted Guiche far away from Paris and Henrietta, had him banned from court and sent off to join the army at Nancy. The lovers had one last rendezvous in Henrietta's apartments with Montalais keeping watch outside the door as usual. When Philippe paid an unannounced visit to his wife's rooms, the resourceful maid of honour shoved Guiche into a large fireplace but this cunning ruse almost failed when Philippe, who was munching on an orange at the time, went to throw the peel into the hearth which, fortunately for Guiche, was not lit. Anticipating disaster, Montalais claimed to be inordinately fond of orange peel and begged him to let her have it before swallowing it whole.

Unfortunately, another maid of honour, Mademoiselle d'Artigny, who had been in love with Guiche before he turned his attentions to Henrietta and now absolutely detested him, got wind of the secret meeting and hurried off to tell Queen Anne all about it, which resulted in the dismissal of Montalais, who made sure to steal Henrietta's secret correspondence with her brother and Guiche before she left. In retaliation, Henrietta demanded that Artigny, who was best friends with Mademoiselle de la Vallière, should also be sacked from her household, which naturally dragged Louis into the whole sorry affair when his mistress begged that her friend be spared the indignity of being sent away from court in disgrace. She may well have got her own way had the unmarried and hitherto allegedly virginal Mademoiselle d'Artigny not proved to have once become pregnant by an unknown gentleman of the court, which strengthened Henrietta's case for her dismissal. In the end it was Vardes, who was still presenting himself as Guiche's best friend while simultaneously trying to ruin his relationship with Henrietta, who managed to persuade her to keep Mademoiselle d'Artigny, which appeased Louise and the king and restored some much needed harmony to her Palais Royal apartments. Even her relationship with Philippe improved and become relatively cordial once Guiche was out of the picture and the two were often seen together at court events during this time.

In the absence of both Henrietta Maria and Guiche, she found herself turning to the Marquis de Vardes, apparently so sensible, so affable and so entirely on her side, for advice and gradually began to trust him so much that she confided all her secrets in him and even, rather foolishly, showed him her private correspondence with her mother and brother Charles. As the latter had recently decided that Henrietta, who was still very friendly with Louis despite the recent drama, would make a far better intermediary in his quest to persuade Louis to ally with him against the Dutch, this was a very dangerous lapse of judgement as their letters would from this point onwards increasingly discuss matters of state alongside all the usual personal family matters and gossip about their mutual friends. In late 1662 the two exchanged letters about the financial affairs of Charles' old flame and Henrietta's very good friend 'Bablon', the widowed Duchesse de Châtillon, who was short of funds and had asked if Charles could grant her a licence to import potassium alum, which was used by fashionable French ladies to whiten their delicate complexions, from England. Henrietta wrote most winningly to her brother about the matter, informing him that:

'I am almost glad of giving you an opportunity of doing Bablon a service. She has begged me to recommend her affair to you, and I assure you, I do it most willingly, for I am very fond of her, and know that she is much attached to both of us, which is a good reason that you should do your best for her, even if you have forgotten old days.'

To the delight of all concerned, the licence was granted a few weeks later, and Bablon was saved from financial ruination.

The winter of late 1662 and early 1663 was particularly terrible with severe frosts and heavy snowfall. In London, both Henrietta Maria and Charles fell ill with colds, although the latter was apparently well enough to watch his courtiers enjoy ice skating on the frozen Thames. In Paris, the French court kept itself warm with a constant round of gaiety and entertainments and Henrietta was at the very forefront of it all as Queen Maria Theresa was temporarily incapacitated by the birth of a daughter, Anne Élisabeth, in the middle of November. When the baby died just over a month later, the court went into mourning but the festivities continued, albeit in a rather more low-key way, with the first ever performance of Molière's comedy *L'Ecole des Femmes*, which took place in the Palais Royal theatre on Boxing Day 1662, being a particular highlight – especially for Henrietta, who was a great admirer of Molière and was delighted to have the performance dedicated to her. She had her own chance to shine on stage not long afterwards in a court masque called *Ballet des Arts,* which she had conceived and designed herself with help from the Duc de Saint Aignan, Benserade and Baptiste, who provided the script, and Lully, who composed the music. Henrietta naturally claimed the starring role of the chief shepherdess for herself, while Louis danced opposite her as the chief shepherd, and later on in the production she appeared again as Pallas Athene, wearing a costume so becoming that she would have herself painted in it. Attending her were her four most lovely maids of honour - Louise de la Vallière, who could hardly be left out even if Henrietta wished it; Athénaïs de Mortemart, who had recently become betrothed to the Marquis de Montespan; Françoise-Marguerite de Sévigné, the extremely beautiful daughter of the popular *salonnière* Madame de Sévigné, and Gabrielle-Louise de Saint-Simon, eldest daughter of the Duc de Saint-Simon. This most enchanting spectacle turned out to be so popular that it was performed several times that winter, while Lully's beautiful score has survived to this day as a reminder of just how lovely these court spectacles must have been.

However, this hectic lifestyle took its toll on Henrietta and in the spring of 1663 she suffered a miscarriage, which forced her to forgo her usual pleasures and take better care of her health. As Queen Anne was seriously ill with what would soon be diagnosed as breast cancer, the court remained in Paris that summer with excursions out to their country estates when the weather became too swelteringly hot to be borne. Henrietta enjoyed visits to Saint Cloud with her husband and daughter and on occasion accompanied Louis and his most favoured courtiers to his hunting lodge at Versailles, which he was beginning to expand into a more suitably palatial residence. Louis had hated and feared his Parisian subjects ever since the events of the Fronde when he had been forced to flee at night from his own capital and then had not been able to return for over a year. Having also subsequently developed a taste for absolute power, he was naturally unwilling to find himself at the mercy of the Parlement and his unruly subjects ever again and so concluded that it would be to his advantage to move the royal court out of Paris on a permanent basis. The old royal palace of Fontainebleau was of course the natural choice for a new power base outside the capital but Louis wanted something modern and far more magnificent than the rather ramshackle Renaissance façade of Fontainebleau. He had also fallen in love with both the building and location of Versailles and was determined that this should be the site of his enormous, brand new palace which was to house not just the royal family and their households but also most of the court, Louis having come to the conclusion that the best way to keep his bored and occasionally mutinous courtiers out of trouble was to keep them away from the dangerous influence of the Parisian intelligentsia.

Although there had been many visits to Versailles over the years, it was during 1663 that Louis and his immediate circle began to spend more time there as his building work, which would continue for several decades, began. Louis and his gentlemen loved clambering around the building site, discussing the plans with his architect Louis Le Vau and generally making a nuisance of themselves, while the ladies, led by Henrietta, enjoyed the gardens which were beginning to take shape under the care of André Le

Nôtre, who was also responsible for the lovely gardens at Saint Cloud. Sadly, Henrietta was not destined to see Versailles when it was finally finished but she was able to enjoy it at the very beginning of its story when it was still in the process of being transformed from a pretty little hunting lodge into a magnificent palace surrounded by wonderful gardens and had not yet sprawled out of control into the vast and inelegant behemoth that it would later become and which visitors see today. The Versailles that Henrietta knew was far more charming and she spent many happy days there that summer although her happiness was always tempered by the sadness of her recent miscarriage and the absence of so many people that she cared about. She kept up a constant flow correspondence with her mother and Charles and there were even very occasional letters from Guiche when he could find a way of getting one into her hands without detection. Naturally none of this was any compensation for actually having them physically close and in her loneliness she turned even more towards the thoroughly unscrupulous Marquis de Vardes, who encouraged her to think of him as her loyal servant, while at the same time dripping poison into her ears about the absent Guiche, even trying to convince her that he was the father of Mademoiselle d'Artigny's dead child.

However, disaster could strike even in the beautiful surroundings of Versailles and in May 1663, Louis alarmed everyone by falling seriously ill with a bout of measles, which was so severe that at one point his physicians thought that he might actually die. Most of the royal family were banned from his bedside for fear of contagion but Henrietta, who had already had the disease at the end of 1660, refused to comply and bravely forced her way into his sick room to keep him company. Mademoiselle de la Vallière was of course nowhere to be seen during his illness so it was down to Henrietta to keep his spirits up with amusing tales about the latest court gossip and funny little stories that she had picked up from her intellectual *précieuse* friends in the capital. Although their romantic relationship had now come to an end and they had had some issues since, the friendship between Louis and Henrietta would always remain deeply warm and he would make allowances for her that were accorded to very few other people in his circle. Luckily, Louis eventually made a full recovery and he would almost certainly never forget that Henrietta had been one of the few people to defy his physicians and visit him during his illness – even though her own health was hardly hearty at this time.

Anxious about her ongoing health problems and keen to promote a gentler pace of life, her brother had sent over a magnificent gift of a beautiful barge, painted blue and gold with blue velvet curtains and furnishings, in which Henrietta and her ladies could take trips on the Seine, often sailing from Paris to Saint Cloud. Henrietta loved to be near water and this thoughtful present exactly suited her current mood and got plenty of use that summer. On one occasion, she and her husband encountered a party of well-heeled English visitors on a barge close to Saint Cloud and invited them up to the château to admire her newly furnished rooms with the beautiful Mignard ceiling paintings and exquisite furnishings before the party enjoyed an impromptu stroll through the famous gardens and picnic on the terrace with its wonderful view across the Seine towards Paris. It was a rare *heure exquise* for Henrietta and Philippe, who were almost always at odds with each other and spent most of their time apart. It was certainly unusual for Philippe, who was always such a stickler for etiquette, to be so accommodating to such unexpected visitors but it seems as though he played the perfect host while Henrietta blossomed with the excitement of showing off her lovely home to a small group of her brother's subjects, whom she clearly hoped would return to England and tell everyone all about their great adventure at Saint Cloud, which at this time was even lovelier than Versailles.

This brief period of rapprochement between Henrietta and Philippe resulted in another pregnancy in the autumn of 1663 and this time she was determined to take better care of her health and embrace a quieter, less hectic lifestyle. In this admirable aim she was, however, thwarted by the usual round of melodramatics in her household, this time provoked by the Marquis de Vardes, who had finally made a move to seduce Henrietta in the early autumn and had been soundly knocked back, which was apparently such an enormous blow to his ego that he became her implacable enemy from that point onwards. His enmity was increased by the favour that she continued to show the absent Guiche and the artless way that she flirted with various other gentlemen of the court, including the Prince de Marcillac, son of the Duc de Rochefoucauld and the Comte d'Armagnac, who was yet another one of Philippe's handsome young men. When Vardes let Philippe know that Armagnac had fallen in love with Henrietta, he was naturally incensed and extremely jealous that he had apparently lost yet another of his admirers to his own wife. Determined to do Henrietta a mischief, he ganged up with his mother as well as the slighted Madame d'Armagnac, who had once enjoyed a brief love affair with the Marquis de Vardes, and Henrietta's former friend Athénaïs, who was newly married to the Marquis de Montespan, and retaliated by insisting that she dismiss her dear friend Bablon from her household. Understandably infuriated by this spiteful behaviour, Henrietta lost no time in dismissing both Madame de Montespan and Madame d'Armagnac instead and then appealing to Louis for support, which he gladly gave, annoying Philippe even more. This tiresome impasse would eventually only come to an end when Philippe found that he missed the two dismissed ladies in waiting so much that he was willing to agree to Bablon's reinstatement in exchange for their return. The damage was already well and truly done though and once again Henrietta found herself wondering who she could really trust in her own household and was forced to conclude that despite all the flattery and fawning that she received as sister-in-law to the king of France, there were actually very few people that she could truly rely upon.

Despite her best efforts to avoid physical over-exertion, Henrietta still managed to have an accident at a masked ball held in her mother-in-law's apartments in the Louvre. This latest pregnancy was progressing much better than her last two and she had felt well enough to join in the party until she tripped on one of the long ribbons hanging from the front of her bodice and fell, narrowly avoiding hitting her head on a silver fire grate thanks to a certain Monsieur Clérambault, one of King Louis' musicians, who had the presence of mind to catch her before any serious damage was done. Henrietta was very much shaken by the incident and took to her bed for over a week afterwards, terrified that she might have accidentally done some damage to her baby. Fortunately, all was well and by the end of February 1664 she was back on her feet again, much to the relief of her brother, who wrote to say that he 'was in great paine to heare of the fall you had, least it might have done you prejudice, in the condition you are in, but I was as glad to find by your letter, that it had done you no harm.' For the rest of her pregnancy, Henrietta felt well enough to involve herself in Charles'

Right: 'The Greate Peece': Charles I, Henrietta Maria and their Two Eldest Children, Anthony Van Dyck, 1631–2. (*Royal Collection Trust / © Her Majesty Queen Elizabeth II 2017*)

Below: The Five Eldest Children of Charles I and Henrietta Maria, Anthony Van Dyck, 1637. (*Royal Collection Trust / © Her Majesty Queen Elizabeth II 2017*)

Charles I at his Trial, Edward Bower, 1649. (*Royal Collection Trust / © Her Majesty Queen Elizabeth II 2017*)

Henrietta Maria, Studio of Anthony Van Dyck, c.1633. (*Royal Collection Trust / © Her Majesty Queen Elizabeth II 2017*)

The Execution of Charles I, 1649. (*Royal Collection Trust / © Her Majesty Queen Elizabeth II 2017*)

Oatlands Palace, Surrey, 1548. (*Royal Collection Trust / © Her Majesty Queen Elizabeth II 2017*)

Anne of Austria, Queen of France, Jean Petitot, c.1643. (*Royal Collection Trust / © Her Majesty Queen Elizabeth II 2017*)

Louvre Palace in the 17th Century, Jacques Rigaud, 1729. (*Metropolitan Museum of Art, New York*)

VÛE DE LA GRANDE FACADE DU VIEUX LOUVRE.

Palais Royal in the 17th Century, Stefano della Bella, c.1649. (*Metropolitan Museum of Art, New York*)

Anne Marie Louise de Bourbon, Peter van Schuppen, 1666. (*Royal Collection Trust / © Her Majesty Queen Elizabeth II 2017*)

Henrietta Anne, Anonymous, c.1660. (*Royal Collection Trust /
© Her Majesty Queen Elizabeth II 2017*)

The widowed Henrietta Maria,
William Faithorne, c.1649. (*Royal
Collection Trust / © Her Majesty
Queen Elizabeth II 2017*)

The young Charles II, c.1649. (*Royal Collection Trust /© Her Majesty Queen Elizabeth II 2017*)

CAROLVS II. MAG. BRIT. FRA.
ET HIBERNIÆ. REX.

Prince Henry, Duke of Gloucester, British School, c.1650. (*Royal Collection Trust / © Her Majesty Queen Elizabeth II 2017*)

Prince James, Duke of York,
Sir Peter Lely, c.1665. (*Royal
Collection Trust / © Her Majesty
Queen Elizabeth II 2017*)

Princess Mary, Princess of Orange,
Adriaen Hanneman, 1660. (*Royal
Collection Trust / © Her Majesty
Queen Elizabeth II 2017*)

LA GLOIRE DE LA FRANCE.

LE ROY   M. LE DVC DANIOV

Délices des humains, Prince Auguste et charmant,   Frere vnique du Roy, nous esperons qu'un jour,   Et quayant tout vaincu par force ou par amour
Si desja tout pompeux vous marchez en campagne.   Vous mettrez les françois dans le rauissement.   Vous combattrez sous luy comme vn foudre de guerre.   Entre vous deux enfin vous partirez la Terre
                                                        Et settrez; loffroy dans le sein de l'Espagne.

PHILIPPE DE BOVRBON   DVC DORLEANS, Frere
Vnique du Roy, Fils de Louis XIII   Roy de France et de Nauarre, et
et d'Anne d'Austriche Naequit à St   Germain en Laye le 21.Septbre 1640
et a Espouse Henriette Stuard   Fille de Charles Stuard Roy d'An =
gleterre le 31.mars 1661, Laquelle est decedée à S.Cloud le 29.Iuin 1670 ·

A Paris chez P.Bertrand Rue St Iacques a la Pomme d'or Proche St Seuerin.   Auec Priuil. du Roy.

Henrietta Anne, Jean Petitot, c.1660. (*Royal Collection Trust /
© Her Majesty Queen Elizabeth II 2017*)

Phillip Duke of Anjon and his Princes.

Philippe and
Henrietta Anne,
c.1661. (*Royal
Collection Trust /
© Her Majesty Queen
Elizabeth II 2017*)

Left: Philippe, Duc d'Orléans, Francois de Poilly, c.1650. (*Royal Collection Trust / © Her Majesty Queen Elizabeth II 2017*)

Below: The young Louis XIV, Robert Nanteuil, 1661. (*Metropolitan Museum of Art, New York*)

Above: Charles II enthroned, John Michael Wright, c.1676. (*Royal Collection Trust / © Her Majesty Queen Elizabeth II 2017*)

Maria Theresa of Austria, Queen of France, after Nicolas Mignard, 1664. (*Royal Collection Trust / © Her Majesty Queen Elizabeth II 2017*)

Henrietta Anne, French School, c.1665. (*Royal Collection Trust / © Her Majesty Queen Elizabeth II 2017*)

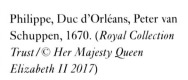

Philippe, Duc d'Orléans, Peter van Schuppen, 1670. (*Royal Collection Trust / © Her Majesty Queen Elizabeth II 2017*)

Saint Cloud, Victor Jean Nicolle. (*Metropolitan Museum of Art, New York*)

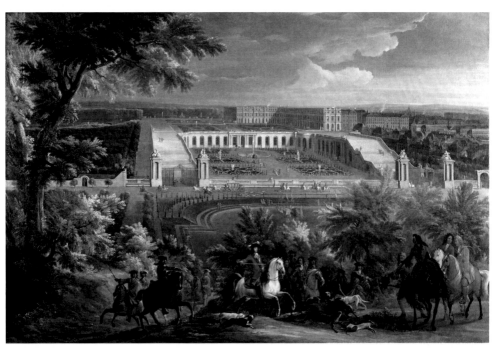

A Stag Hunt at Versailles, Jean–Baptiste Martin, c.1700. (*Royal Collection Trust/© Her Majesty Queen Elizabeth II 2017*)

Saint Cloud, William Wyld, 1855. (*Royal Collection Trust /© Her Majesty Queen Elizabeth II 2017*)

Anne of York, painted during her time in Henrietta's household, French School, c.1668. (*Royal Collection Trust /© Her Majesty Queen Elizabeth II 2017*)

Henrietta Anne, Nicolas de Larmessin, c.1661. (*Royal Collection Trust/© Her Majesty Queen Elizabeth II 2017*)

Henrietta Anne and her eldest daughter Anne Marie d'Orléans, engraving after a lost original portrait, 1841. (*Royal Collection Trust/© Her Majesty Queen Elizabeth II 2017*)

Jacques-Bénigne Bossuet, Robert Nanteuil, 1674. (*Metropolitan Museum of Art, New York*)

negotiations with the French over his impending war against the Dutch as well as petty issues caused by the new French Ambassador to London, the Comte de Comminges, who made few friends with his haughty, snobbish ways. Lord Holles, the new English Ambassador to the French court was just as troublesome however. Henrietta spent just as much time ironing out the issues that his incompetence caused, emboldened by the fact that her brother had secretly informed her that he considered her to be his actual ambassador to Louis' court as she was by far a better statesman than poor, bumbling Holles, who was almost pathetically grateful to her for sorting out his many mistakes and for easing his passage through the often tricky world of the Sun King's court.

Henrietta's daughter, Marie Louise, had turned two in March 1664 and was a most delightful and mischievous child. Her mother's initial apathy had long since vanished and she now absolutely adored her little girl, whose charm and dark, sparkling eyes reminded her of Charles. When she wrote to inform him of this, he replied that he hoped:

'it is but in a compliment to me, when you say my niece is so like me, for I never thought my face was even so much as intended for a beauty. I wish, with all my heart, I could see her, for at this distance I love her.'

The bright and lively little girl was absolutely idolised by Philippe, who even had himself painted proudly holding a portrait of her. Marie Louise was also adored by Queen Anne, who took a particular interest in her wellbeing and in fact took over her upbringing at this time. It was noted at court that King Louis also showed particular favour to Marie Louise, adding fuel to the inevitable rumours, which were almost certainly false, that he and not Philippe was the little girl's true father. It's more likely though that Louis was simply taken by her dark haired prettiness and sparkling personality, which were so very different from the fair haired, dull, stolidity of his own son, the Dauphin.

Henrietta's baby was due at the end of June but eventually surprised everyone, as second babies are wont to do, by waiting until 16 July to make an appearance after a labour that lasted less than an hour. To the great delight of the proud parents, their family and most of the court, the new baby was a splendid boy, who was christened Philippe Charles and given the grand old title of Duc de Valois. Philippe wasted little time before writing to Charles, who was to be the child's godfather, to announce the birth, Henrietta obviously being too preoccupied to immediately do so herself:

'I should fail in the duty which I owe Your Majesty, if I did not hasten to inform you, that your sister was this morning safely delivered of a very fine boy. The child seems to be in excellent health, and will, I hope, grow up worthy of your Majesty's friendship, which I ask you to bestow upon him. I wish you the same joy with all my heart.'

His brother Louis, who was pleased to see the Bourbon dynasty strengthened by the birth of another boy as his own only son was worryingly sickly, also wrote to Charles straight away:

'We have this morning received the accomplishment of our wishes, in the birth of a son, whom it has pleased God to give my brother; and what renders this blessing the more complete is the favourable state of health of both mother and child. With all my heart I congratulate Your Majesty, and to understand my joy, you need only be pleased to consider the greatness of your own, for my tenderness towards my brother and sister is not less even than that of your Majesty.'

Although this should have been one of the happiest and most contented times of her life, Henrietta had barely recovered from childbirth before she found herself embroiled in yet another tiresome court drama. She had become quite friendly with Olympe Mancini, Comtesse de Soissons, over the past few years and so probably was not too surprised when the Comtesse, who had fallen seriously ill and was confined to her bed, asked her to visit. Always warm hearted and keen to do her friends a service, Henrietta went at once to the Comtesse's Paris residence, to find Olympe, who believed that she was close to dying, in a contrite and confessional mood. To Henrietta's astonishment, the other woman began to pour out a full account of Vardes' iniquity and her own collusion in his plans to destroy both Henrietta and Guiche, who was still banned from the court and currently fighting with the Polish army. To Henrietta's horror, Olympe revealed that Vardes had been writing to Guiche and making up all sorts of stories about her various flirtations, even embellishing some of them to make it seem as though she was actively taking lovers and had completely forgotten about the unfortunate young Comte, who had been exiled because of his love for her. This was all bad enough but worse still and even more dangerous was the revelation that Vardes had secretly gone to Louis and informed him that Henrietta's letters to Charles, many of which she could not deny that he had seen when they were still close friends, were treacherous and revealed French state secrets as well as discussing Louis in the most belittling manner.

When Vardes inevitably heard that Olympe had told Henrietta everything, he immediately hastened to the Palais Royal and begged for one final interview. Henrietta really should have refused to see him but once again her soft heart got the better of her judgement and she allowed Vardes into her presence, whereupon he immediately threw himself at her feet and begged for her forgiveness. He even managed to squeeze out a few tears but Henrietta, who had turned twenty in June 1664, had grown up a lot over the last twelve months and gave his tearful excuses very short shrift, whereas once upon a time she might well have believed everything that he said. Realising that his theatrics were having no effect, Vardes then tried to give Henrietta a letter that had allegedly been entrusted to him by the Comte de Guiche. Although she no doubt longed to take it, especially as news that the Comte had been severely injured and lost three fingers while fighting in Poland had just arrived in Paris, she distrusted Vardes so much by now that she refused to accept it and immediately ordered him out of her rooms, never to return. Naturally fearing that the wily and malicious Vardes would go to Louis with yet another pack of lies, Henrietta then hastened across to the Louvre, determined to get her version of events in first before Vardes could completely destroy her reputation. Luckily, she managed to get to Louis before the Marquis and, relieved to find him inclined to be sympathetic to her plight, poured the whole sorry tale out, sparing herself none of the blame but making sure that he knew that the true villain of the piece was Vardes. Moved by her obvious distress and convinced by her sincerity and frankness, Louis assured Henrietta that she could rely on him to deal with Vardes and would no longer pay the slightest bit of attention to his lies.

In the meantime, the injured Guiche was on his way back to Paris from Poland. As a favour to his father, the venerable old Duc de Gramont, Louis had agreed to allow the Comte to return to court so long as he promised not to see Henrietta or attempt to contact her in any way. Guiche had been absent from court for over two years and much had happened in that time. Henrietta was now the mother of two children and thanks to the unhappiness of her marriage and the sorrow of losing a pregnancy, had lost much of the youthful bloom that had attracted so many admirers to her in the past. Meanwhile, Guiche had been distinguishing himself in the Polish army – the handsome playboy had turned out to be a truly courageous soldier with the gift of inspiring loyalty in his men. Although his wife, who disliked him intensely, was less than thrilled to have him back in Paris again, Henrietta was delighted to hear of his return, even if they were not allowed to meet. Naturally, Guiche did his best to contravene the terms of his return by trying to contact Henrietta and arrange a clandestine meeting but she dutifully refused to either see him or accept his notes. Somehow though, despite the best efforts of Henrietta and Louis to keep it quiet, the sordid tale of Vardes' failed seduction of Henrietta and subsequent attempts to ruin her reputation and closest relationships reached Guiche's ears and the hot-headed young Comte immediately went off and challenged his former friend to a duel. This rash action might well have made everything much worse and caused an enormous scandal had Guiche's father not intervened and had his troublesome eldest son sent back to his regiment in Nancy before matters got dangerously out of hand.

After Guiche had left Paris, Henrietta gladly accepted an invitation to spend some time with Louis and Maria Theresa at the Château de Vincennes on the outskirts of Paris, while Philippe and their two children remained at the Palais Royal. Maria Theresa was pregnant again and as her last baby had died, the court physicians had advised that she should have plenty of rest and Henrietta was yet again deputised to act as hostess in her stead. While at Vincennes, Henrietta was visited by her brother's ambassador Lord Holles, who reported back that Henrietta:

'looks as well as ever I saw her look in my life, that is as well as possible; and is grown so fat, that my compliment to her yesterday was, it was well she had good witnesses, else nobody would believe she had brought forth such a lusty young duke, to see her in so good plight so soon, and the young duke is as lusty and fine a child as ever I saw.'

She rejoined her family again at the start of autumn for a month-long visit to their château at Villers-Cotterêts in the Aisne region of northern France. This lovely old Renaissance palace had been a favourite residence of François I but was not much liked by Henrietta, who no doubt thought that it was a little too far away from Paris for comfort, especially as Philippe was also accompanied as always by his usual annoying gaggle of handsome young men. Isolated from her own friends, lonely and rather bored, Henrietta began to lose weight and became so run down and miserable that her physicians recommended a diet of goat's milk to build up her strength. Thanks to their ministrations, she was well enough towards the end of their stay to entertain Louis, Maria Theresa and some favoured courtiers at the château, treating them to an opulent fête, crowned by a special performance of the new comedy *Tartuffe* by Henrietta's favourite playwright Molière, with whom she was so friendly that she had agreed to be godmother to his eldest son Louis in February 1664.

Chapter Eleven

War

1664–1666

During the last few months of 1664, Henrietta was much preoccupied with the threatened war between the English and Dutch and it is a testament to both her intelligence and the absolute trust that her brother had in her that he felt able to write to her with astonishing frankness about the impending crisis, telling her that he would do:

> 'what is wise and best for the honour and good of England and will be very steady in what I resolve, and if I be forced to a war, I shall be ready with as good ships and men as ever was seen, and leave the success to God.'

As would later happen with the First World War, this conflict looked set to become something of a personal family issue for Charles and Henrietta as their thirteen-year-old nephew, William, Prince of Orange, was at least the nominal ruler of Holland, although as a minor his hands were tied in this conflict, which was directed by the States of Holland, and both sides were actively engaged in scrambling to enlist the support of King Louis, who was also related to all concerned. He had signed a treaty with the Dutch in 1662 which promised military assistance if they went to war but naturally both Charles and Henrietta, who had close personal ties to Louis, hoped that he would go back on his word and instead back England. Such delicate negotiations could clearly not be trusted to the bumbling and easily offended Lord Holles and so it fell to Henrietta to act as a go between for her brother and Louis during this difficult time.

'I have shown your last letter to the King [Louis] who commanded me to tell you in reply to what you write to me concerning the Dutch that if you are willing to treat his subjects in England like the English he will consent to do the same for the English in France except for the 50 sols [a tax of 50 sold per ton imposed on all foreign ships coming in to French ports]. I am not clever enough to understand what this means, but they are the very words which the King told me to repeat to you. If this is what you want, reply as soon as you can, for if you do not quickly end all this, you will not gain time, as you both appear to wish, and this will drag on to infinite lengths!'

Henrietta may have been very self-effacing about her political acumen but it is clear from her letters that she relished this chance to involve herself in state affairs and dabble in the fine art of courtly diplomacy, a skill that she was proving particularly adept at, to the great pride of her brother. In October she accompanied Louis and his entourage to Versailles, which was still the grandest building site in Europe, and while there she continued to subtly work on her brother-in-law, who certainly seemed inclined at that time to favour his English relatives over his agreement with the Dutch. However, as both Henrietta and Charles knew to their cost, Louis had previous form for saying one thing then doing quite another and so absolutely nothing could be certain until he made a decisive move to support them. Henrietta was keen to encourage Charles and Louis to come to a secret agreement, recognising that it would injure Louis' honour to publicly break his agreement with the Dutch and urged her brother to:

'lose no time in obtaining a promise from the King not to help the Dutch. You understand that he cannot bind himself publicly, owing to his engagements with them, although we all know these are only worth what he chooses to make them. For, as with everything else in this world, it is necessary to keep up a good appearance. You must, therefore, content yourself with a private agreement, which is likely in fact to be more lasting, and I promise to see that this is done in good faith, for I fear the contrary so much.'

The secret discussions between Henrietta and Louis were briefly interrupted in November by the sudden illness of Maria Theresa, who was eight months pregnant. Henrietta reported to Charles that:

'The King seems much distressed, although we are assured there is no danger at present, either for her or her child. I think you had better send someone to inquire after her, for this is not a little illness which will be over today or tomorrow.'

Her gloomy prognosis turned out to be accurate for Maria Theresa's feverish state only worsened and a few days later she gave birth prematurely to yet another baby daughter, Marie Anne, who lived for just over a month. Henrietta wrote to let Charles know that:

'the Queen is much better, but as for the little Madame, she has suffered from such violent convulsions during the last ten days that her death is hourly expected, so the congratulations you are going to send on her birth will, I fear, have to be changed to condolences for her death.'

When she returned to Paris, Henrietta was delighted to make the acquaintance of a new arrival in the capital – Elizabeth Hamilton, Comtesse de Gramont, a beautiful and extremely vivacious Irish noblewoman who had married Guiche's half uncle, the Comte de Gramont in London earlier that year, disappointing several gentlemen, including Henrietta's brother James, in the process. Charles himself recommended Elizabeth to Henrietta, writing with his usual droll candour to say that:

'I cannot choose but again desire you to be kind to her, for besides the merit her family has, on both sides, she is as good a creature as ever lived. I believe she will pass for a handsome woman in France, though she has not yet, since her lying in, recovered what good shape she had before, and I am afraid never will.'

Naturally, Henrietta was thrilled to have a new friend, especially one that came so well recommended and who could furthermore give her much longed for news of her mother, brothers and other friends at the English court. However, this happiness was as usual tempered by the behaviour of the circle that surrounded her husband, which seemed to become increasingly vicious with each passing year as Henrietta's already scant influence over Philippe continued to decrease and theirs, in comparison, only became stronger. His latest favourite was the handsome but extremely ruthless and spiteful Chevalier de Lorraine, a younger brother of the Comte d'Armagnac, who had made such a nuisance of himself when he fell in love with Henrietta a few years earlier. The Chevalier was in no danger of falling for her charms however and having realised that the one sure way to lose Philippe's favour was to pay too much attention to his wife, he instead cultivated an air of hostile insolence whenever he found himself in her presence. Not that he was entirely immune to the allure of other female household members in the Palais Royal – he was conducting an affair with one of Henrietta's maids of honour, Françoise du Bois de Fiennes, daughter of the Comte de Chaumont.

On one occasion when the boastful Lorraine was regaling some of his equally dissolute friends with the sordid details of his latest rendezvous with Mademoiselle du Bois de Fiennes, Vardes, who was standing nearby, loudly chimed in with, 'I don't see why anyone would bother with the maid when any man can have the mistress whenever he likes'. Of course, this being the French court, it did not take long before his spiteful remark reached the ears of Henrietta, who was absolutely outraged and immediately hurried to tell Louis all about it, demanding that Vardes be disgraced and banished from court. However, before the king could do anything, Vardes, who this time realised that he had finally gone too far, surprised everyone by taking himself off to the Bastille and demanding to be imprisoned, pre-empting Louis' order for his arrest. When Vardes was released a few days later, he and his jubilant cronies spread it around court that his punishment had not been so very great because Louis himself could not deny that what he had said about Henrietta was true, which naturally sent her straight back to Louis' apartments again with another demand for Vardes' immediate banishment. When Louis hesitated, she wrote to her mother and brother in London, regaling them with the whole sorry tale and asking them to also urge her brother-in-law to do the right thing and send Vardes away from court for good:

'I will only say that the thing is so serious, I feel that it will influence all the rest of my life. If I cannot obtain my object, it will be a disgrace to feel that a private individual has been able to insult me with impunity, and if I do, it will be a warning to all the world in future, how they dare to attack me. I know that you were angry that he was not punished for the first affair, which makes me ask you this time to write a letter to the King, saying that although you feel sure he will give me every possible satisfaction, and finish as well as he has begun - for it will never do for us to let him see that we are displeased with him - yet, out of love for me you cannot help asking him to do so ... as I have already told you, it is a business which may have terrible consequences, if this man is not exiled. All France is interested in the result, so I am obliged to stand up for my honour, and leave you to judge what might happen.'

To Henrietta's great delight, Vardes was ordered to leave court and banished to his estates at Aigues-Mortes before her anguished letters had even arrived in London, and there he would remain for eighteen years before being allowed to return to Versailles, still wearing the exact same, now hilariously outmoded, clothes as he was wearing when he departed. 'When one has displeased your Majesty, one is not only wretched but ridiculous,' he informed the astonished king. Olympe, Comtesse de Soissons, was incensed when she was told of Vardes' banishment and forgetting her earlier pretence of cordiality towards Henrietta, decided to get her revenge by going to Louis, who must have been thoroughly fed up with all this tale telling by now, and telling him that she had it on good authority that Guiche and Henrietta had been conspiring together to forcibly seize Dunkirk and present it to Charles. Luckily, Louis had heard enough of Vardes' lies to be able to recognise one by now and sent the Comtesse packing as well. In truth, he had long since had enough of Olympe and her husband, who were a pair of inveterate trouble-makers, and had been looking for an excuse to banish them from court. Now that one presented itself, he wasted no time in sending them both off into exile to their estates in Champagne. They would be back eventually but for now Henrietta was free of two of the biggest thorns in her side and for the first time in years, she felt able to relax, relieved of the constant worry of what Vardes and Olympe were saying about her behind her back.

Her happiness was only increased by a chance encounter at a masked ball held by the Duchesse de Vieuville during the Christmas festivities. As Henrietta, heavily disguised beneath the traditional mask and cloak went up the stairs, she stumbled and might have fallen if not for the swift response of a passing gentleman, also masked, who caught her in his arms then pulled her even closer when he caught a whiff of the distinctive carnation scented hair pomade that she used on her ringlets and realised who she was. A second later, Henrietta noticed the gentleman's missing fingers and realised that after two years of separation, she was back in Guiche's arms once again. The two only had time to exchange a few hurried words before Philippe appeared and they were forced to part once again. It was to be the last time they ever spoke to each other as all of Guiche's subsequent attempts to meet her before he returned to his regiment were frustrated by Henrietta's determination to stick to her word and not see him again. On one occasion, the unfortunate lovesick Comte disguised himself as a servant in the Palais Royal livery and attempted to accost Henrietta when she was carried past in her sedan chair but was so overcome with nerves that he collapsed and fainted away before he could speak to her.

The departure from Paris of Guiche, Olympe and Vardes at the end of 1664 gave Henrietta a chance to take stock of her life and start again. She was only twenty, had already been married for three years, borne two children and lost another. Besides those two short romantic interludes with Louis and Guiche, she had never really known true happiness and thanks to the machinations of the Marquis de Vardes, she had experienced far too much of the ugly side of human nature. She was loved though, by her family and her many friends both in England and France, and now that her greatest enemy was banished had every hope that her life would be much happier and more carefree from now on:

'She lived on better terms with the Queen, her mother-in-law, and took her part in the necessary diversions of the Court, with no wish but to make herself pleasant to all, [her mother's friend Madame de Motteville recalled later on about this time] as she had much genius and penetration, and could talk well on every subject, those who had the honour of knowing her best, noticed that she was beginning to recognise, by her experience, how little the pleasures she had sought so eagerly, were capable of satisfying the human heart, but she hardly grasped the truth in all its fullness, as yet she only saw it dimly and from afar.'

At the very end of 1664, a great comet made an appearance in the skies over Europe, fascinating scientists, amateur astronomers (like Charles, who was very keen to get a good look at it), royals and commoners alike. To many it was a portent of disaster, presaging war, destruction, famine and death, while to others, including Charles, it was an omen of success and better times to come, encouraged by the fact that it was seen in the sky above Germany before the Turkish army was defeated at the Battle of St Gotthard:

'By the letters from Paris, I perceive that the blazing star hath been seen there likewise, [Charles wrote to Henrietta in December] I hope it will have the same effect here as that in Germany had, and then we shall beat our neighbouring Turks [the Dutch], as well as they beat theirs.'

Both Charles and Henrietta were much preoccupied at this time with the imminent war between the English and Dutch, with Henrietta continuing to act as a go-between for her brother and Louis, who was currently entertaining the Dutch ambassador, Van Benninghen, who had negotiated the 1662 treaty between France and Holland, in Paris and apparently on the most friendly terms with him. On Boxing Day, Charles wrote to his sister, enclosing:

'a printed paper, which will clearly inform you of the state of the quarrel between me and Holland, by which you will see that they are the aggressors and the breakers of the peace, and not we: I pray read it with care that you may be fully instructed, for I do not doubt but Van Benninghen will use all sorts of arts to make us seem the aggressors, and I would be glad that you might be able to answer anything that may be objected in that matter.'

The rest of his letter was taken up with yet more talk about the comet but it is clear that the Dutch crisis was very much on Charles' mind as 1664 came to an end and that he was becoming increasingly pessimistic both about his chances of enlisting Louis' support and also maintaining a long-term friendship with the French if they insisted upon taking the side of the Dutch. For now, all he could do was continue to press his case that the Dutch were the aggressors in this current crisis and as such had lost their right to Louis' support.

Naturally, Henrietta enthusiastically supported her brother in this, although her position was a precarious one. It would become still more difficult however if Louis insisted upon supporting the Dutch and relations between France and England broke down as a result. Like Charles, she was very well aware that Louis disliked the Dutch just as much as they did but at the age of just twenty-six, he was already an astute, pragmatic and dispassionate politician, motivated entirely by self-interest and, unlike the close-knit Stuarts, remarkably unsentimental about familial connections. Although both Charles and Henrietta proved themselves to be adept politicians, at heart they both believed that Louis' first loyalty should be to them, as close family members, rather than to the Dutch. Louis however was loyal only to his own interests and those of France and right now he was also playing a long game, waiting for his ailing father-in-law Philip IV of Spain to die so that he could lay claim to large chunks of the Spanish Netherlands, particularly in Flanders, nominally on behalf of his wife but really for himself. It would therefore suit him very well to have the Dutch occupied elsewhere in a war against the English when he was ready to make his move against them.

In the meantime, Louis continued to treat Henrietta with great affection, even asking her to take charge of the latest court ballet, a performance of *La Naissance de Vénus*, which was put on at the Palais Royal on 26 and 29 January and had music composed by Lully. Henrietta took the part of Venus with her husband playing the morning star, Phosphorus, and other starring roles taken by Madame de Montespan, Mademoiselle de Sévigné, the Comte d'Armagnac and the Duchesse de Bouillon, who was yet another one of the ubiquitous Mancini sisters. In the final act, Louis himself appeared as Alexander the Great, accompanied by Henrietta, this time in the guise of his consort Roxana. The ballet was an enormous success but Henrietta became very ill during rehearsals and for a while it was thought that she was suffering from exhaustion until it was revealed that she was actually pregnant again. Charles was delighted by the news and wrote to congratulate her that her 'indisposition of health is turned into a great belly' before adding that:

'I hope you will have better luck with it than the Duchess (of York) here had, who was brought to bed, Monday last, of a girl. One part I shall wish you to have, which is that you may have as easy a labour, for she dispatched her business in little more than an hour. I am afraid that your shape is not so advantageously made for that convenience as hers is, however a boy will recompense two grunts more.'

Clearly Charles had forgotten that Henrietta's last labour had been as quick and easy as that of her sister-in-law Anne Hyde and had, moreover, resulted in the much longed for son.

On 4 March, Charles officially declared war on Holland, which naturally caused his sister much anxiety both about the outcome of this conflict and the effect that it would have upon English relations with the French. At the start of April, she wrote to tell Charles that she did not think it desirable for Louis to take the side of the Dutch and to ask of him if he could not:

'consider if some secret treaty could not be arranged, by which you could make sure of this, by giving a pledge on your paper that you would help in the business he will soon have in Flanders, now the King of Spain is ill, and which will certainly be opposed by the Dutch, but will not be contrary to your interests.'

Aware that she was taking a huge risk in daring to write to him in a way that could be massively misconstrued should her letter fall into the wrong hands, she then went on to adjure him to:

'think this over well, I beg of you, but never let anyone know that I was the first to mention it to you, only remember that there is no one in the world who would so willingly serve you, or who wishes for your welfare as heartily as I do. My enemies here look so suspiciously on all I do, that soon I shall hardly venture to speak your affairs! So, when you wish me to say something, send me word, and when I have a message to give from you, I shall have a right to speak on the subject.'

The unnamed enemies that she mentions in this letter were her own husband Philippe, who was extremely resentful of the time she spent closeted alone with his brother and the confidence that both Charles and Louis had in her diplomatic acumen, and his friends, who were keen to seize on anything that might discredit Henrietta in the eyes of the king. Certainly, she was very afraid at this time that her letters to Charles were being opened and read by hostile eyes and in May, wrote to warn her brother that their letters were being tampered with.

As the war with Holland advanced along with her pregnancy, Henrietta became increasingly anxious and dejected, both about the inevitable clash that would soon happen between the Dutch and English navy, the latter of which would be commanded by her brother James in his capacity as Lord High Admiral, and also her imminent childbirth, a prospect that struck dread into the hearts of most women of her time, no matter what their station might be. At the same time, Queen Anne's cancer worsened and the royal family were warned to prepare themselves for the worst as she was not expected to live for much longer. Henrietta had had her various clashes with Anne over the years, particularly about her relationship with Louis, but ultimately, she had known her for virtually her entire life and had, moreover, almost always experienced nothing but kindness and affection from her. Anne's illness therefore caused her a great deal of worry and she and Philippe, who was absolutely devoted to his mother, spent much of their time at her bedside, which at least distracted Henrietta a little from wondering what was happening at sea after the English fleet set sail at the end of May with the intention of taking on the Dutch navy.

At the beginning of June, the French merchants and pro-Dutch faction at the French court began to spread the news that the two sides had clashed on 3 June and the ensuing battle off the coast at Lowestoft had resulted in a terrible defeat for the English side, with James and many of his officers being blown into pieces along with their ship. When this entirely uncorroborated piece of gossip reached Henrietta's ears, she collapsed in shock and had to be taken to her bed in a state of hysterics. She was at Mass in the royal chapel at Saint Germain when the news broke that the battle had in fact resulted in a resounding victory for the English and that James, Duke of York was in fact alive and well, although sadly various other gentlemen that Henrietta knew personally had been killed in the action. On 22 June, she wrote a letter full of jubilant congratulations and wise advice, that belied her youth and comparative inexperience, to Charles, urging him to come to secret terms with Louis and bring the war to an end now that he had secured his victory against the Dutch:

'We cannot delay any longer, Monsieur and I, to send you this gentleman to congratulate you on your victory, and although I know you will easily believe my joy, I must tell you how much it has been increased, owing to the repeated frights we have had received from the false reports of the merchants, who all wish the Dutch well. But, on the other hand, the whole court and all the nobility appear most anxious to show that your interests are as dear to them as those of their own King. Never has such a crowd been seen here, as Monsieur and I have had to congratulate us on this occasion! And indeed you should be grateful to Monsieur for the interest which he has taken in the whole thing, and for the way in which he stands up for all that concerns you. The Comte de Gramont was the first to bring us the news yesterday. We were at Mass, and there was quite a sensation. The King himself called out to his ministers who were in the tribune: 'We must rejoice!' which I must say surprised me not a little, for although at the bottom of his heart he wishes you every possible success, I did not think he would care to declare this in public, owing to his engagements with the Dutch. But I hope that the result of this success will be to give you a second, by enabling you to bring the war to an end in so honourable a way that thirty more such victories would not add to your glory. I assure you this is the opinion of all your friends here, who are very numerous, and also that of common sense, since now you have shown, not only what your power is, and how dangerous is is to have you for an enemy, but have also made your subjects see how well you can defend their interests and greatness; you may now show the world that your true desire is for peace, and triumph by clemency as well as by force. For this is what gains hearts, and is no less remarkable in its way than the other, besides being a surer thing than trusting to the chances of war. And even if the results of a long war were certain, you will never be in a position to derive from advantage from success than you are at present, when you might win over people, who, I can assure you, ardently desire your friendship, and are in despair at feeling that their word is already pledged. I have spoken of this several times, and always find the King most reasonable, and since I do not think that your feelings have changed, I have good hopes of such a result as your best friends would desire. But if I am so strongly on the side of peace, do not think that it is from a sense of fear, as is the case with most women. I can assure you that I only desire your good, and since you have nothing more to win by force, you must seek glory in another way, and try to secure friends, of whom none can be more important than the King, without entering on a perpetual war of chicanery. This is what I most passionately desire.'

Sadly, on 9 July, while staying at Versailles, Henrietta went into labour and gave birth to a stillborn daughter, who was buried in the royal necropolis at Saint Denis. Completely devastated by the loss of her child and debilitated by what had been a lengthy and painful birth, Henrietta did not feel well enough to leave her bed for quite some time and, unsurprisingly, became very dejected. The arrival a few days later of Henrietta Maria, who was planning to reside in France for six months, did much to revive her spirits though and eventually she was sufficiently recovered to accompany her mother to Colombes for a period of gentle convalescence in the countryside while her husband went off with the rest of the court back to Saint Germain. Henrietta and her mother were visited by King Louis, who rode over to privately discuss the Dutch crisis with them both. As Charles was still refusing to end hostilities with the Dutch, relations between England and France, who were still pledged to assist Holland, were becoming increasingly strained, which would inevitably make life more difficult for Henrietta, especially if war should break out between the two. Not that Charles was unconcerned about the effect that his foreign policy would potentially have upon his sister – his letters show that he was deeply worried about her but also confident that she was well able to look after both her own interests and those of England should war break out.

Queen Anne's breast cancer took a turn for the worse at the end of 1665 and once again Henrietta found herself spending a great deal of time at her mother-in-law's bedside. The social whirl of the court went on as always though that Christmas and as usual she often found herself called upon to act as official court hostess instead of the retiring, sickly Maria Theresa, who was also in mourning for her father, Philip IV of Spain, who had finally passed away in September. One of the high points of the season was a splendid gala held by Henrietta and Philippe in the Palais Royal on the eve of the feast of Epiphany. The beautiful palace was illuminated by hundreds of candles and torches and the hostess, always very attractive, looked especially lovely that evening, although the most dazzling sight of the whole event was undoubtedly King Louis, who arrived dressed in beautiful violet velvet spangled with diamonds and pearls. The constant round of balls, concerts and entertainments did much to take Henrietta's mind off her worries about both Queen Anne and the threat of war breaking out between England and France, although she could do nothing about the increasingly tense atmosphere at court. On 5 January, the Venetian Ambassador to France reported to the Doge that:

'They are beginning to experience at Court the sorry preludes of the rupture with England. Madame, the sister of that king, become the object of unfriendly glances and the butt of bitter words, was able for some time to put up with the unpleasantness, rebutting the strokes with modesty and affecting deafness. But when the queen here spoke of the ill will of the English to this crown, a quarrel began between the two ladies. When Monsieur came in he said that his advice would be to wage war directly against Spain, the real root of these troubles. The queen could not stand this and ordered him out, Monsieur obeying her promptly.'

He added that King Louis had later attempted to comfort Henrietta but that:

'through distress and melancholy (she) has taken to her bed, rather from sickness of the spirit than from any physical ailment.'

In the middle of January, she was well enough to write to her brother to inform him that Philippe had written a long letter attempting to mediate between the two sides but that:

'as for me, I confess that I do not care to attempt what is useless, so that I only pray God to guide you in all your actions to do what is best.'

She also added that her mother-in-law was still very ill and that the court doctors were 'greatly alarmed' and in fact, by the time her letter arrived in London, Queen Anne was already dead. Philippe was at her side in her bedchamber in the Louvre palace when the end came just before dawn on 20 January and was absolutely devastated by her loss. He and Henrietta retired to Saint Cloud to mourn in private, only appearing in public again for the private interment of Queen Anne's heart at her beloved Val de Grace convent, which was followed by an opulent state funeral at Saint Denis on 12 February, during which Henrietta acted as chief mourner, wearing a seven-foot-long train. In her will, Anne had left the majority of her enormous fortune to her granddaughter, Marie Louise d'Orléans, who was now returned to the care of her parents, while Henrietta was the fortunate recipient of the crucifix that her mother-in-law had been holding when she died and much of her famous jewel collection, which included fabulous ropes of pearls, rubies and sapphires.

On 26 January and with a great public show of reluctance, Louis declared war on England, explaining that his agreement to support the Dutch still stood and that he could not find any just cause to abandon them. This was a terrible blow to Henrietta, who was devastated to see her adopted country at loggerheads with the land of her birth, while she herself would undoubtedly find herself caught between her brother and brother-in-law and would have to draw on her considerable diplomatic skills in order to navigate the potentially thorny situations that lay ahead, not least the questions that would now inevitably arise about where her own loyalties lay. There were more personal considerations too about how best to keep her correspondence with

Charles going now that their countries were at war. Charles wrote to her at the end of January, after war had been declared:

> 'I cannot tell what kind of correspondence we must keep with letters, now that France declares war with us. You must direct me in it, and I shall observe what you judge convenient for you, but nothing can make me lessen in the least degree, of that kindness I always have had for you, which I assure you is so rooted in my heart, as it will continue to the last moment of my life.'

Chapter Twelve

The Chevalier

1666–1668

1666, the *annus horribilis* of both Henrietta and Charles, started badly with the death of their aunt Queen Anne and the declaration of war between France and England, and would continue to get worse with each passing month. The only ray of hope on the horizon was the fact that the terrible plague that had swept through London the previous year was finally showing some signs of abating, although not before it claimed over 100,000 victims, a quarter of the capital's population, in just eighteen months. Paris was mercifully pestilence free but Henrietta still suffered vicariously along with her brother and his people. The Dutch crisis and subsequent declarations of war had reignited her hitherto latent patriotism and even though she had accumulatively spent less than three years in the country of her birth, at this low point in its fortunes, she still felt herself to be entirely English.

Another consequence of recent events was that Henrietta, previously dismissed as an utterly charming but ultimately ineffectual court butterfly, was now gaining a great deal of respect for her sharp intelligence, erudition and diplomatic abilities. Even the Venetian Ambassador wrote about her in the most admiring way, informing his master, the Doge that:

'Monsieur the king's brother is married to the sister of the King of England, a lady of high spirit, fit for every turn of affairs. He has a seat in the secret council and to him, before the others, they communicate the events and from him they receive advice. This serves not only to keep him detached and far from any turbulent humour, which might easily rise in this country, but also to conciliate a lady of a noble and masterful spirit, much inclined to authority and command. In the existing circumstances it is highly important to keep her satisfied and content.'

This vivid description of Henrietta is a marked contrast to the more fawning panegyrics of her friends both at court and in Parisian literary circles, which emphasise her sweet nature and that famously beguiling Stuart charm, and yet it is perhaps even more compelling, painting instead a picture of a confident and self-assured young woman who was finally beginning to come into her own and become a force to be reckoned with at the French court.

One such flattering description comes from the pen of Daniel de Cosnac, Bishop of Valence, who had officiated at Henrietta's wedding in 1661 in his capacity as Grand Almoner to her husband Philippe and over time had become one of her closest allies. He was to write of her that:

'Madame had a clear and strong intellect. She was full of good sense, and gifted with fine perception. Her soul was great and just. She always knew what she had to do, but did not always live up to her convictions either from natural indolence or else from a certain contempt for ordinary duties, which formed part of her character. Her whole conversation was filled with a sweetness which made her unlike all other royal personages. It was not that she had less majesty, but she was simpler, and touched you more easily, for, in spite of her divine qualities, she was the most human creature in the world. She seemed to lay hold of all hearts, instead of treating them as common property, and this naturally gave rise to a mistaken belief that she wished to please people of all kinds without distinction. As for the features of her countenance, they were exquisite. Her eyes were bright, without being fierce, her mouth was admirable, her nose perfect, a rare thing, since nature, unlike art, does its best in eyes and worst in noses. Her complexion was white and clear beyond words, her figure slight, and of middle height. The grace of her soul seemed to animate her whole being, down to the tips of her feet, and made her dance better than any woman I ever saw. As for the inexpressible charm which, strange to say, is so often given to persons of no position, 'ce je ne sais quoi', which goes straight to all hearts. I have often heard critics say that in Madame alone this gift was original, and that others only tried to copy her. In short, everyone who approached her agreed in this, that she was the most perfect of women.'

Cosnac's support became especially invaluable to Henrietta at the start of 1666 when he comforted her during her period of mourning for Queen Anne. He also retained a large amount of influence over her husband and took this opportunity to encourage the young Duc to mend his ways, turn his back on his dissolute friends, make peace with his wife and support his brother in any way he could. Philippe was two years old when his father died and unlike Louis, who seems to have found the lack of a paternal male influence liberating, had a tendency to strive for the approval of older males, such as Charles, Cardinal Mazarin and now Cosnac, who even induced him to take up the study of mathematics and at least attempt to give up his favourite pastime of gossiping with his wife's ladies in waiting. Inevitably though, Philippe quickly began to fall once again under the pernicious influence of his latest favourite, the Chevalier de Lorraine and within months most of his good intentions were forgotten and everything was back to normal once again at the Palais Royal.

Cosnac was to remain an invaluable ally to Henrietta though and when a libellous pamphlet entitled *Les Amours du Palais Royal* was anonymously printed in Holland, it was he who immediately despatched one of his subordinates to forcibly suppress its publication, then buy the entire first edition of 1,800 copies and bring them back to Paris, where they were all ceremoniously burnt to ashes in front of a gleeful and very thankful Henrietta. This spiteful and highly embellished piece of work professed to tell the true story of her doomed romance with the dashing Comte de Guiche and bore enough vague elements of the truth as to make it appear almost plausible. Although it was for a long time believed to be the work of Henrietta's friend Roger de Rabutin, Comte de Bussy, it was almost certainly authored by a certain Monsieur Malicorne, an old friend of Guiche's, who was now the lover of Henrietta's disgraced former maid-of-honour Mademoiselle de Montalais, who still retained the letters that she had stolen upon her dismissal from royal service a few years earlier and had almost certainly used them to add some credible colour to the booklet.

Although war was now inevitable, Henrietta and her mother were still doing their best to negotiate with Louis and in April, the three held a secret conference at Saint Germain along with the English Ambassador, Lord Holles and the French Secretary of State for Foreign Affairs, Hugues de Lionne. Although this meeting would ultimately be fruitless for all concerned, Henrietta and her mother refused to give up and would continue to mediate between the two and actively work towards reconciliation. Louis was particularly sorry not to be able to oblige his aunt as he was most sincerely fond of her and had over the years grown to regard her as another mother, whereas his feelings for Henrietta had become rather more distant over the months, thanks once again to yet another court drama involving her maid of honour, Louise de la Vallière, who was now quite visibly pregnant with his child, much to the disgust of Maria Theresa. The little Spanish Queen who had until now either been in total ignorance of his affair with Mademoiselle de la Vallière or had decided to turn a dignified blind eye, now suddenly demanded that Louise be dismissed from court. As Mademoiselle de la Vallière was still a part of Henrietta's household, the final decision rested with her and although she knew that Louis relied upon her to provide Louise with an official function that would keep her at court, she decided on this occasion to support her sister-in-law and ask for Mademoiselle de la Vallière's resignation. Louis was predictably furious and insisted that his mistress remain at court, which Henrietta was forced to comply with. Nonetheless, even though she did as he asked, thus disappointing Maria Theresa, Louis now became noticeably cooler towards her.

In July, the Venetian Ambassador reported to the Doge that Louis:

'recently entertained Monsieur, his brother, and Madame at a sumptuous banquet. He proposed to drink to the felicity of the Lords States and to the health of their Admiral Ruiter. Madame made no response, but with downcast eyes showed her disapproval. The King added that it behoved them to rejoice at the good fortune of their friends, the Dutch. Madame replied that she would always hear with pleasure of the felicity of France, but that she must always prefer England to Holland.'

In the same missive, Ambassador Giustinian also related a far more damaging allegation that Henrietta:

'receives letters from her brother every week in which biting remarks against the Dutch may be read, and in particular they deny the victory won by the latter over the English. By several letters scattered abroad and by false and made-up accounts they would like to misrepresent the issue. Madame takes care to avail herself of these and distributes them freely everywhere. The king complains about it. He has intimated that it would be better to retire to St. Cloud, than to fill the Court with lies. These altercations serve to bring to light personal sympathies and to disclose character.'

As her correspondence with Charles had been somewhat curtailed by the war, with none being sent or received between May and October of that year, it seems likely that the Venetian Ambassador was either exaggerating or misinformed. That Henrietta felt that she was caught between the two warring nations is undeniable though and this was to be a particularly awkward time for her, not least because she could no longer rely on her brother's support against Philippe and his cronies, who were making life as difficult as ever for her, despite the efforts of Cosnac to force Monsieur to be a better husband.

Philippe's infatuation with the handsome Chevalier de Lorraine was to become perhaps the most significant love affair that he ever had and the two men quickly became inseparable, with the Chevalier accompanying the couple wherever they went, much to Henrietta's discomfort. He had always been extremely insolent towards her but now he became absolutely hostile, making no effort to hide his hatred of her and even encouraging Philippe to be rude to her face, whereas before he had always treated his wife with at least some semblance of courtesy and respect. This was all rather easier to bear when they were residing in their Parisian residence, the Palais Royal, where at least she had her mother and friends nearby for support, but when they travelled to stay at one of their country residences, she had very few people around her that she could trust and consequently felt extremely isolated and less able to defend herself against the Chevalier's sly and bullying behaviour. It would perhaps have been easier for her if Philippe had agreed that they should discreetly live apart, as was the custom at the time in such cases, but he had somehow developed a weird and toxic possessiveness towards

Henrietta and so could not bear to let her out of his sight, while the mere suggestion that she might take another lover was enough to send him off into frightening paroxysms of jealous rage and make him threaten to have her packed off to the countryside for the rest of her days.

Nonetheless, although Philippe was completely besotted with his handsome Chevalier, Henrietta's regular pregnancies show that he was at least still doing his duty as a husband, even if his visits to her bedchamber were entirely perfunctory and begrudging. Philippe still adored their eldest child, Marie Louise, who was now a bright and lively six-year-old and by all accounts a bit of a handful, while her younger brother, the two-year-old Duc de Valois was an altogether more sweet-natured child and definitely his mother's favourite. After Queen Anne's death, Louis had suggested to Philippe that the little Duc be raised and educated alongside his first cousin, the Dauphin, a scheme that his ambitious and adoring parents had naturally agreed to with enormous enthusiasm. Louis' only legitimate child, the Dauphin was an extremely sickly boy, always coming down with colds and other ailments and not very bright either, much to the disappointment of his exacting father. If he died before producing an heir of his own then there was a very good chance that first Philippe and then the little Duc de Valois would eventually be called upon to mount the throne as Louis' successors, which rendered it imperative that Henrietta's son should have a suitably regal education to ready him for the great responsibility that might well lie ahead in his future.

It was a great shock to everyone, therefore, when the little Duc de Valois, who up until that point had been exceptionally sturdy, was taken seriously ill at the start of November. Henrietta was at Saint Germain, practising for the upcoming performance of Benserade, Lully and Molière's latest court entertainment, *Les Ballet des Muses* when her son's devoted governess, Madame de Saint-Chaumont, who was the aunt of the Comte de Guiche, sent a message from Saint Cloud to let her know that the boy had fallen ill with a fever. Extremely frightened by this news, Henrietta immediately abandoned the rehearsals and travelled post haste to her son's side. It was thought at the time that his fever was due to teething problems – a diagnosis that seemed justified when he began to recover after a few days of having his mother and governess fussing over him. When Henrietta returned to the

Palais Royal, she took her son with her and as soon as she felt certain that he had made a full recovery, she went back to Saint Germain on the evening of 2 December to take part in the first performance of the ballet. Louis had decreed that there were to be no *grand divertissement* for a year while the court was in mourning for his mother and as this performance would be the first such event in almost twelve months, it was to be especially spectacular. Henrietta took the part of a shepherdess, dressed in a delightful costume and carrying her favourite spaniel, Mimi, who is featured in at least two of her portraits by Mignard, in her arms. Alongside her danced Louise de la Vallière, now recovered from the birth of her daughter Marie Anne the previous October, and Athénaïs de Montespan, Henrietta's former friend, who was rumoured to be Louis' new mistress. Louis himself took the part of a shepherd, dancing opposite the three ladies and partnering each one, his past, present and future loves, in turn.

Although the *Ballet des Muses* was performed a few times more, this was destined to be Henrietta's final performance. The following day, she received a message from Madame de Saint-Chaumont, informing her that despite all her precautions, the Duc de Valois had caught a cold and was once again feverish and very ill. Greatly alarmed, both Henrietta and Philippe hurried back to Paris where they found their beloved son desperately sick and the royal physicians pessimistic about his chances of recovery. According to tradition, royal children were not baptised and officially given Christian names until they reached the age of twelve, instead going by their official titles, but when his son took a turn for the worse a few days later, Philippe insisted that the baptism could not be delayed any longer and it was duly performed by the deeply sorrowful Cosnac, in his capacity of Bishop of Valence, in the chapel of the Palais Royal on 7 December. The newly baptised Philippe Charles d'Orléans, Duc de Valois, died the following evening with both of his parents at his side. He was just two years old.

Everyone at court was deeply touched by the loss of Henrietta's son, who was felt to have been a most promising and delightful boy. Even Louis, usually so stoic about the death of close family members, was so distressed that it took him over a fortnight to pen a short and poignant note of condolence to Charles II, who had never met his sister's only son but was still utterly distraught to hear of his death.

'The common loss we have had at the death of my nephew the Duc de Valois touches us both so closely that the only difference in our mutual grief is that mine began a few days sooner than yours.'

Their countries were still at war but this shared sorrow did much to bring Louis and Charles closer together again, albeit temporarily. None of Henrietta's letters from this time have survived, but we know from contemporaries that she was completely devastated by her son's death. Once his small body had been laid to rest in the crypt of Saint Denis, she withdrew from court life for a period to mourn his loss, confiding only in her mother, the faithful Cosnac and Madame de Saint-Chaumont, who was a precious link to both her dead son and the absent Guiche, and as such was absolutely loathed by Philippe, who was desperate to find a reason to get rid of her. The realisation that she was pregnant again must have offered some bittersweet comfort as well.

Although their meetings were naturally tinged with sorrow, the secret gatherings to negotiate peace terms between England and France still continued throughout the spring of 1667. They were presided over by Henrietta Maria, who was authorised to act on her son's behalf and attended by Louis and Henrietta, who no doubt relished the opportunity to think about something other than her own troubles for a short time at least. The war was not going well for either side and as neither Louis nor Charles had the appetite to let it drag on for much longer, they were both keen to work out an honourable way out of it. Charles was particularly eager to bring it to an end as soon as possible – he had run out of money and the Great Fire that had destroyed much of London in September 1666 had had an extremely parlous effect on both morale and resources. In April, a secret treaty was signed by both cousins, effectively bringing the war to an end although the main official treaty was to be signed at Breda in July. The Dutch, getting wind of this new development, were naturally rather miffed to have been left out of the secret negotiations and also, quite rightly, fearful that, with the English as his allies, Louis would now go after the disputed territories in the Spanish Netherlands (effectively present day Belgium), which he insisted were his in lieu of the dowry of 500,000 gold écus that the Spanish had failed to pay as compensation for his wife Maria Theresa giving up her claim to the Spanish throne at the time of their marriage.

As the Dutch feared, within a month of the French and English making peace, the great Marshal Turenne, who was still the hero of Henrietta's brother James, was marching on the disputed territories with an army of 50,000 men, while Louis and another army headed for Peronne in northern France. Encouraged by Cosnac, who convinced him that proving his military prowess would impress his brother and also hoped that army life would curb his more markedly effeminate tendencies, Philippe also went to the front, where to everyone's surprise he managed to distinguish himself with his hitherto unexpected courage and leadership skills. As the French army made its way into the disputed territory, they encountered so little resistance that what was intended to be an invading force became more like a victory parade. Indeed, it was so lacking in dangerous encounters that Maria Theresa and various court ladies, including both Louise de la Vallière and her great rival Athénaïs de Montespan, decided to join them. Henrietta was not having an easy pregnancy and so decided to stay behind at Saint Cloud, where she eagerly kept up to date with the latest developments from the front, especially delighting in reports about her husband's bravery and popularity with the troops. However, although he even managed to impress Turenne with his military prowess, Philippe had quickly grown bored with army life and was keen to return to Paris. When Henrietta wrote to inform him that she was suffering a miscarriage, he jumped at the chance to leave his troops and gladly hurried back to her side, doubtless assuming that she would already be up and about again, only to find that she had lost so much blood that she had almost died and was still confined to her bed.

As soon as Henrietta was well enough to travel to Villers-Cotterêts with her mother for the summer, Philippe unwillingly returned to the army. Military life still bored him but the arrival of the Chevalier de Lorraine did much to reconcile him to his situation, although Cosnac was naturally horrified by the ridiculous way that they both cavorted about the camp and obviously spent their nights together. When Philippe joined Henrietta at Villers-Cotterêts later that summer, Lorraine turned up like a bad penny a few days later and she was unnerved to witness just how delighted her husband was to be reunited with the other man. When they returned to Paris, Lorraine went with them and was installed in his own apartments in the Palais Royal, where Philippe would spend hours closeted alone with him. It is impossible to know just how much Henrietta understood about the nature of her husband's obviously extremely close relationship with the Chevalier de Lorraine. Her upbringing had been very sheltered and although her mother may well have been aware of such matters, it seems likely that she would have done her best to ensure that Henrietta remained in absolute ignorance. On the other hand, she was no fool and must have realised that there was something peculiar about Philippe's friendship with the Chevalier de Lorraine. She was very well aware that her brothers and other male friends and relatives kept mistresses and was even able to frankly discuss these relationships in her letters to her brother – it must have occurred to her that her own husband apparently did not, as far as she knew, keep a mistress and that further, his close male friendships had a clearly amorous element about them.

Confused and distressed by the strange atmosphere that prevailed at the Palais Royal now that the Chevalier was permanently in residence and throwing his weight around more than ever, she turned to her friends Cosnac and Madame de Saint-Chaumont for support. Deeply suspicious about what was being said about him when the three of them got together and encouraged by the Chevalier, who was keen to oust his avowed enemy Cosnac from his position in the Orléans household, Philippe began to turn against his former mentor. Aware that his position was becoming more precarious with each passing day, Cosnac asked Henrietta to give him permission to withdraw back to his diocese, telling her that it was up to her to let him leave by the door before her husband threw him out of the window. Henrietta was so dependent upon him though that she refused to let him go and so the sorry situation continued, with Philippe and the Chevalier becoming increasingly hostile and vindictive towards both Cosnac and Henrietta. In the end, it was the Chevalier's clandestine relationship with Henrietta's maid of honour Mademoiselle du Bois de Fiennes that brought about Cosnac's downfall. When Philippe found out about this affair, he reacted with predictable fury and immediately dismissed the girl from his wife's service and threw her out of the Palais Royal. In her haste to be gone, Mademoiselle du Bois de Fiennes left behind a casket stuffed full of her love letters from the Chevalier, which quickly made its way into Henrietta's hands. Cosnac apparently stayed up all night reading the letters, which contained many unflattering remarks about both Henrietta and Philippe, before selecting the most incriminating to be shown to the king and returning the rest to Mademoiselle du Bois de Fiennes. When she realised that some of the letters were missing, she immediately alerted the Chevalier of their loss and he, in turn, went to Philippe, pre-emptively informing him that Cosnac was planning to cause trouble for them with Louis and insisting that he be dismissed at once, a request that Philippe was only too pleased to grant.

Henrietta was deeply upset by Cosnac's departure, feeling, quite rightly, that she had lost one of her most loyal and faithful supporters and was now even more at the mercy of the petty malice of Lorraine and her husband, who now set their sights on her other confidante, Madame de Saint-Chaumont. Luckily for Henrietta though, the fearless governess proved much more difficult to dislodge and she would remain with the household as an essential source of advice and support for her beleaguered mistress for a few more years. When Philippe and Lorraine's behaviour became intolerable to the point that it was actually abusive, she alone of Henrietta's friends was brave enough to risk incurring Philippe's wrath by begging Louis to intervene. Predictably, though, his remonstrations only made Philippe behave even more badly towards his wife, at one point even forcibly removing her to Villers-Cotterêts, and so in the end even Madame de Saint-Chaumont fell silent. Her stressful living situation was almost certainly a major contributor to the terrible, debilitating migraines that Henrietta suffered at the end of the year, which became so severe that her physicians prescribed a course of bleeding.

'Madame begs me to excuse her to you that she does not write, [Philippe wrote to Charles on 20 October] but for six days she has had headaches so violent that she has had her shutters always closed. She has been bled in the foot and has tried many other remedies, but they have not relieved her at all.'

At the start of 1668, Henrietta was much cheered up by the arrival of her nineteen year old nephew, James Scott, Duke of Monmouth, the illegitimate son of Charles and his former mistress Lucy Walter. Extremely handsome and replete with that infamous Stuart charm, James was a great success at the French court and even managed to win Philippe and Lorraine over, which, temporarily at least, made life much more bearable for Henrietta. Charles was keen that his son, of whom he was extremely proud, should acquire some Parisian polish and Henrietta wholeheartedly threw herself into this project, buying the boy new clothes from the most fashionable Parisian tailors, taking him with her wherever she went and introducing him into the very cream of French society with a series of balls held at the Palais Royal in his honour. 'I cannot enough thank you for your kindness to James,' Charles wrote to her on 4 February. 'I hope he is as sensible of your goodness to him as I am.' However, as always, it was only a matter of time before the Chevalier de Lorraine, who absolutely hated to see Henrietta happy and was also extremely jealous of Philippe's obvious liking for the handsome young duke, was doing his best to spoil things. When he noticed that Henrietta and her nephew were in the habit of speaking English together in private, doubtless because she was somewhat rusty and needed the practice, he convinced Philippe that they were conspiring together and even hinted that they might be having a clandestine, incestuous affair. After all, he reasoned, Henrietta was just five years older than her nephew and did he not strongly resemble her brother, the person that she loved most in all the world? Although his spiteful allegations were almost certainly false, they were enough to drive yet another wedge between husband and wife and sour the last precious weeks of James' visit.

Once again, Henrietta fell victim to another mysterious illness, this time of an intestinal nature which forced her to travel to her mother's favourite spa at Bourbon for treatment. When that failed, Charles sent over his own personal physician Dr Alexander Frazier, who brought with him a supply of pills made to a formula invented by the very same, but now sadly deceased, Dr Mayerne who had so begrudgingly overseen Henrietta's birth twenty-four years earlier. Although Charles had enough problems of his own to contend with, not least his recent romantic rejection by the beautiful Frances Stewart and yet another failed pregnancy with his wife Catherine, he still took the time to worry a great deal about his sister's poor health, writing in April to tell her that it was:

'a matter which I am more concerned with than anything in this world … I see by your letter … that you are consulting your health with a physician, which I have a very ill opinion of in that affair, which is yourself. I must confess I have not much better opinion of those you were governed by before, not believing they understood the disease you have so well as they do here. I have therefore sent Doctor Fraser to you, who I will dispatch tomorrow, who is well acquainted with the constitution of your body, and I believe is better versed in those kind of diseases, than any man in Paris, for those kind of obstructions are much more here than in France.'

It is not known precisely what ailed Henrietta in the spring of 1668 but it is possible that she was either suffering from a form of irritable bowel syndrome, provoked by the stressful nature of her living arrangements or that these were the first symptoms of the disease that would eventually take her life.

Whatever the cause of her illness, Henrietta had made a full recovery by the start of May, probably thanks to Mayerne's pills, although her mother tried to claim that her prayers had done the trick:

'I will not go about to decide the dispute between Mam's masses or Monsieur de Mayerne's pills, [Charles wrote to her in May] but I am sure the suddenness of your recovery is as near a miracle as anything can be, and though you find yourself very well now, for God's sake have a care of your diet, and believe the plainer your diet is, the better health you will have. Above all, have a care of strong broths and gravy in the morning.'

A month later he lifted her spirits still further by once again commending his son James to her care – the boy had obviously had such a good time in Paris during the previous visit that he decided to return again as soon as possible, although this was somewhat hard on his wife Anne, who had managed to fracture her thigh while dancing at a court ball and had to undergo the horror of having it set and then reset again a few days later with what Charles described to his sister as 'all the torture imaginable'. Although Henrietta welcomed James back with open arms, for she was genuinely extremely fond of her nephew, his presence did little to improve the grim atmosphere that hung over the Palais Royal as Philippe was still inclined to be jealous of the close relationship that they enjoyed. However, when Henrietta tried to explain this to her brother, he sagely referred to Philippe's behaviour as the result of a 'ridiculous fancy', before changing the subject to the happier one of the reunion that the siblings hoped to have later that year. Although Charles and Henrietta had maintained an affectionate and often astonishingly frank correspondence over the years, they had not actually set eyes on each other since the early spring of 1661, over seven years previously, and were longing to see each other again. However, they were continually being thwarted by war, political circumstances and the constant jealousy of the envious and peculiarly possessive Philippe, who could not bear the thought of Henrietta being the centre of attention at her brother's court.

The high point of her nephew James' visit to Paris was a trip to Versailles on the evening of 18 July for the splendid *Le Grand Divertissement Royal*, a night of magnificent and ruinously expensive entertainments ostensibly designed to celebrate the recent signing of the Treaty of Aix-la-Chapelle, which had ended the war between France and Spain, but actually being held to showcase the king's latest serious love affair with the fiery aristocratic beauty, Athénaïs de Montespan, whose years of scheming and throwing herself at him had finally paid off now that she had managed to supplant Louise de la Vallière as Louis' chief mistress. Poor Louise's star had well and truly fallen over the past few years and even Henrietta, who had reasonable cause to dislike her, must surely have pitied her former maid of honour, who had been emotionally bullied into acting as a decoy for her former lover's affair with the married Madame de Montespan, whose husband, unusually for the French court, was far from thrilled about the fact that his wife was sleeping with the king. On the plus side, Louise had been richly compensated for her years of faithful devotion with the title of Duchesse – an honour that the ambitious Athénaïs would never achieve thanks to her disgruntled husband's deliberate refusal to accept any ennoblement. Henrietta had once been very good friends with Athénaïs until the latter had been lured over to Philippe's camp and could therefore no longer be trusted. Her current ascendancy over Louis, who was completely infatuated with her, was no doubt extremely troubling to Henrietta, who relied upon her brother-in-law to keep her husband in check when his behaviour became so outrageously spiteful that even Louis, who normally tried his best to keep out of the marital disputes of his family and courtiers, could no longer turn a blind eye and was forced to intervene. However, now that he was apparently completely under the thrall of one of Philippe's closest female friends, it seemed entirely likely that he might no longer be quite so sympathetic to Henrietta's plight.

On that memorable July night though, Henrietta, her little daughter Marie Louise and James, who was due to return to England the following morning, arrived at Versailles determined to enjoy themselves and indeed it would have been impossible not to for Louis and his army of designers, musicians and writers had left nothing to chance and had managed to truly excel themselves. It would take a great deal to surpass the exquisite loveliness of the last extraordinarily lavish major court entertainment *Les Plaisirs de l'Ile Enchantée*, which was held at Versailles over six days in May 1664 and intended to honour Mademoiselle de la Vallière, but somehow they managed to achieve this in just one night of fireworks, music, dancing, theatre and feasting, all held in the magical new palace gardens. Louis had spent the enormous sum of 117,000 livres on the evening's entertainments, which began with a promenade around his new Dragon Pool followed by a sumptuous buffet dinner in the Star Grove, which had a giant marzipan palace as the centrepiece. After they had eaten, the six hundred fortunate guests climbed into their sedan chairs and went off to another grove where the Saturn Fountain now stands, decorated with tapestries and dozens of chandeliers and tented with a blue cloth spangled with gold fleur de lys, where they were treated to the first ever performance of Molière's *Georges Dandin*, a comedy about a peasant who marries a woman of a much higher social class than his own, only for it all to go horribly awry.

The play was followed by a wonderful supper, this time held in a large open air room at the future location of the Flora Fountain, where the ladies of the court sat down to eat at ten different tables. Henrietta and her daughter were seated at the Queen's table, which was reserved for the princesses of the blood. After this everyone promenaded to a vast outdoor ballroom, designed by Le Vau and decorated with porphyry, marble, gilt and crystal so that it gleamed in the soft amber light cast by the dozens of torches and candelabra that illuminated the space. The guests were now free to wander as they pleased through the beautiful avenues, groves and parterres, all of which were lit up with thousands of brightly coloured lanterns strung between the trees, while music played by the king's orchestras floated on the breeze. It was a truly magical evening and one that Henrietta and James, who was naturally agog and could hardly wait to tell his father Charles all about it, would remember for the rest of their lives. The crowning glory though came at the very end when the palace and its beautiful gardens were illuminated by an enormous firework display.

Chapter Thirteen

The Secret Treaty

1668–1670

'I take the occasion of this bearer to say some things to you, which I would not send by the post, [Charles wrote to his sister from Whitehall at the start of August 1668] and to tell you that I am very glad that Monsieur begins to be ashamed of his ridiculous fancies; you ought undoubtedly to over see what is past, so that, for the future, he will leave being of those fantastical humours, and I think the less eclairecissement there is upon such kind of matters, the better for his friend the Chevalier. I think you have taken a very good resolution not to live so with him, but that, when there offers a good occasion, you may ease yourself of such a rival, and by the character I have of him, there is hopes he will find out the occasion himself, which, for Monsieur's sake, I wish may be quickly.'

For some reason, perhaps as the result of yet another one of Louis' reprimands, Philippe's behaviour towards Henrietta had improved so much that she felt compelled to let her brother know, although clearly that of his constant companion, the Chevalier, still left something to be desired. The couple went together to Saint Cloud that year and while there, free for once from stress, Henrietta turned her thoughts to negotiating a closer relationship between her native country England and her adopted home, France. Although they were still at peace, it was an uneasy alliance and could, she felt, be even stronger - especially if her brother finally took the step of converting to the Catholic faith, which she knew that he had been secretly considering for some time.

Henrietta wrote to her brother from Saint Cloud towards the end of September:

'Following the promise I made to you to let you know my opinion and what I have been able to see in this important business I will tell you that the order into which the King [Louis] has put his finances has greatly increased his power and has put him more than ever in a position to make attacks on his neighbours, but so long as England and Holland are united they have nothing to fear from that quarter, and they can even protect their neighbours as they have been seen to do at the time of the last war in Flanders, when they became allied because they were indirectly interested in the preservation of that country.

'It is not surprising that the majority of people who do not know the inside of things judge that the safest part you can play would be not to enter into any alliance against Holland. But the matter takes on a very different aspect, firstly because you have need of France to ensure the success of the design about R [religion], and as there is very little likelihood of your obtaining what you desire from the King except on condition that you enter into a league with him against Holland. I think you must take this resolution, and when you have thought it well over you will find that besides the intention of R, your glory and your profit will coincide in this design. Indeed what is there more glorious and more profitable than to extend the confines of your kingdom beyond the sea and to become supreme in commerce, which is what your people most passionately desire and which will probably never occur so long as the Republic of Holland exists?'

Henrietta continued in this vein for several pages, exhorting her brother to publicly convert to Catholicism and return England to what she believed to be the one true religion, effectively tightening his bonds with Louis so that they could work together to bring about the downfall of the Protestant state of Holland, which was a constant thorn in the side of both of them.

Henrietta concluded her extraordinary letter, which amply demonstrates her sharp intelligence, devotion to her brother's interests and sophisticated grasp of diplomacy, with a graceful and self-deprecating apology, informing her brother that:

'I have become engaged in such a long discussion and my zeal has carried me so far that I no longer dare to direct this letter to you. I only venture to assure you that the same tenderness which leads me into arguments more serious than are becoming to me will always cause me to act in such a manner as to make you admit that there is no one who loves you so much as I.'

As both were aware that their correspondence was liable to be intercepted and read by unfriendly eyes, Charles suggested that they used a cypher in future and more than once, doubtless entirely unnecessarily for she was no fool, impressed upon his sister the need for absolute secrecy about their discussions. Over eight years had passed since Charles' triumphant restoration to the English throne and although he now felt secure enough to at least contemplate conversion to Catholicism, he was canny enough to be aware that such a move might well end in disaster, perhaps even another devastating civil war, and so he knew that he needed to tread carefully. At heart, he had always been deeply attracted to Catholicism and felt a connection to it, thanks to his mother and beloved sister Henrietta, that he did not feel for Protestantism. It is unlikely though that Charles ever really seriously considered restoring England to the Catholic faith, no matter how much he wanted peace with France and to please his sister. He must also have been aware that for all her astuteness and eagerness to foster a closer relationship between their two countries, Henrietta was fatally ignorant of how his people really felt about the French and had no idea just how much most of them loathed the very idea of Catholicism. Her love for England and its people was genuine but she knew next to nothing about them and, as was perhaps understandable for one who spent a great deal of time discussing philosophy and hypotheticals in the elegant drawing rooms of the Parisian *salonnières*, her concept of how this potentially devastating change of religion could potentially come about was based entirely on an absolute intellectual belief in the rightness of their plan and made no concessions at all for the emotional attachment that the English people felt for their way of doing things.

For several months, brother and sister played this diplomatic game, using a special code that assigned different numbers to various people and delighting in hoodwinking people like the Duke of Buckingham, Henrietta's vainglorious great admirer who was keen to be the one to broker a deal between France and England, and their mother's close friend and advisor Henry Jermyn, Earl of Saint Albans, who was not in on the secret but guessed from the many clandestine meetings at Colombes between Henrietta, her mother and Louis that something of great significance was afoot between them all. Even the new English Ambassador to Paris, Ralph Montagu, who was much liked by both Charles and Henrietta, especially since he had managed to negotiate a one off grant of £5,000 for the latter when her husband's extravagance left her perilously short of funds, was kept in the dark about the negotiations. Like all of Charles' other diplomatic envoys to France, Montagu was to form a very high opinion of Henrietta's abilities, writing to Charles' Secretary of State, Lord Arlington, whom, in contrast, Henrietta did not much like, that:

'You may give credit to Madame's intelligence, for some of the most understanding people of France apply themselves to Madame, having a great opinion of her discretion and judgement, and tell her all that they know; and it is not without reason they have that opinion of her, for she has them both in great perfection; besides in England you ought not to slight any advance that comes from her, because she is so truly, compassionately concerned for the King her brother.'

As usual, this period of *rapprochement* with her husband resulted in yet another pregnancy, which she announced to her brother in December, much to his annoyance for he was hoping that she would be able to travel to visit him the following year. As well as her new pregnancy, Henrietta was also somewhat preoccupied with yet another drama brewing in the Palais Royal, this time caused by the handsome younger son of the Duc de Montbazon, Louis de Rohan Guémené, who had been raised alongside King Louis as a child. Like many of the young men at court who were drawn to her delicate prettiness and abundant charm, the Chevalier de Rohan had admired Henrietta for quite some time and had furthermore decided that it was about time someone dealt with the Chevalier de Lorraine, whom he regarded, with good reason, as the sole author of her evident unhappiness. Being a rash and rather audacious young man, he decided that the best course of action was to pick a fight with Lorraine and challenge him to a duel – much to the horror of Henrietta, who was far from flattered and immediately went to Louis, who absolutely hated duelling, to beg him to intervene before there was a terrible scandal. Naturally, she badly wanted rid of the Chevalier de Lorraine as well, but was wise enough to know that this was not at all the way to go about it. Rohan was duly reprimanded but made sure that everyone at court knew that he had withdrawn his challenge under duress and that he was still prepared to die for Henrietta's cause, whether she wanted him to or not. Rohan's rashness would ultimately be the instrument of his downfall though and he would eventually be beheaded in 1674 for participating in a plot to remove his old playmate King Louis from the throne and replace him with his far more malleable son, the Dauphin.

Although she scared everyone by suffering a bad fall in April, the rest of Henrietta's latest pregnancy passed without incident and at Saint Cloud at midnight on 27 August 1669 she gave birth to a second daughter, who was christened Anne Marie in honour of her late mother-in-law. She had spent the pregnancy desperately praying that the new baby would be another little boy and fell into a deep state of depression when her hopes came to nothing. She had turned twenty-five in the middle of June and at that time had no reason to suppose that she did not have many years of childbearing left ahead of her, but with Philippe's behaviour worsening with each passing month as the Chevalier de Lorraine's influence over him grew, she no doubt assumed that it was only a matter of time before he entirely ceased to visit her bed. As if matters were not already bad enough, in the early hours of 10 September her husband visited her in her apartments, where she was still in bed recovering from the birth of her daughter and with admirable and unusual gentleness informed her that her beloved mother Henrietta Maria had been found dead that morning. The Dowager Queen had been ailing for some time, complaining of insomnia, dizzy spells, feverishness and terrible pains in her side but had resisted taking medical advice, telling everyone that she intended to retire to her convent at Chaillot and concentrate on the health of her soul rather than that of her body, until she paid a visit to Henrietta a few days before her baby was born and was persuaded to talk to the fashionable Parisian physicians patronised by her daughter and also King Louis' physician Dr Vallot about her symptoms. Dr Vallot assured Henrietta Maria, who after all was not yet sixty years old, that her illness was unlikely to be fatal and recommended that she take three grains of opium at night to help her sleep. Thanks to the advice of Dr de Mayerne, who was not a fan of narcotics, Henrietta Maria had always avoided taking opiates but after some discussion with her own doctor, who could see no harm in them, decided to see if they would alleviate her terrible insomnia. She dutifully swallowed the three grains, mixed in egg yolk to make them more palatable and then fell into a deep sleep, watched over by her own doctor who had agreed to stay with her. She never woke up again.

Henrietta was completely devastated by her mother's death, which worsened the depression that she had fallen into after the birth of her daughter. Her unhappiness was only increased by the behaviour of her husband, who had lost no time before laying claim to his mother-in-law's property, declaring that according to French law her goods belonged to Henrietta, as she was the only one of Henrietta Maria's remaining children who lived in the same country. The fact that the Dowager Queen had failed to write a will only complicated matters even further, although Henrietta did her best to defuse the situation by distancing herself from Philippe's avaricious actions and insisting that she would do nothing until she knew the wishes of her brother who was actually the legal beneficiary of their mother's estate. Charles was pleased to immediately bestow Colombes on his sister, along with most of its furniture and the amazing pearls that had been Henrietta Maria's pride and joy. To Philippe's great annoyance the splendid art collection, which had been collected by Charles I and included some real masterpieces, was crated up and shipped off to England to be added to the royal collection there. On the plus side, Henrietta and Philippe had a treasure restored to them in the person of their eldest daughter Marie Louise, who had been staying with her grandmother at Colombes at the time, keeping her four-year-old cousin, Lady Anne of York company. Lady Anne, the younger of the two daughters of Henrietta's brother James and his wife Anne Hyde, was in France in order to be treated by eye specialists in Paris – they failed to cure her but the three years that Anne spent in France first with her grandmother and then with her aunt Henrietta were to be invaluable in other ways.

The body of Henrietta Maria was buried alongside that of her father, Henri IV, in the royal necropolis of Saint Denis after lying in great state for six weeks on a black velvet dais in the centre of the nave. Her heart, at her request, was laid to rest in the chapel of the convent she had founded at Chaillot and it was there on 16 November that the entire court gathered to listen in rapt attention as the celebrated preacher Jacques-Bénigne Bossuet, who was said to be one of the greatest orators of the age, delivered Henrietta Maria's *oraison funèbre*, a magnificent and rousing piece of prose that struck the perfect balance between being a sermon and a panegyric about the Dowager Queen's life, qualities and achievements. Reminding the congregation that the marriage of Henrietta Maria and Charles I had been not just a romance but also a means of keeping the peace between the great nations of France and England, he then directly addressed their daughter Henrietta and her husband Philippe and extolled them to remember that it was their destiny to continue this great work and by uniting their blood, promote peace not just between their own native countries but throughout all Europe as well.

In the weeks after her mother's death, Henrietta remained in retirement at Saint Cloud while she struggled to reconcile herself to her great loss. She had the three little girls, her two daughters and her niece, to distract her from her sorrows and there were also frequent visits from her friend Madame de la Fayette, who took this opportunity to resume writing her biography of Henrietta's life, thinking that reminiscing and talking about the past would help her to come to terms with the death of her mother. The two young women had originally started working on this book a few years earlier but had been forced to put it aside because of time constraints – now though they had many spare hours to just sit in the gardens of Saint Cloud and talk. Although the majority of the book is Madame de la Fayette's work, Henrietta became so enthusiastic about the project that she insisted upon writing some of it herself. Another frequent visitor was the preacher Bossuet, who became a very dear and close friend of Henrietta's. They would spend hours talking together about religion, spirituality and philosophy and it was under his gentle direction that her faith, already very strong, became even more profound. 'I am afraid that I have thought too little of my soul,' she said sadly to him during one of their long conversations. 'If it is not too late, help me to find the way of salvation.' This, Bossuet, who cared very deeply about her, was only too happy to do and she would later commission a splendid emerald ring for him as a token of her sincere gratitude.

Her old friend Daniel de Cosnac, Bishop of Valence was also a comfort to her. Although he had been banished from court and she had been forbidden by Philippe to contact him in any way, she had resumed their correspondence that summer, using Madame de Saint-Chaumont as a go between, and heavily relied upon him for advice and succour, especially as he was very well aware of the terrible indignities that she endured at the hands of her husband and the Chevalier de Lorraine. In the wake of her mother's death, she obviously felt that she needed him more than ever and begged him to come to her as soon as possible so that they could meet in person and talk properly. She also asked him to bring with him the love letters from the Chevalier de Lorraine that he had extracted from the large collection amassed by Mademoiselle du Bois de Fiennes. Cosnac was naturally resistant, as he knew that Louis, who had banned him from entering Paris, would be deeply displeased if he ever found out about such a meeting but in the end was unable to resist Henrietta's pleadings and so he travelled to Paris in disguise in order to meet her after her mother's funeral. However, the unfortunate bishop was taken ill shortly after his arrival in the capital and was promptly arrested by Louis' secret police, who had been spying on him the entire time, and imprisoned before being exiled once again, only this time on much stricter terms. All of which, Philippe was delighted to be able to personally inform his wife about so he could enjoy her reaction first hand. Henrietta was horrified that such an indignity had befallen her old friend and entirely blamed herself as, after all it was she who had enticed him back to Paris. Worse was to come though as although Cosnac had managed in the nick of time to smuggle most of the papers that he brought with him out to Henrietta at the Palais Royal, several others had been seized at the time of his arrest. Amongst them was a compromising letter from Madame de Saint-Chaumont, the governess to the Orléans girls and one of Henrietta's closest friends.

Louis might well have overlooked this indiscretion on the part of the Orléans governess had she not fallen out with Athénaïs de Montespan, who was now agitating for her dismissal. Unable to refuse Montespan anything, aware that his brother Philippe would also be pleased to see the back of Saint-Chaumont and not a little suspicious that Henrietta might be plotting against him with her brother, he ordered Marshal Turenne to do his dirty work for him and sent him to Henrietta with the order that she must immediately dismiss her governess. All of Henrietta's arguments and pleading were in vain and Madame de Saint-Chaumont was duly sacked, to be replaced by Madame de Clérémbault, who was chosen by Philippe, rather than Madame de la Fayette, who would have been Henrietta's choice. Deeply distressed to have lost one of her closest confidantes, humiliated by the high handed behaviour of both Louis and her husband and infuriated by the spiteful behaviour of the Chevalier de Lorraine, who was going about Paris telling everyone that his credit with Philippe was so high that he was personally responsible for getting rid of her best friends and that Henrietta herself would be sent packing soon as well, she appealed to the English Ambassador Ralph Montagu to act on her behalf, which he duly did by writing an indignant letter to Charles, imploring him to finally take action before the situation in the Orléans household escalated into a diplomatic crisis between France and England:

'I suppose your Majesty has, by Madame's own letter ... had an account of the disgrace of Madame de St Chaumont, which has been done with so many unkind circumstances, and so little consideration of whose daughter and whose sister she is, that I do not see how your Majesty can avoid doing something that may show the world that you both intend to own her and right her when occasion shall serve, which will make them here for the future use her at another rate, when they see that your Majesty lays her concerns and interests to heart. By all the observation that I have made since I have been in this country, nobody can live with more discretion than Madame does both towards the King and Monsieur, and the rest of the world; but she is so greatly esteemed by everybody that I look upon that as partly the occasion of her being so ill used both by the King and her husband. To remedy this, I would humbly propose to your Majesty what Madame has already discoursed to me of, which is, that your Majesty would tell the French Ambassador in England that you know the Chevalier de Lorraine is the occasion of all the ill that your sister suffers, and that she is the one that you are so tender of that you cannot think the French King your friend, whilst he suffers such a man about his brother, by whose counsels he doth every day so many things to Madame's dissatisfaction.

'The King here is sufficiently convinced of all the impertinences and insolences of the Chevalier de Lorraine, and doth at this time both desire and stand in need so much of your friendship that I believe in a little time he may be brought to remove him from about Monsieur, if he sees it is a thing your Majesty really insists upon. If, Sir, you shall ever think fit to say this to the French Ambassador, at the same time a letter from you to the King here would be very necessary, with some instruction to me to speak to him in it too.

'In case your Majesty doth not approve of this way, nothing could be more for Madame's comfort, as well as credit, than that your Majesty should desire her to have her make a journey to you into England in the spring. I think there needs not many arguments to persuade your Majesty towards the seeing of one that you love so well. If you shall think this improper too, Madame would then desire that you would let fall to the French Ambassador that you are informed how unkindly she is used here, but that she has desired you to take no notice of it, but only, if you please, not live so freely, nor do the French Ambassador so much honour, as you use to do.

'Your Majesty may perhaps think me very impertinent for writing of this, but I assure you, Sir, not only all the French, but the Dutch, the Swedish, and Spanish Ministers are in expectation of what your Majesty will do in this business, for they all know that Madame is the thing in all the world that is dearest to you; and they whose interest it is to have your Majesty and the King here be upon ill terms, are very glad that he has done a thing which they think will anger you. I believe the King is now sorry that he has done this, though he be of a humour not to own it. This is a conjuncture of that consequence for the quiet and happiness of the rest of Madame's life, that I thought I should be wanting both in the duty I owe your Majesty and the zeal I have for her service, if I did not give you the best account I could of what concerns her, which I hope you will pardon.'

Although Charles had always been fairly sanguine about the unusual domestic arrangements in his sister's household and until now had considered the Chevalier de Lorraine to be relatively harmless, albeit extremely annoying, he was absolutely incensed to hear just how badly she was being bullied – especially at a time when she had just given birth and lost her mother all in the space of a few weeks and therefore ought to be treated with the greatest of care. It was Louis' behaviour that infuriated him most of all though as he could hardly believe that their cousin was so in thrall both to his brother and Madame de Montespan that he would allow himself to be manipulated to act against Henrietta, who was so absolutely necessary, and even more so now that their mother was dead, to the secret negotiations between their two countries. As Montagu had advised in his letter, Charles immediately demanded an audience with the French Ambassador, Charles Colbert, Marquis de Croissy, and furiously harangued him at great length about his sister's plight, ordering him to relay his anger back to his master Louis along with a demand that instant reparation be made to Henrietta for the insults that she had endured at his hands and those of Philippe and Lorraine, whose dismissal from the French court he also insisted upon. As Montagu had already predicted, Louis was no doubt already deeply regretting his actions when this choleric message arrived from England and immediately agreed that Lorraine would be dismissed as soon as the opportunity to do so arose. He had to tread carefully though as his brother's attachment to the Chevalier was absolute and he had no wish to either cause him pain or give him cause to blame Henrietta for Lorraine's departure, which would only end in more poor treatment.

He was unable to prevent word that Lorraine was on borrowed time leaking out into the court though and Philippe fell into a great panic when he realised that he and his favourite had gone too far this time and were in very real danger of being separated. Convincing himself that this was entirely Henrietta's fault, he informed her, through her confessor Father Pierre Zoccoli, that this was all her own doing and that if she did not make an effort to reconcile with Lorraine and let it be known both to Louis and her brother that she had done so then he would no longer visit her bed:

'He has long since lost the use of his native tongue, [Henrietta wrote to Cosnac at the end of December 1669] and can only speak in the language which has been taught to him by the Chevalier de Lorraine, whose will he follows blindly, and the worst is, I have no hope that he will ever mend his ways. You will understand how happy this certainty is likely to make me, and what hours I spend in bitter reflections! If the King keeps the promises [to remove Lorraine] which he daily repeats to me, I shall in future have less cause for annoyance, but you know how little I have learnt to trust such words … As for good Père Zoccoli, he implores me every day to be kind to the Chevalier de Lorraine, and blames me for refusing to receive his insincere advances. I tell him that, in order to like a man who is the cause of all my sorrows, past and present, I ought at least to have some esteem for him, or else owe him some debt of gratitude, both of which are absolutely impossible, after the way in which he has behaved.'

In the end, she did not have to do anything at all for it was Philippe himself who inadvertently brought about Lorraine's downfall by offering him the enormously valuable gift of the living of two abbeys that had just fallen vacant. However, when he asked Louis for the necessary permission to do so, he was astounded when his brother absolutely refused to hear of it, even going so far as to say that it was inappropriate for a person who lived as badly as the Chevalier did to receive any church funds. Philippe completely lost his temper with Louis, which almost never happened, and informed him that he never wanted to see him again before storming off to vent his rage at his favourite, who joined in with quite a few choice and unflattering remarks about the king as well. Unluckily for him, he was overheard and his comments were repeated to Louis, who immediately gave the order for his arrest, delighted to have an excuse to do so at last. When the Comte d'Ayen arrived to arrest the Chevalier, Philippe had hysterics then fainted dead away – his histrionics left Louis entirely unmoved though and, for now at least, the Chevalier was gone.

Unable to accept that he and Lorraine had been the authors of their own destruction, Philippe naturally found it much easier to blame Henrietta for everything and began to treat her even more badly than before. Nonetheless, Henrietta wrote jubilantly to Madame de Saint-Chaumont at the end of January 1670:

'You will need all your piety to enable you to resist the temptation, which the arrest of the Chevalier will arouse in you, to rejoice at the evil which has befallen your neighbour. You will soon hear how violently Monsieur has acted, and I am sure you will pity him in spite of the ill treatment which you have received at his hands. But, even if I had time to tell you all that has happened, I would prefer to speak of the injustice that you do me, in ever thinking that I can forget yo. I love you, and you must, I am sure, know this. I have never tried so hard to help anyone as I have tried to help you, and as often as ever you wish, I am ready to tell you that I care more for you than for any of my friends. After this, do not judge what I wish to do by what I can do, and believe that my only wish is to find out how to please you.'

Her delight was to be short lived though, for the very next day, Philippe declared that he was taking Henrietta away to Villers-Cotterêts, a château that she had never been very fond of and which was particularly bleak in the dead of winter, and that they were going to remain there in isolation until the Chevalier was released and restored to him. As she sadly wrote to her old friend Turenne before her departure:

'Things have come to such a pass that, unless the King detains us by much affection and a little force, we go today to Villers-Cotterêts, to return I know not when. You will understand what pain I feel from the step which Monsieur has taken, and how little compared with this I mind the weariness of the place, the unpleasantness of his company in his present mood, and a thousand other things of which I might complain. My only real cause of regret is having to leave my friends, and the fear I feel that the King may forget me. I know he will never have to complain of me, and all I ask him is to love me as well in my absence as if I were present with him.'

Henrietta was forced to remain in the countryside with her husband for almost a month, enduring his bad moods, spiteful comments and terrible temper tantrums, during which he relentlessly blamed her for the exile of his beloved Chevalier. His behaviour only got worse when his repeated pleas to Louis that Lorraine be released only resulted in his favourite being incarcerated in an even less salubrious prison and banned from sending or receiving any letters. As negotiations between Louis and Charles advanced at the start of 1670 it became more imperative than ever that Henrietta, who was essential to the success of their plans, was at liberty to return to Paris and, eventually, travel to England ostensibly to visit her brother but really to complete the negotiations and oversee the signing of their secret treaty. It was Louis' plan that Henrietta should make the journey across the Channel in the spring while the court was in Flanders inspecting the French crown's newly gained territories there, but as the weeks went by and Philippe showed no sign of relenting, it became increasingly imperative that he be cajoled into bringing her back to court again before this opportunity was missed and another had to be fabricated. To this end, Lord Falconbridge, the English Ambassador to Venice, Florence and Savoy and his secretary Doddington paid visits to Henrietta at Villers-Cotterêts, where they found her in unexpectedly good spirits and keen to talk both about her problems with Philippe and the issue of how to bring about her visit to England. Doddington reported to his superior after his visit in late February,:

'Madame received me with all imaginable kindness, much beyond what a man of my figure could pretend to, and did me the honour to give me a full hour's private discourse with her and, perceiving that I was not unacquainted with her affairs, and flattering herself that I had address enough, or, at least, inclination, to serve her, she was pleased to tell me she had designed to see the King, her brother, at Dover, as this Court passeth by Calais to Flanders; that this King [Louis] had received the motion with all kindness, and conceived the ways of inducing Monsieur to accomplish it, which was that both her brothers and my Lord of St Albans should write to Monsieur to that effect, which they had done; but the letters, coming hither a day or two after the Chevalier de Lorraine's disgrace, Monsieur fell into so ill a humour with Madame, even to parting of beds, that the King of France had commanded the letters should not be delivered to Monsieur, until he was better prepared to receive such a motion. That, since coming to Villers-Cotterêts, he began to come to himself, and that she thought, if the King of France approved of it, that the letters might now be delivered ... The King of France is extraordinary kind to Madame, and hath signified it sufficiently in all this affair of the Chevalier de Lorraine, who he disgraced on her account, and on hers also is is that Monsieur is now invited to Court, although he seems not to take notice of it. She is even adored by all here, and questionless, hath more spirit and conduct than even her mother had, and certainly is capable of the greatest matters.'

Lord Falconbridge's despatch from Villers-Cotterêts was also glowing with admiration for the winsome Henrietta:

'Madame's reception was obliging beyond expression. She has something of particular in all that she says or does that is very surprising. I found by her that, although Monsieur were at that time in better humour than he had of late been, yet he still lies apart from her; that she wanted not hopes of inducing his consent to her seeing of the King, my master, at Dover or Canterbury this spring, as this Court passes into Flanders, nor is this King (Louis) unwilling to second her desires in that particular; and, to say the truth, I find she has a very great influence in this Court, where they all adore her, as she deserves, being a princess of extraordinary address and conduct.'

The very next day, Louis' trusted Minister of Finances, Jean Baptiste Colbert, arrived with a veritable treasure trove of gifts for Henrietta, including jewels, diamond garters, scented gloves and 2,000 gold coins, which he pretended she had won as prizes in the annual court lottery but were in actuality intended to compensate for her poor treatment at his brother's hands. At this delicate stage, it was imperative that Philippe, always so quick to be roused to jealousy and so resentful of any sign that his wife was receiving more attention than himself, was kept in the dark about Henrietta's diplomatic importance and the true purpose of her planned visit to England. To that end, Colbert informed him that the Chevalier had been released from prison and instead sent into exile in Italy and that once he was there, they could resume their correspondence without hindrance.

Convinced that Louis' change of heart was entirely due to the affection that he had for himself and nothing to do with Henrietta, he allowed himself to be appeased by this and graciously agreed that Henrietta could return to Paris the following day, much to the joy of her friends, one of whom, Madame de Suze, had lamented during her absence that:

'Since Madame left us, joy is no longer seen at St Germain. Everyone here is very dull in Madame's absence, and unless she returns soon I cannot think what we shall do with ourselves. Nobody thinks of anything else but of writing to her, and the ladies of the Court are to be seen, pen in hand, at all hours of the day. She alone can bring us back the spring-time.'

Although her two English visitors had given the impression that Henrietta was as high spirited, beguiling and attractive as ever, her friends in Paris were struck by how ill and withdrawn she appeared when she returned from her exile in the countryside. Even her cousin Anne-Marie-Louise, who was by now very fond of her, was shocked by her altered appearance, the openly contemptuous manner in which her husband treated her even in public and the resigned and entirely uncomplaining way in which she seemed to accept this as her due. Henrietta had always had something of the long-suffering martyr about her, no doubt because of her often difficult upbringing, but she had at least been cheerful and good natured in her submissiveness to the extent that it only added to her charm. Now, however, she had the shrinking, constantly apprehensive nervousness that nowadays would characterise a victim of emotional abuse, which of course, is what she was even if it was not a complaint that was recognised at the time. She wrote to her friend Madame de Saint-Chaumont upon her return to court at the start of March:

'Monsieur still persists in believing that it is all my doing, and forms part of the promises which I made you. That is an honour of which I am unworthy, excepting so far as wishes go, and I was not guilty in this respect, if indeed it can be called guilt, to desire the ruin of a man, who has been the cause of all my troubles. In your piety, you seem to have ceased to wish for vengeance. That is a pitch of perfection to which

I confess I cannot attain, and I am glad to see a man, who had never done justice to anyone, get his deserts. The bad impression which he left on Monsieur's mind still lasts, and he never sees me without reproaches. The King has reconciled us, but since Monsieur cannot at present give the Chevalier the pensions which he desires, he sulks in my presence, and hopes that, by ill treating me, he will make me wish for the Chevalier's return. I have told him that this kind of conduct will never answer. He replies with those airs of his which you know well.'

Chapter Fourteen

Homeward Bound

1670

Plans for Henrietta's visit to England advanced through the spring of 1670, with both Louis and Charles being very careful to hide the true reason for her visit from everyone, even her husband, a notorious chatterbox who could not be trusted to keep any secrets at all, let alone one of such international importance. However, this naturally meant that there was no easy way of managing his petty little jealousies and demands, all of which were designed to ruin Henrietta's pleasure in the anticipated visit and perhaps even, he clearly hoped, cancel it completely. Philippe had always been insanely envious of the close relationship that his wife enjoyed with his brother and deeply resented any special attention that was paid to her, which he always felt was entirely at his own expense. Therefore, this current state of affairs, which involved Henrietta and Louis spending hours closeted alone together in a room near his own apartments in Saint Germain discussing the diplomatic aspects of her visit and the treaty that she would be secretly carrying with her, was deeply displeasing to him and it was no surprise to anyone when he eventually threw one of his tantrums and informed his brother that he absolutely refused to let Henrietta go. When Louis tried to appeal to his better nature, pointing out that almost ten years had passed since she last set eyes on her own brother, Philippe confounded him by insisting that in that case she could go but that he would be accompanying her. This was obviously better than nothing but even so, both Louis and Henrietta were horrified by the prospect of the woefully indiscreet and temperamental Philippe going with her to England, where he would doubtless ruin everything that they had worked so hard to achieve.

In the end the crisis was averted when Louis put his foot down and informed his brother that Henrietta would be making the journey alone but

Philippe still managed to extract a promise that the visit would last no more than three days and that she would not be allowed to visit London but instead remain in the vicinity of Dover, which even in the seventeenth century was hardly the most amusing spot on earth. There was no real reason for this last edict other than pure spite but they had no option but to acquiesce to his demands. Henrietta wrote to Madame de Saint-Chaumont from the Palais Royal at the end of March:

'All that Monsieur does, concerns me so nearly that it is impossible his actions should not fall back upon me. He has been very angry at the wish which the King, my brother, has expressed that I should go and see him. This has driven him to lengths which you would hardly believe, for, regardless of what the world may say, in his wrath against me, he declares aloud that I reproached him for the life he led with his favourite, and many other things of the kind, which have been very edifying hearing for our charitable neighbours. The King has worked hard to bring him to reason, but all in vain, for his only object in treating me so ill is to force me to ask favours for the Chevalier, and I am determined not to give in to blows. This state of things does not admit of any reconciliation, and Monsieur now refuses to come near me, and hardly ever speaks to me, which, in all the quarrels we have had, has never happened before ... I am, on the whole, content with what the King has hitherto done, but I see that, from the ashes of Monsieur's love for the Chevalier, as from the dragon's teeth, a whole brood of fresh favourites, are likely to spring up to vex me. Monsieur now puts his trust in the little Marsan and the Chevalier de Beuvron, not to speak of the false face of the Marquis de Villeroy, who prides himself on being his friend, and only seeks his own interests, regardless of those of Monsieur, or of the Chevalier. All I can do, is to spend the rest of my life in trying to undo the mischief which these gentlemen have done, without much hope of remedying the true evil that lies at the root of it all. You will understand how much patience I shall need for this, and I am quite surprised to find that I have any left, for the task is a very hard one. As for my journey to England, I do not despair that it may yet take place. If it does, it will be a great happiness for me.'

Perhaps the most remarkable thing about this correspondence is the clear affection and concern that Henrietta still, despite everything, felt for Philippe. They were still first cousins after all and had known each other for virtually their entire lives, growing up in fairly close quarters and playing together as children and if she could not love him in a romantic sense, she certainly cared a great deal about him, even to the extent of feeling genuinely sorry for him when the Chevalier was banished from court and worrying about the malign influence that his male companions were having upon him as they used him in order to serve their own selfish ends.

On 6 April, two days before the baptism of her infant daughter Anne Marie in the Palais Royal chapel where she had been married just over nine years earlier, Henrietta wrote to her friend that her husband:

'still declares that he cannot love me, unless his favourite is allowed to form a third in our union. Since then, I have made him understand that, however much I might desire the Chevalier's return, it would be impossible to obtain it, and he has given up the idea, but, by making a noise about my journey to England, he hopes to show that he is master, and can treat me as ill in the Chevalier's absence as in his presence. This being his policy, he began to speak openly of our quarrels, refusing to enter my room, and pretended to show that he could revenge himself for having been left in ignorance of these affairs, and make me suffer for what he calls the faults of the two Kings. However, after all this noise, he has thought fit to relent, and said he would make peace if I would make the first advances. This I have done gladly enough, through the Princesse Palatine [the widow of Henrietta's cousin Edward]. He accused me of saying a thousand extravagant things, which I should have been mad ever to dream of saying! I told him that he had been misinformed, but that I was ready to beg his pardon, even for what I had not said. Finally he became more tractable, and after many promises to forget the past, and live more happily in future, without even mentioning the Chevalier's name, he not only agreed that I should go to England, but proposed that he should go there too ... I will own to you that, however fair things appear outwardly, I do not always see the kindness which I hope for in certain quarters. When you think me happiest, I often meet with terrible disappointments, of which I tell no one, because it is of no use to complain, and, besides, I have no one whom I can speak to now.'

Although Henrietta's departure was certain and scheduled for the end of the month, Philippe still continued to make trouble for her right up to the time she was due to leave for England, even going to the lengths of resuming his visits to her bedchamber every night in the hopes that she might get pregnant and therefore not be able to travel. Although Louis was adamant that he would never give permission for the Chevalier to be given the rents from the two abbeys and had furthermore promised Henrietta that he would not be allowed to return to France for eight years, the infatuated Philippe still hoped that he could bully and intimidate his wife into forcing Louis to speed up his return. Henrietta wrote to Madame de Saint-Chaumont from Saint Germain in the middle of April:

'Although Monsieur is somewhat softened, he still tells me there is only one way in which I can show my love for him. Such a remedy [the return of Lorraine], you know, would be followed by certain death! Besides, the King has pledged his word that the Chevalier shall not return for eight years, by which time it is to be hoped Monsieur will either be cured of his passion, or else enlightened as to his favourite's true character. He may then see what faults this man has made him commit, and live to hate him as much as once he loved him. This is my only hope, although, even then, I may still be unhappy. Monsieur's jealous nature and his constant fear that I should be loved and esteemed will always be the cause of trouble, and the King does not make people happy, even when he means to treat them well. We see how even his mistresses have to suffer three or four rebuffs a week. What then must his friends expect?'

If Henrietta had ever had doubts as to the nature of her husband's relationship with the Chevalier, it is clear that at some point she had become fully appraised of the facts and now knew that they were sexually involved. It is notable that, although according to the mores of the day homosexuality was universally frowned upon as a moral deficiency as well as a mortal sin, she makes no actual judgement about her husband's proclivities nor expresses any disgust about them. Of course, we do not know what she privately thought about the matter but it seems unlikely that she would conceal such feelings, if she had them, from such a trusted correspondent as Madame de Saint-Chaumont.

On 28 April, the royal party, accompanied by the ubiquitous Madame de Montespan, several other courtiers and an army of 30,000 men, set out for Flanders. It was to be a most trying journey, hampered by waterlogged roads, mudslides and appalling weather which caused a river they were due to cross to flood its banks and sweep away the only bridge for several miles, forcing the royal party to take refuge overnight in a miserable little farmhouse where they all slept together on the floor. Henrietta, who was feeling increasingly poorly at this time, found it especially difficult and entirely lost her appetite as a result of the stress. Before leaving Paris, she had learned from Louis that the Chevalier de Lorraine's claims that Philippe was trying to divorce her were actually grounded in fact for her husband, encouraged by Lorraine, had indeed approached his brother to ask about the possibility of getting rid of her and this new piece of information had hurt her deeply, even though she held the Chevalier rather than her husband entirely responsible. 'I told him that he must see the necessity of never allowing the return of this man, who would only do far worse in the future,' she wrote to Madame de Saint-Chaumont. Nonetheless she hid her distress well, even though Philippe seemed determined to behave more badly than ever, even informing her in front of everyone that an astrologer had told him that he was fated to have several wives and so he did not think that she had very long left to live. She must have been greatly relieved therefore to finally reach Courtray in Flanders, where she was greeted by the English envoy who was to escort her to Dunkirk, where Lord Sandwich and his fleet were waiting for her. However, even as she was preparing to say her goodbyes, Philippe felt compelled to throw yet another one of his tantrums and inform Louis that he had changed his mind and she was not allowed to go after all, reducing Henrietta to tears and scandalising the rest of the party, who could hardly believe how badly he was behaving, although they may have speculated that the recent rumour that his beloved Chevalier had become the lover of his brother's former love

Marie Mancini, Princess Colonna, who was also residing in Italy, might have had something to do with his terrible mood.

As if to make up for his earlier poor treatment, Louis did his best for Henrietta by providing her with 200,000 crowns to pay her expenses and buy new clothes for her journey and allowing her friends, the Comte and Comtesse de Gramont to accompany her to England as part of her large entourage, which almost certainly enraged Philippe, who would doubtless have liked to surround her with his own spies. Henrietta was escorted to Lille by Louis and her husband who behaved badly right up until the moment that they had to say their goodbyes - no doubt enraged by the attention that was being paid to her both by his brother and the various diplomats who visited her before her departure, all of whom were astounded by Henrietta's sharp understanding and intelligence, which entirely belied her fragile and rather frivolous appearance. Although Philippe behaved like a spoilt child much of the time, he was also no fool and had no doubt long since worked out that there was some special purpose to Henrietta's visit to England that he was being excluded from - but he was also completely self-centred and clearly did not care one jot that the success of any secret mission might well be jeopardised by his jealous tantrums. All he cared about was the fact that his brother, whom he adored, seemed to prefer his wife to him and one of the chief tragedies of Philippe's life is that his fatal self-absorption and egocentrism totally blinded him to the fact that his behaviour only served to push them both even further away.

Philippe's tantrums and last ditch attempts to prevent Henrietta from leaving were to no avail and after taking her leave of him at Lille, where he could barely bring himself to speak to her, she went on to Dunkirk, where the English fleet was waiting to take her to Dover. As impatient to be reunited with her as she was to see him, Charles was already waiting there for her and she could barely control her excitement as she boarded her ship on the evening of 24 May and they set sail for England. Elated to be finally free of Philippe if only for a few days and excited to be finally seeing her beloved brother for the first time in nine years, Henrietta could hardly sleep that night and was up at dawn in time to catch her first glimpse of the white cliffs of Dover, illuminated by the sunrise. Her brother also spent a sleepless night and was up as soon as the report came in that her fleet had been sighted off the English coast. Unable to wait for her to reach land, he ordered that the royal barge be launched and he, James, the young Duke of Monmouth and their cousin Prince Rupert all set off to meet her en route. The nine years that they had been apart had not been entirely kind to Charles and Henrietta – they had lost their mother, friends, relatives and even some children, suffered romantic disappointments and endured war, plague and fire, as well as various personal dramas. When they last met, she was a fresh-faced sixteen-year-old, betrothed to a handsome young prince whom she had known almost her entire life and with the whole world at her feet while he was the thirty-year-old newly restored king, full of vitality and optimism about the future. However, although the lives that they looked forward to back then may well have proved dispiriting and even painful in so many different ways, they could never be disappointed by each other and their mutual delight as they greeted each other on the deck of Henrietta's ship was wholeheartedly joyous and set the tone for the entire visit.

The royal party travelled together to Dover, where Henrietta was to be lodged once again in the forbidding old castle overlooking the Channel. Although they were thrilled to be in each other's company again and keen to enjoy themselves as much as possible in the few days that Philippe had granted to them, there was still business to be done first and discussions about the treaty immediately began, not that Henrietta had to do much persuading, for her brother had already made up his mind to accept both Louis' condition that he convert to Catholicism and the gold that was to compensate him for this act. Nonetheless, negotiations took rather longer than anticipated and after an appeal by Henrietta, Louis gave his permission for her visit to be extended for another twelve days, much to the satisfaction of the reunited brother and sister. In the event this extra time was not really required for the secret treaty was signed on 1 June by Lord Arlington, Lord Arundel, Sir Richard Bellings and Sir Thomas Clifford on behalf of the English and by the French Ambassador Charles Colbert, Marquis de Croissy on behalf of the French. According to the terms of the treaty, Charles and Louis agreed to immediately declare war on the Dutch with the English taking responsibility for the war by sea, assisted by French sailors and ships and the French being in charge of any fighting on land, assisted by English troops. Charles also agreed to convert to Catholicism, although he could delay the public announcement of this fact for as long as he chose (and indeed he managed to successfully delay it until he was on his deathbed) and in return would receive the sum of £160,000 from Louis as well as an annual payment of £200,000 for as long as the war with the Dutch continued.

Once a signed copy of the treaty had been sent off to Louis, who was waiting for it at Dunkirk, Henrietta and Charles were free to enjoy themselves for the time that was left to them. As soon as permission had been granted for her stay to be extended, Charles had sent word to London that his wife, Catherine, and sister-in-law, Anne, Duchess of York should join them at Dover with their suites, which would make their party even merrier. Henrietta was already acquainted with Anne, whom she had first encountered when she was the lady-in-waiting of her sister Mary, Princess of Orange during her visit to Paris in 1656 and whose youngest daughter Anne was still residing in her household in France, but this was the first time she had met Queen Catherine, although she had read a great deal about her in the letters of her brother. Like her, Catherine had suffered the loss of more than one pregnancy and had been forced to endure her husband's obvious preference for the company of his favourites, and so it is hardly surprising that Henrietta found herself drawn to her shy young Portuguese sister-in-law and upset on her behalf to see her brother paying a little too much attention to the winsome Breton beauty Mademoiselle de Kérouaille who had accompanied her as part of her suite. She was also delighted to be reunited with her old friend Frances Stewart, now Duchess of Richmond and still one of the greatest beauties of the age, although her glow had been somewhat diminished by a bout of small pox the previous year.

Although Philippe was still spitefully refusing to give Henrietta permission to visit her brother's capital city, they were able to make the best of things and very much enjoyed their sojourn in the Kent countryside, where there were plenty of pastimes to amuse them. Both Charles and Henrietta adored sailing and so naturally they took several trips off the coast in the royal yacht, even paying a visit to the fleet where they were very well entertained by the sailors, who were delighted to have the king and his sister on board. 'Madame is as bold as she is on land,' one of her entourage commented admiringly after watching her clambering along the side of her yacht, 'and walks as fearlessly along the edge of the ships as she does on shore.' There was also an excursion to Canterbury to watch Thomas Shadwell's comedy, *The Sullen Lovers*, which was based on *Les Fâcheux* by Henrietta's protégé and friend, Molière. The highpoint of the visit though were the long hours that Henrietta and Charles were able to spend alone, talking over matters too personal to be committed to paper even by them and simply enjoying each other's company until this precious time came to an end far more quickly than either would ever have wished for and before they knew it, they were saying goodbye yet again. Charles presented Henrietta with the generous gift of 6,000 pistoles as well as a set of beautiful jewels to remember him by. In return, she asked Louise de Kérouaille to fetch her own jewellery box so that her brother could choose something for himself, only for Charles to take the blushing Louise by the hand and declare that she was the only jewel that he desired. Torn between amusement and exasperation at her brother's boldness, Henrietta gently pulled Louise away and informed her brother that she had promised to return Mademoiselle de Kérouaille to her parents in France and as she had no wish to disappoint them, he would have to choose a different gift for himself.

Along with Princes James and Rupert, Charles accompanied Henrietta on board her ship to a mid-point in the Channel, where they said their final goodbyes before boarding the royal yacht and returning to Dover. The siblings clung together for several minutes, barely able to bring themselves to let go before finally Charles, who was seen to have tears in his eyes, felt able to release her and walk away. Although promises were made to see each other again soon, they both knew that the mood swings of Philippe would most likely make such a venture impossible and so had no idea if they would ever see each other again. Although one of their acquaintances, Hortense Mancini, who had once been proposed to by Charles during his exile, had recently run away from her abusive husband, this was still considered a highly unusual step at the time and one that unfortunately tended to reflect more badly on the abused spouse than her abuser. Although Charles would undoubtedly have preferred to have his sister remain safely with him in England, he knew that there was no way that she could ever really leave Philippe as to do so would entail losing not just her reputation and social standing but also her children, who would have to remain with him in France and would probably be forbidden from ever seeing her again. As for Henrietta, she had long since accepted her situation, painful and difficult as it undoubtedly was, and had no wish to escape it.

After Henrietta had landed at Calais, she travelled in great pomp to Beauvais where she was met by the English Ambassador, Ralph Montagu, who accompanied her the rest of the way to Saint Germain, where the court was waiting to welcome her back. Louis had originally planned to travel to Beauvais as well but had been foiled by yet another one of Monsieur's tantrums during which he absolutely refused to greet his wife, which meant that no one else could either. He did his best to destroy the happiness of her reception, by sulking and once again pestering her to use her influence to have the Chevalier de Lorraine recalled to court, but ultimately was unable to entirely ruin her triumphant reunion with Louis, who was thrilled by the success of her secret mission and gave her another gift of 6,000 pistoles to match that presented to her by her brother. He also invited her to stay with him at Versailles while she recovered from the ordeal of her journey but Philippe refused to let her go and so instead she took to her bed at Saint Germain until she had recovered enough to go to the Palais Royal, where she was reunited with her daughters and Anne of York, who was no doubt keen to hear how her parents were doing. While resting in Paris, which was stiflingly hot that summer, Henrietta paid Sir Thomas Clifford, who had signed the treaty in Dover, the great honour of writing to him in English – the only letter that she ever wrote in her native language and which is so charmingly idiosyncratic in its phrasing and spelling that it must have absolutely delighted its recipient, although Charles, whose requests that she at least attempt to write to him in English rather than French had been ignored, must have felt rather piqued when he heard about it.

'When i have write to the King from Calais i praid him to tel milord Arlington an you what he had promised mi for bothe. his ansers was that hi gave me againe his word, that hee would performe the thing, but that hi did not thing it fit to exequte it now.

'I tel you this sooner than to Milord Arlington because i know you ar not so hard to satisfie as hee. I should be so my self, if I was not sure that the King would not promis mee a thing to faille in the performance of it.

'This is the ferste letter I have ever write in inglis. you will eselay see it bi the stile and tograf. prai see in the same time that i expose mi self to be thought a foulle in looking to make you know how much I am your frind.'

After a few days in Paris, the Orléans household travelled to Saint Cloud, where she would be able to escape the terrible heat and recuperate properly from her great adventure. Henrietta had been thoroughly exhausted by her travels and was in need of some rest and cosseting before she felt able to rejoin the hectic social whirl of the French court. Some of her friends joined her at Saint Cloud and she spent the next week quietly enjoying her beautiful gardens, which she had spent so much time designing with Le Nôtre, playing her prettily beribboned guitar, eating freshly picked strawberries and swimming in the deliciously warm waters of the Seine. To her relief, Philippe kept out of her way as much as possible and without the pernicious and toxic presence of the Chevalier, the air at Saint Cloud must have felt fresher and more invigorating than ever. She wrote to her friend Madame de Saint-Chaumont that week:

'I knew you would understand the joy which my visit to England gave me. It was indeed most delightful, and, long as I have known the affection of my brother, the King, it proved still greater than I expected. He showed me the greatest possible kindness, and was ready to help me in all that he could do. Since my return, the King here has been very good to me, but as for Monsieur, nothing can equal his bitterness and anxiety to find fault. He does me the honour to say that I am all powerful, and do everything that I like, and so, if I do not bring back the Chevalier, it is because I do not wish to please him. At the same time he joins threats for the future with this kind of talk. I have once more told him how little his favourite's return depends upon me, and how little I get my own way, or you would not be where you are now. Instead of seeing the truth of this, and becoming softened, he took occasion of my remark to go and complain of you to the King, and tried, at the same time, to do me other ill offices. This has had a very bad effect, together with the letter that you wrote to my child [Marie Louise, Madame de Saint-Chaumont's former charge], and which, they pretend, was delivered to her secretly, and has, I fear, increased the King's unfavourable opinion of you … I have often blamed you for the tender love you feel for my child. In God's name, out that love away. The poor child cannot return your affection, and will alas be brought up to hate me … Since my return from England, the King has gone to Versailles, where Monsieur would not follow him, lest I should have the pleasure of being with him'

In the end, even Philippe was unable to refuse the next royal summons that arrived from Versailles and so the warring and increasingly estranged couple set off to spend the day with Louis and his court.

In 1670, Versailles was quite transformed from the pretty but relatively humble hunting lodge that Louis had visited with Louise de la Vallière in the first flush of their romance but was still not quite the magnificent, impersonal and overwhelming monolith that it would eventually become. In fact, it might be said that it would never look more attractive than it did in the summer of 1670, when Henrietta visited it for the last time, when it was still the grandest and most elegant palace in Europe and had not yet sprawled out of control, losing all vestiges of charm and beauty in the process. Certainly, she would have enjoyed strolling through the gardens before her private meeting with Louis, who wished to have a full debriefing about her visit to England and the discussions that had occurred before the signing of the treaty. Feeling left out as usual, Philippe burst in on them, perhaps hoping to find them *in flagrante* so that he finally had something concrete to complain about, but instead only discovered them deep in conversation, which they broke off as soon as he entered, much to his annoyance, which he naturally vented by carrying her off back to Saint Cloud as soon as possible.

On 28 June, Henrietta was joined at Saint Cloud by her dear friend Madame de la Fayette, who strolled with her in the lovely gardens until midnight as it was too unbearably warm to remain indoors. Despite the heat, Henrietta managed to get some sleep that night before she gave up and got up early in order to write a long letter to the Princess Palatine, the widow of her cousin Edward, who had asked her to intercede on her behalf with Charles in order to get a promised pension paid to her:

'I will confess that, on my return, I had hoped to find everyone satisfied, instead of which, things are worse than ever. You remember telling me that Monsieur insisted on three things: first, that I should place him in confidential relations with the King, my brother; secondly, that I should ask the King to give him his son's allowance; thirdly, that I should help the Chevalier de Lorraine. The King, my brother, was so kind as to promise that he would willingly trust Monsieur with his secrets if he would behave better in future than he had done with regard to my journey. He even offered to give the Chevalier de Lorraine a refuge in his kingdom till affairs should have calmed down here. He could do no more for him … I have said all this to him, expecting it would be well received, but since there is no prospect of the Chevalier's immediate return, Monsieur declares that all the rest is useless, and says I am never to be restored to his good graces until I have given him back his favourite. I am, I must confess, very much surprised at this behaviour on his part. Monsieur wishes for my brother's friendship, and, now I offer it to him, he accepts it as if he were doing the King a favour … If he reflects at all, it is impossible for him to go on in this manner, and I can only suppose that he is bent on quarrelling with me. The King was good enough to assure him, on his oath, that I had no part in the Chevalier's exile, and that his return did not depend upon me. Unfortunately for me, he refused to believe the King, who has never been known to utter a falsehood … Of the three things which Monsieur desired, I can obtain two and a half, and he is angry because I cannot do more, and counts the King, my brother's, friendship and his own advantage all as nothing. As for me, I have done more than I could have hoped. But if I am unhappy enough for Monsieur to go on treating me so unkindly, I declare, my dear cousin, that I shall give it all up, and take no more trouble as to his pension or his favourite's return, or his friendship with the King, my brother … If he desires me to act I will do it joyfully, for I have no greater wish than to be on good terms with him. If not, will keep silence and patiently bear all his unkindness, without trying to defend myself. His hatred is unreasonable, but his esteem may be earned. I may say that I have neither deserved the first, nor am I altogether unworthy of the last, and I still console myself with the hope that it may some day be obtained.'

It is perhaps fitting that nothing could be more redolent of Henrietta's great unhappiness and desperation to be reconciled with her difficult husband than this missive, which was fated to be her last ever letter.

After writing, she paid her customary visit to her husband in the morning, no doubt to patiently endure still more of his self-centred and childish harping on about the return of the Chevalier de Lorraine and his accusations that she was not doing enough to bring it about, after which she escaped to Mass with her friend Madame de la Fayette, who had stayed the night, informing her afterwards that 'she would not be in such a bad humour if she could talk with me; but that she was so weary of all the people who surrounded her. She could not endure their presence'. They then went together to one of the salons, where Henrietta's daughter Marie Louise was being painted by an English artist, perhaps one that had been sent over by her uncle to capture her image so that he could see for himself just how much she resembled him. After this diverting pastime, the two ladies went to dinner with the Duc, after which Henrietta, who had eaten more than usual, decided to have a nap on some cushions that had been arranged on the floor at Madame de la Fayette's feet while the others continued chatting. Resting her head on her friend's lap, she drifted off to sleep but as she dozed, both her husband and Madame de la Fayette noticed with some concern that she was not looking at all well, before coming to the conclusion that she was still exhausted from her recent travels. Henrietta woke up suddenly soon afterwards, complaining of a sharp pain in her side and calling for a glass of chicory water, a favourite cold drink that was specially made for her with iced water and served in a silver cup. Almost as soon as she had taken a sip, she screamed with pain and insisted that she must have been poisoned. Madame de la Fayette and her ladies immediately unlaced her gown, hoping to relieve some of her discomfort then, when that did not work and she still continued to cry out in pain, they whisked her off to her bedchamber, followed by a bewildered Philippe, who was supposed to be travelling to Paris but postponed his trip until his wife was settled.

The couple's physicians were called to Henrietta's bedchamber, where she continued to writhe and scream in pain in between frantically telling her terrified ladies that she must surely have been poisoned for why else would she be suffering such terrible torments of agony? The suspicious Madame de la Fayette watched Philippe's face as he bustled about his wife's chamber, hardly knowing what to do with himself, but was forced to concede that she saw only the same genuine confusion and alarm as she herself felt as he implored the doctors, who believed that she was suffering from a severe but not mortal case of colic, to do their best for her. When Henrietta continued to insist that she must surely have been poisoned for only that could explain the terrible pain that she was suffering, it was Philippe who suggested that the chicory water be given to one of her pet dogs, although surely not her beloved Mimi, before volunteering to try some himself out of the very same cup that she had used. Her *femme de chambre*, Madame des Bordes, who had been with her since she was a little girl, also courageously offered to drink out of the cup, as did her old friend Bablon, now Duchess of Mecklenburg-Schwerin since she married a German prince in 1664, who had arrived to pay a visit just as the commotion began. Although all three drank the chicory water with no ill effect, Henrietta still continued to insist that she must have been poisoned and was dying, despite all the best efforts of the physicians to assure her that her life was not in any danger. Ignoring them and clearly preparing herself for death, she asked her bewildered and deeply distressed husband to come to the bedside, took his hand and whispered, 'Alas, Monsieur, a long time has passed since you ceased to love me. That was unjust of you as I have never failed you.' As he wept, realising at last just how badly he had treated her, her agonies began to increase until she was screaming in pain once again and it was decided to send a messenger to Versailles to inform the king that she was dying.

Horrified by this unexpected news, Louis immediately took a carriage to Saint Cloud, accompanied by his wife, cousin Anne-Marie-Louise and the Comtesse de Soissons, who had returned from her exile. It was very late at night when he eventually arrived at the château, almost exactly twenty-four hours after Henrietta had been enjoying her moonlit stroll through the gardens with Madame de la Fayette, and he immediately ran to her bedside, where he found her looking very ill indeed and obviously near death. Bursting into tears, he gathered Henrietta into his arms, and implored her physicians, who had by now conceded that this was no ordinary case of colic and that she was indeed dying, to save her life. Word of her fatal illness had quickly spread through the royal apartments at Versailles and a great crowd of Henrietta's friends began to gather in her rooms, hoping to either give her some comfort with their presence, say a final goodbye or simply spectate at what was no doubt destined to be one of the most infamous and dramatic spectacles of the year. Her former maids-of-honour Athénaïs de Montespan and Louise de la Vallière were both there, united for once by this most terrible mutual loss as they watched their old mistress pass away, too exhausted now by the incessant pain to do more than whimper and writhe around in the most miserable fashion. Guiche was still away fighting, but his father, the doughty old Duc de Gramont, who was exceedingly fond of Henrietta, was present along with his friends Turenne and the Duc de Condé, both of whom had adored her. If she had felt able to look around, she would have seen a whole host of familiar faces, many of whom she had known since childhood or at least since she had joined the French court as the new bride of the Duc d'Orléans. Not all of them had treated her very well over the years but at that moment as she suffered her final agonies and they prepared to say goodbye for the very last time, she would have seen only sadness and regret.

Anne-Marie-Louise, the Grande Mademoiselle, who had taunted the young Henrietta so terribly when she had been a mere poor relation, surviving on handouts on the very fringes of the court, was horrified and deeply moved by the spectacle.

'When we arrived at Saint Cloud we found almost everybody afflicted [she wrote later] Monsieur seemed to be very bewildered. Madame lay on a little bed with her nightdress unfastened and her hair loose, her face was deathly pale; she had the air of a dead person. Monsieur was saying to her: "Madame, do your best to vomit, so that this bile does not suffocate you."'

Not long after this, Henrietta said her final farewells to her relatives, telling Anne-Marie-Louise that, 'You are losing a good friend, who was beginning to know and love you,' and gently chiding Louis with the words, 'Ah, do not weep, Sire, or you will make me weep too. You are losing a good servant who has always feared the loss of your good graces more than death itself.' After the king, still weeping bitterly, had left her chamber along with the rest of the royal party, a stern and unsympathetic Jansenist priest, Monsieur Feuillet, who had been sent for by Madame de la Fayette, entered to take Henrietta's last confession and perform the last rites before, to the horror of all still present, haranguing her about her lack of faith during life, telling her that she had 'offended God for twenty six years' and deserved to suffer for her sins – an accusation that she meekly accepted.

When the English Ambassador Ralph Montagu, who had seen her only the previous day, arrived, he was horrified by how ill she looked and immediately realised that she was very close to death. 'I have always loved my brother above all things in the world, and my only regret in dying is to leave him,' she whispered to him, as he knelt, weeping, at her bedside. When he discreetly asked her in English if she truly believed that she had been poisoned, Henrietta beckoned him closer and whispered, 'Do not tell this to the king my brother; he must be spared that grief. Above all do not let him take any vengeance on the king here, for he at least is not guilty.' She then removed a ring from a finger, which she gave to Montagu with instructions that he should pass it on to Charles along with a casket of his letters, which were in the safe keeping of her *femme de chambre* – however, when he later went to her study to retrieve these precious missives, they had already been whisked away by Monsieur.

In the early hours of the morning of 30 June, Henrietta decided that it was time to say her last goodbye to her husband Philippe, who made a great deal of fuss and eventually had to be forcibly removed from her side as his histrionics were making her painfully agitated. The couple had not always been very happy but they had been married for over nine years and had known each other for much longer than that and despite everything her death clearly moved him very much and, it is hoped, forced him to realise just how badly he had treated her. After he had gone, Henrietta was left alone with a small group of her closest friends, including the faithful Madame de la Fayette and Ralph Montagu, who all sank to their knees as the Jansenist Feuillet prepared to pray over her. However, before he could begin, the bedchamber doors burst open and her friend, the Abbé Bossuet entered the room and advanced towards the bed where Henrietta now lay very close to death. Her eyes lit up and she even managed one of her sweetest smiles as the formidable Abbé, a true gentle giant, knelt beside her and placed her crucifix into her hands before performing the final sacrament. 'Madame,' he said, weeping to see her in such terrible pain, 'you believe in God, you hope in God, you love God?' 'With all my heart,' Henrietta whispered in reply, before closing her eyes and quietly passing away, her agonies, both physical and emotional, over at long last.

Chapter Fifteen

Madame est Morte

1670

'My Lord, I am sorry to be obliged by my employment, to give you an account of the saddest story in the world, and which I have hardly the courage to write,' Ralph Montagu wrote to Lord Arlington only a few hours after he had witnessed Henrietta's death, no doubt already anticipating the terrible furore that his tragic news would cause once it arrived in London:

> 'She continued in the greatest tortures imaginable, till 3 o' clock in the morning, when she dyed … God send the King, our master, patience and constancy to bear so great an affliction. Madame declared she had no reluctancy to die, but out of grief that she thought it would be to the King, her brother … Never anybody died with that piety and resolution, and kept her sense to the last. Excuse this imperfect relation, for the grief I am in. I am sure all that had the Honour to know her will have their share for so great and general a loss.'

Rumours that she had been murdered and conjecture about who might have done such a terrible deed, began to sweep through the richly decorated corridors of Saint Cloud and out into the world before Henrietta had even drawn her last breath. The fact that she herself had insisted that she had been poisoned and that her attendants also obviously entertained the idea only served to fuel the speculation, much to the alarm of her brother-in-law Louis, who had no wish to see his recently signed treaty with England jeopardised by a domestic drama. After privately ascertaining that his brother really had nothing to do with Henrietta's death, Louis ordered that a post mortem be carried out in front of around a hundred witnesses, both French and English, who were able to see for themselves that his sister-in-law had died of natural causes. The Venetian Ambassador in France, Zuane Moresini, had much to say about the crisis in the report he sent back to his master, the Doge about Henrietta's last terrible hours and repeated the ever-increasing rumours about her demise, which would, as he pointed out, no doubt be fanned and spread even further by the Dutch in their efforts to undermine the relationship between France and England. The suspicious death of the English king's beloved sister, who was well known to be unhappily married to the brother of the king of France was a godsend to anyone who wished to cause mischief between the two nations and the canny Venetian was right to assume that they would not waste any time in taking advantage of this unexpected bounty:

'The strained relations which existed in the last months of her life between her Highness and her husband and the instantaneous manner of her death after she had taken the water as mentioned has caused the people, who always take the worst view, to conceive the suspicion of poison. This opinion has got such a hold on the populace that the demonstrations carried out by the royal order, although very vigorous, have not sufficed to uproot it. It was accordingly decided, with the unanimous consent of the royal House, that the body should be opened with all possible speed in the presence of ten of the most celebrated physicians of this city with the assistance of the British ambassador and other English subjects staying at this Court, so that the true cause of the mischief and of death might be known and that all those present might convince themselves of the falsity of the present rumours and put an end to the world's belief in them, so far as it depended upon them.

'The operation was carried out yesterday. The intestines were found to be all ulcerated and the lungs in particular almost completely putrified so that it was established in the general opinion that Madame had only a few months more to live; that an abscess had already formed and by the excessive cold of the water it had suddenly burst and was probably the sole cause of so sudden a death. For the rest there was a complete absence of anything that gave any sign of poison or that would justify the unjust and ill considered report among the common people ... Since her death the duke, her husband, has been in this city in no state to receive consolation and the exhaustion and physical languor by which he is prostrated afford the clearest testimony to this.

'When the king heard of the death of his sister in law, he abandoned his sojourn at Versailles declaring that at a moment so unhappy he did not wish to stay any longer in a place that had been chosen above all others for relaxation and ease. From St. Germain where his Majesty was staying at the time, he proceeded yesterday with all the royal House to this city to console Monsieur in his present affliction. As soon as he has become visible the foreign ministers will perform this duty and I will try to assure him of the deep sympathy of your Excellencies over such a loss. The desire of the government here, for reasons already given to your Serenity, to be united with the British king and the hope it had conceived of succeeding in the present design through the most efficacious means of the deceased, causes the accident of her death to be most severely felt. Moreover the knowledge that the Dutch will not leave any means untried to encourage estrangement from this side in the mind of the British king, even confirming the common report of poison, is a severe blow to the royal feelings. The king is considering with his Council in what ways they may take steps to counter the negotiations which they foresee. In the mean time the Marshal de Bellefond will leave for London to-morrow in the capacity of royal envoy extraordinary to assure the British king and the princes of that royal House of the sorrow of the king and princes here at this present loss. He also has definite instructions to disabuse their minds of every suspicion of poison at such a sudden death, taking with him the most ample attestation of the physicians and letters from the British ambassador here, with assurances thereon.'

The news of Henrietta's death reached London within a few days and, as anticipated, completely devastated Charles, who immediately exclaimed that it was all the fault of 'that damned villain', his brother-in-law Philippe then took off to his private chambers, where he remained in total solitude for five days with just his dogs for company. Although he had indulged himself with a myriad romantic passions during his life, Charles' one true love was undoubtedly his youngest sister, who understood and cared for him in a way that no other woman ever could and had, furthermore, never disappointed him or let him down unlike all his other loves. She had been his most faithful and adoring supporter and companion since childhood and it would be fair to say that when Henrietta died, Charles lost an essential part of himself and would never be quite the same again. However, although his initial reaction was to recall Ralph Montagu and demand reparation for his sister's death, this skilled and pragmatic politician, perhaps the finest statesman of his age, knew that it was better to hold his peace – although he allowed himself the petty satisfaction of refusing to see the French Ambassador for several days. Meanwhile, as in France, the English court was rife with speculation about the cause of Henrietta's death, with it generally being assumed that her husband and his male companions had almost certainly poisoned her and very little credence being given to the official report made at her post mortem, which stated that she had died of natural causes. There were even some demands for Charles to declare war upon the French, most notably from Henrietta's former admirers, the Duke of Buckingham and her cousin Prince Rupert, both of whom were denounced by more sensible, level headed courtiers, who reminded them that, like her mother, Henrietta had always been sickly and prone to unexplained illnesses and aches and pains and so cautioned the more hot-headed nobles to hold their fire and let the two kings work it out between them.

To be fair, the timing, as Charles' lord in waiting, the poet courtier and infamous rake Lord Rochester noted in a letter to his wife at this time, looked very bad indeed for Philippe.

'Monsieur, since the banishment of the Chevalier de Lorraine (of which he suspected Madame to be the author) has behaved himself very ill in all things, threatening her upon all occasions that if she did not get Lorraine recalled, she might expect from him the worst that can befall her.'

Rochester concluded his letter in his usual humorous and irreverent style with the wry comment that:

'she died the most lamented (Both in France and England) since dying has been the fashion. But I will not keep you too long upon the doleful subject, it is enough to make most wives in the world very melancholy.'

His meaning is clear and as Rochester both knew Henrietta fairly well and was a friend and protégé of Charles, who regarded him as akin to a foster son in many ways; he was almost certainly in a position to know intimate details about the state of her marriage. Then again, he was also prone to hyperbole and, if not outright lies, then certainly plenty of gossipy embellishment. However, Rochester's version of Henrietta's death was one that was quickly gathering momentum and spreading throughout Europe, where it was gleefully seized upon by enemies of the Anglo–French alliance.

As the Venetian Ambassador in England, Piero Mocenigo reported to his master, the Doge:

'The antipathy of the English for France leads the generality of them, when looking into the causes of Madame's death, to have recourse to suspicion and political reflections, which in themselves are unworthy of the notice of the Senate, but I feel bound to mention the matter so that your Excellencies may know how much inflammable material is ready for the kindling and how inclined men are to put the worst interpretation upon whatever happens. The king in his prudence, even in the very depths of his grief, has never given expression to any sentiments except those of the utmost piety and resignation to the Divine will; and the ministers, dumbfounded, do not utter a word.'

Meanwhile his counterpart in France was reporting similarly alarming developments there:

'With the return from London of the courier sent from this Court with the sad news of the sudden death of the duchess of Orleans the king has received various despatches from his Ambassador Colbert which have very greatly disturbed the government here. The ambassador reports the very bitter feeling of the British king over this loss, the reports published broadcast in the city there of the use of poison for such a sudden death, and the arrival of a secret despatch from the Ambassador Montagu here confirming this opinion in the British Court. All this serves to increase ill feeling and discontent in the king here and his royal House. Your Excellencies will receive fuller particulars from the spot. Here in the mean time they spare no effort to remove from the mind of the British king a suspicion so injurious and so hateful His Majesty has written an affectionate letter in his own hand to the king there in order to make him fully realise the grief that is felt here and to remove from his mind every thought of violence. In the mean time the king strongly resents the mischievous change in the sentiments of the English ambassador here. In the first days, immediately after Madame's death, he agreed with the others in declaring it to be natural. A few days later he changed his mind, withdrew this truth and by harmful offices is inspiring mistrust and ill feeling between these governments … The Marshal di Bellefond has been sent on a special mission and has already started, charged with the necessary instructions to act as a counterpoise and so far as is possible to put an end to the detraction and the mischief against this side.'

Both Ambassadors reported that the Dutch were losing no time in capitalising on Henrietta's death and that in fact letters had been intercepted stating that:

'the death of the duchess of Orleans has occurred very opportunely, as with the impression already formed in the mind of the king and of the whole kingdom generally that it was due to poison, the sentiments of that Court are completely estranged from the interests of France' and that furthermore and more explictly, 'The loss suffered by France in Madame may be considered a notable gain for the United Provinces.'

However, although Charles would never cease to believe that his sister had been poisoned if not by her husband then almost certainly by his favourites, he was too wise and far too invested in the Treaty of Dover, which Henrietta had worked so diligently to bring about, to let the crisis imperil the always fragile friendship between France and England. Besides, putting his own self interests and those of his country aside, it would have seemed to him to be an unpardonable insult to Henrietta's memory to allow the unfortunate circumstances of her death destroy the alliance that she had desired with all of her heart for so long and which should now stand as a memorial to her diplomatic skills, hard work and intelligence. He therefore agreed to receive the French Ambassador and accept his condolences before diplomatically appearing to go along with the French official line that her death had been entirely due to natural causes – effectively quashing any rumours to the contrary. Nonetheless, Henrietta's cousin Charlotte Elizabeth of the Palatine, who became Philippe's second wife a year later, would later claim that Louis took her aside shortly after her marriage to reveal that Henrietta had indeed been poisoned by the Chevalier de Lorraine and the Marquis d'Effiat, another one of Philippe's minions, but that her husband had known absolutely nothing about the plot and had been just as shocked as anyone by the fate that had befallen her predecessor. He also added that had he truly believed his brother to be a poisoner then he would never have allowed him to marry again, which more than anything convinced Liselotte that he was telling the truth for she adored Louis and had an extremely high opinion of his personal integrity, particularly in his dealings with close family members. To be fair to Philippe, he may have been a terrible husband but he was almost certainly not a murderer, not least because he would never have dared to do anything that might imperil his precious relationship with his brother Louis.

Although contemporary reports indicate that Philippe was, at least at first, exceedingly upset by Henrietta's death, he was sufficiently in command of himself to order his household to go into mourning (along with the entire French and English courts) and also request that visitors arriving to pay their condolences should do so not just to him but also to both of his daughters, the youngest of whom was just ten months old, as well as his deceased wife's five year old niece who was still residing with the Orléans household, although not for much longer as her parents removed her from Philippe's care before the end of the summer. Not only that but the three girls, including the baby, were all provided with elaborate violet velvet mourning capes, an attention to detail that Philippe delighted in and which caused his brother Louis some much needed amusement in the midst of what was to be one of the saddest periods of his entire life. Although their relationship had not always been smooth, Louis had been genuinely fond of Henrietta and was fully aware of the great debt that he owed her for her skilful and remarkably discreet handling of the negotiations prior to the signing of the Treaty of Dover. He therefore resolved to give her a grand send off with an elaborate and extremely costly state funeral in the royal basilica of Saint Denis on the outskirts of Paris, where her mother and son had both been interred the year before.

After her death, Henrietta's body lay in state in her bedchamber under a black velvet cloth while her embalmed heart was placed in a gold vase and ceremoniously placed with that of Queen Anne in the beautiful church attached to the convent she had founded at Val de Grâce. At midnight on 4 July, her doleful cortège set out from Saint Cloud, led by her eight-year-old daughter Marie Louise, who was followed by the Princesse de Condé, five duchesses and her entire household, all of them dressed in black. As was fitting for a daughter of the etiquette- obsessed Philippe, Marie Louise almost ruined the solemnity of the occasion by having a most undignified row with the chief mourner, the Princesse de Condé, about precedence at the head of the procession. At the centre of the procession was Henrietta's embalmed body, encased in several coffins and covered in a magnificent ermine lined cloth of gold with her mantle and coronet displayed on top. When the cortège reached Saint Denis, the coffin was carefully carried through the nave, which was draped with black velvet held up by seven foot tall imitation marble skeletons and into the choir, where massive torches and four huge statues representing Youth, Nobility, Poetry and Music surrounded an elaborate dais with four elaborate incense vases on each corner, each releasing scented smoke into the air. The coffin was carried up the eight steps of the dais and carefully placed on an imitation black marble plinth supported by four bronze lions, the symbolic animal of her native country, and there it remained for the next six weeks as arrangements were finalised for what was to be one of the most elaborate funerals of the age.

The funeral of Henrietta-Anne Stuart, Duchesse d'Orléans, took place on 21 August 1670 and was a most magnificent affair, attended by virtually the entire court although, according to etiquette, King Louis, Philippe and Anne-Marie-Louise were all absent. Little Queen Maria Theresa, who had grown to love her cousin Henrietta over the years, attended incognito though, her face hidden beneath a black veil as she took her seat beside the English Ambassador, Ralph Montagu. For over two hours, the courtiers fidgeted during the interminable Latin service and the musical interludes, although as Henrietta had adored music more than almost anything else, Louis made sure that the pieces chosen for her service were the most beautiful and uplifting possible. They all sat to rapt attention though when Bossuet, simply dressed in a black cassock and stole and with the emerald ring that Henrietta commissioned for him, which had been presented to him after her death, flashing on his finger, stepped forward to give his much anticipated *oraison funèbre*. The splendid oration that he had given at the funeral of Henrietta's mother, just a year earlier, still lingered in the minds of those fortunate enough to witness it but the one he gave for the daughter was an astonishing and passionate piece of prose and perhaps even one of the greatest pieces of writing of the entire age.

'Oh disastrous night! Oh terrible night! When suddenly like a roll of thunder, resounded this amazing news: Madame is dying! Madame is dead! Who among us felt himself struck by this blow, as if some tragic accident had stricken his own family? At the first sound of this strange evil, we rushed to Saint Cloud from all sides; and we found everything in uproar, except for the heart of this princess. Everywhere we hear shouts; everywhere we see pain and despair, and the image of death. The King, the Queen, Monsieur, all of the court, all of the people, everything is defeated, everything is desperate; and I think that I see the fulfilment of the prophet's words: the king will mourn, the prince will be sorry and the hands of the people will fall in sadness and astonishment.

'But the princes and people did groan in vain; in vain did the King hold Madame in his arms. Then they could tell one and another, along with Saint Ambrose: *Stringebam brachia, sed quam jam amiseram tenebaum.* I clenched my arm, but had already lost what I held.

'The Princess escaped these tender embraces as the more powerful death carried her away from these royal hands. What! Was she to perish so soon? In most men, the changes are made gradually as death usually prepares them for the final blow. Madame, however, passed from morning to night like the flowers in the field. In the morning, she bloomed, with all the graces that you know so well and in the evening we saw her turned to dust.'

Bibliography

ACKROYD, Peter, *Civil War: The History of England Volume III*, Macmillan, 2015.

ADAMSON, John, *The Noble Revolt*, Orion, 2007.

BARKER, N.N., *Brother to the Sun King*, Johns Hopkins University Press, Baltimore, 1989.

BEVAN, Bryan, *Charles II's Minette*, Ascent, 1979.

BONE, Quentin, *Henrietta Maria: Queen of the Cavaliers*, Peter Owen, 1973.

BOUYER, Christian, *Henriette-Anne d'Angleterre*, Paris, 2006.

CARTWRIGHT, Julia M.C.A., *Madame, a Life of Henrietta, Daughter of Charles I and Duchess of Orleans*, New York, 1901.

DRAZIN, Charles, *The Man Who Outshone the Sun King: Ambition, Triumph and Treachery in the Reign of Louis XIV*, William Heinemann, 2009.

DUNLOP, Ian, *Louis XIV*, Sinclair-Stevenson, 1999.

DUNLOP, Ian, *Royal Palaces of France*, Hamish Hamilton, 1985.

FRASER, Antonia, *King Charles II*, Weidenfeld and Nicholson, 1979.

FRASER, Antonia, *Love and Louis XIV: The Women in the Life of the Sun King*, Orion, 2007.

HAMILTON, Elizabeth, *Henrietta Maria*, Hamish Hamilton, 1976.

HILTON, Lisa, *Athenais: The Life of Louis XIV's Mistress, the Real Queen of France*, Little, Brown, 2002.

HINDS, A.B. (ed), *Archive of State Papers Relating to English affairs in the Archives of Venice, vols 18–32, 1912–31*.

HUNT, Tristram, *The English Civil War At First Hand*, Orion, 2011.

LAFAYETTE, Madame de, *Histoire de Madame, Henriette d'Angleterre*, 1988.

LATHAM, R.C and MATTHEWS, W. (eds), *The Diary of Samuel Pepys, 11 vol, 1670–83*.

MARSHALL, Rosalind K., *Henrietta Maria: The Intrepid Queen*, Stemmer House, 1990.

MITFORD, Nancy, *The Sun King*, Harper and Row, 1966.

NORRINGTON, Ruth, *My Dearest Minette: Letters Between Charles II and His Sister Henrietta, Duchesse d'Orleans*, Peter Owen, 1996.

OMAN, Carole, *Henrietta Maria*, 1936.

PLOWDEN, **Alison**, *Henrietta Maria: Charles I's Indomitable Queen*, Sutton, 2001.

PURKISS, Diane, The English Civil War: A People's History, HarperPress, 2007.

SACKVILLE-WEST, **Vita,** *Daughter of France: The Life of Anne Marie Louise d'Orléans, Duchesse de Montpensier 1627–1693*, 1959.

UGLOW, **Jenny**, *A Gambling Man: Charles II and the Restoration*, Faber and Faber, 2009.

WHITAKER, **Katie,** *A Royal Passion: The Turbulent Marriage of Charles I and Henrietta Maria*, Weidenfeld and Nicholson, 2010.

Index

Aix-la-Chapelle, peace 154
Alexander VII, Pope 93
Alfonso VI, King of Portugal 78
Anne of Austria, Queen of France 13, 21,
    24–25, 27–30, 34, 42–44, 46–47, 51, 54, 56,
    58, 63–64, 66, 74–78, 86, 92, 101, 103–104,
    115, 117, 121, 131, 135, 138–139, 141, 143,
    146, 161, 199
Anne Gonzaga, Princess Edward of the
    Palatinate 83
Anne Stuart, Princess 3
Arlington, Henry Bennet, Earl of 160, 180,
    183, 192
Armagnac, Comte d' 119–120, 129, 133
Artigny, Mademoiselle d' 114–115, 118
Arundel, Henry, Lord 180
Ayen, Comte d' 168

Ballet des Arts 116
Ballet des Muses 146–147
Ballet des Saisons 103–104, 107
Bartet, Monsieur 86
Bellefond, Maréchal de 194, 197
Bellier, Catherine 77
Bellings, Sir Richard 180
Benserade, Isaac de 103, 116, 146
Berkeley, Sir John 16–17, 19, 41
Béthune, Marguerite Louise Suzanne de,
    Comtesse de Guiche 107, 124
Beuvron, Chevalier de 175
Bordes, Madame des 188
Bossuet, Abbé 163–164, 190, 200
Breda 70, 148
Brégis, Madame de 62
Buckingham, George Villiers, 1st Duke
    of 2–3, 16
Buckingham, George Villiers, 2nd Duke
    of 86, 90–92, 160, 195
Buckingham, Mary Fairfax, Duchess of 86,
    90
Burnell, Dr Lawrence 16

Canterbury 171, 182
Catherine of Braganza, Queen of
    England 108, 112–113, 152, 181
Catherine Stuart, Princess 3
Catherine Howard, Queen of England 17
Chaillot 43–44, 58, 61–62, 72, 93–94, 161,
    163
Chantilly 69
Charles I, King of England 1–9, 11–13,
    16–17, 19, 22, 27–28, 30–32, 34–35, 49,
    60–61, 65, 70, 83–86, 90, 162–163
Charles II, King of England 16, 35, 37–39,
    44, 47, 49, 62, 65, 77–79, 81–82, 84–90,
    116, 122, 132, 151, 156, 185
    Appearance 3, 42
    Childhood 1, 3, 13, 24
    Dutch wars 120–121, 126–127, 132–134,
        136–137, 139, 141
    French war 137, 139–141, 145, 148
    Marriage 80, 108, 112–113, 151, 181
    Military career 7, 11, 16–18, 24, 40–42
    Mistresses 16, 80, 97, 108, 115, 151,
        181–182
    Personality 3, 28–29, 41, 51, 67, 76, 181,
        195
    Prospective brides 25, 39, 42, 67, 72–73,
        80, 91
    Reaction to Henrietta Anne's death 194–
        198
    Relationship with Henrietta Anne 16, 23,
        29, 37, 40–41, 57, 59, 68–69, 71, 86–88,
        94–95, 107–108, 115, 118, 120–121, 123,
        126, 128, 130, 134–135, 137, 145, 147,
        151, 153–154, 157, 159–160, 162, 165,
        167, 179–183, 190, 194–195
    Relationship with his mother 28–29, 35,
        37, 39–40, 45, 50, 53–54, 59, 68, 83, 148,
        162
    Relationship with Louis XIV 24, 51, 57,
        73, 95, 108, 115, 122, 126–127, 132–134,
        136–137, 139, 143, 147–148, 158, 167,
        170, 174, 180

Relationship with Philippe 76, 122, 143, 194, 197
Restoration to the throne 67–68, 70–73, 82
Secret Treaty 127, 157, 159, 170, 174, 180–181
Time in France 21, 23, 25, 28–29, 39–42, 48, 51–52, 68–69
Châtillon, Elisabeth Angélique 'Bablon', Duchesse de 40, 97, 115–116, 120, 188
Chevreuse, Madame de 102
Chimerault, Françoise de 104
Choisy, Abbé de 96
Clarendon, Edward Hyde, Earl of 18, 37, 79, 89
Clérambault, Monsieur de 120
Clérémbault, Maréchale de 165
Clifford, Sir Thomas 180, 183
Colbert, Jean Baptiste 171
Colombes 61, 64, 68–69, 97, 103, 113, 137, 160, 162
Comminges, Gaston Jean Baptiste, Comte de 121
Condé, Louis de Bourbon, Prince de 30, 32, 34, 45–46, 68–69, 189
Condé, Claire-Clémence de Maillé-Brézé, Princesse de 199
Conti, Armand de Bourbon, Prince de 56
Conti, Princesse de see Martinozzi
Cosnac, Daniel de, Bishop of Valence 94, 142–143, 145, 147–151, 164, 167
Croissy, Charles Colbert, Marquis de 167, 180
Cromwell, Oliver 31, 49–51, 54, 65, 70, 85
Cromwell, Richard 65, 67

Dalkeith, Anne Villiers, Countess of (later Countess of Morton) 16–23, 35, 38, 41, 50
Dampierre 102
Doddington, John 170
Dover 6, 19, 70–71, 81–84, 170–171, 175, 179–182,
Dover, Treaty of 170, 180–181, 183, 197, 199
Dunkirk 108, 130, 178–179, 181
Dyke, Elinor 19

Edgehill 6, 8
Elizabeth I, Queen of England 11
Elizabeth Stuart, Princess 3, 19, 28, 41, 49
Elizabeth Stuart, Queen of Bohemia 27, 61–62, 83, 86
Essex, Robert Devereux, 3rd Earl 11, 14, 16–17
Exeter 12–18, 36

Fairfax, Sir Thomas 11, 17–18, 86
Falconbridge, Thomas Belasye, Lord 170–171
Feuillet, Père 190
Fiennes, Françoise du Bois de 129, 150–151, 164
Fontainebleau 76, 96–97, 99–103, 105, 107, 117
Fouquet, Basile 61
Fouquet, Nicolas 105–106
Frazier, Dr Alexander 152
Frederick Henry, Stadtholder of the United Provinces 4
Fronde, Wars of 26, 29–30, 32, 44–45, 117
Fuller, Dr Thomas 16–17, 36

Gamaches, Père Cyprien de 32, 33, 35, 37, 38, 81, 83
Gloucester, Henry, Duke of 3, 19, 28, 49–55, 59–60, 62, 68–70, 80–81, 83, 89
Gramont, Philibert de Gramont, Comte de 136, 179
Gramont, Elizabeth Hamilton, Comtesse de 128, 179
Gramont, Antoine de Gramont, Duc de 106, 114, 124, 189
Gramont, Françoise-Marguerite du Plessis de Chivré, Duchesse de 106
Greenwich 6
Guiche, Armand de Gramont, Comte de 106–107, 109–110, 112–115, 118–119, 122–124, 128, 130–131, 143, 146, 148, 189

Hague, The 5, 29, 35, 37, 49, 51, 59, 62, 70–71
Hampton Court Palace 28, 90
Harcourt, Henri de Lorraine, Comte d' 9
Henrietta Anne Stuart, Princess, Duchesse d'Orléans Appearance 14, 23, 41, 56, 62–63, 68, 73, 77–78, 86–88, 93, 96, 98–100, 124–125, 142, 172, 179
Adolescence 62–65, 68–73
At Versailles 117–118, 127, 137, 154–155, 185
Birth 9–15, 152
Childhood 16–26, 30–52, 55–61
Children 110–112, 121–122, 124, 131, 139, 146–148, 155, 161–163, 176, 182, 184–185, 187, 198–199
Death 187–191
Diplomacy 126–128, 132–141, 144–145, 148, 157–160, 170–171, 174, 179–181, 183
Education 26–27, 37–38, 58, 63

Enmity of the Chevalier de Lorraine 129,
    143, 145–146, 149–152, 157, 160–161,
    164–178, 183–184, 186–187, 195, 198
First visit to England 79–92
Flight to France 19–25, 43
Friendships 26, 43–44, 58, 74–75, 97,
    105–109, 112–115, 118, 120, 122–123,
    125,128–129, 131, 142–143, 145,
    147, 150–151, 154, 163–165, 169,
    172, 176, 179–182, 184–185, 187–190
Religion 36–39, 43–44, 50, 60, 74, 77,
    85, 102, 157–160, 163–164
Funeral 199–200
Gossip about alleged affairs 86, 90–92,
    119–120, 143, 146, 152, 160–161
Health 14–15, 68, 91–92, 100, 105–109,
    117–120, 124–125, 133–137, 148–149,
    151–153, 161–163, 172, 178, 183–184,
    187, 195
Intellectual pursuits 58, 63, 116, 118, 125,
    159, 163, 182, 184
Issues with the Marquis de Vardes 109,
    112–115, 117–120, 122–124, 129–131
Love affair with Guiche 106–107,
    109–110, 112–115, 118–119, 122–124,
    130–131, 189
Love affair with Louis XIV 97–108, 131
Performances 55–56, 102–104, 107,
    116–117, 133–134, 146–147
Personality 41, 43–44, 55–56, 58, 62–64,
    68, 73–74, 77, 86–87, 98–100, 102,
    111, 114, 123, 131–132, 141–142, 160,
    171–172, 179
Physical activities 58–59, 68, 77, 100–101,
    116, 118–119, 138, 181, 184
Portraits 97, 116, 147
Pregnancies 105–110, 113, 117–122, 124,
    134–135, 137, 148–149, 160–161
Prospective marriages 46, 55–57, 63–64,
    67, 74–75, 78
Relationship with Charles II 16, 23, 29, 37,
    40–41, 57, 59, 68–69, 71, 86–88, 94–95,
    107–108, 115, 118, 120–121, 123, 126,
    128, 130, 134–135, 137, 145, 147, 151,
    153–154, 157, 159–160, 162, 165, 167,
    179–183, 190, 194–195
Relationship with Henrietta Maria 22–23,
    36–38, 40, 43, 55, 57, 64, 74, 95, 103,
    113, 118, 161–162
Relationship with Louis XIV 24–26,
    55–57, 60, 63, 74, 78, 95, 98–105, 107–
    110, 114–116, 118, 120–121, 123–127,
    129–131, 133, 135, 137, 139, 143–144,
    148, 154–155, 161, 165, 167, 171–172,
    174, 177–179, 183, 185, 188–189, 198,
    200
Relationship with her husband Philippe,
    Duc d'Orléans 24, 55, 57, 64, 75–79, 81,
    86, 89, 92–97, 101, 112–115, 119, 129,
    135, 139, 145–146, 149–151, 157, 161,
    164, 167–173, 175–179, 182, 184–185,
    188, 190, 195, 198
Rumours about death 187–188, 190–199
Saint Cloud improvements 97–98, 119,
    184
Second visit to England 170–171,
    174–182
Secret Treaty 127, 128, 136–137, 144, 148,
    170–171, 174, 179–181, 183, 198–199
Wedding 93–95
Henrietta Maria, Queen of England 1, 4–5,
    18–21, 25, 27, 30, 41–42, 45–49, 51–54, 56,
    59, 61–63, 65, 67–70, 72–73, 77, 79–80, 89,
    91, 93–94, 97, 102, 108, 137, 149, 153, 159,
    167, 180
Appearance 15–16
Death 161–164, 199–200
Diplomacy 137, 143–144, 148, 160
Execution of husband 31–36
Flight to France 14–15
Marriage to Charles I 2–3, 5–7, 9–13, 15,
    22, 28, 31, 36, 83, 90, 113, 163
Personality 2, 5–9, 14, 39, 44, 50, 58, 60,
    64, 76, 85, 98
Relationship with Charles II 28–29, 35,
    37, 39–40, 45, 50, 53–54, 59, 68, 83, 148,
    162
Relationship with Henrietta Anne 22–23,
    36–38, 40, 43, 55, 57, 64, 74, 95, 103,
    113, 118
Relationship with Philippe, Duc
    d'Orléans 76, 162
Visits to England 79, 81, 83–86, 88, 113,
    115–116
Henry VIII 17
Holles, Denzil, Lord 121, 124, 126, 143
Hudson, Jeffrey 15
Hugues de Lionne, Monsieur d' 143
Hyde, Anne see York, Duchess of

James I, King of England 65, 86
James II, King of England see York, Duke of
Jermyn, Henry, Earl of Saint Albans 9, 15,
    18, 32–33, 160

Kérouaille, Louise de 181–182

La Fayette, Louise de 43–44, 58
La Fayette, Marie-Madeleine Pioche de la
    Vergne, Comtesse de 58, 75, 97, 163, 165,
    185, 187–188, 190
La Naissance de Vénus 133
Lambert, Thomas 19
La Rochefoucauld, Duc de 119
La Vallière, Louise de 103–107, 109–110,
    113, 115–116, 118, 144, 147, 149, 154–155,
    185, 189
Le Nôtre, André 97, 118, 184
Leopold I, Emperor of Austria 78
Le Vau, Louis 155
Les Plaisirs de l'Ile Enchantée 155
Lille 179
London 6, 8–9, 13–14, 19, 30–31, 41, 68,
    70–72, 81, 84–86, 88, 90–91, 94, 108, 116,
    121, 128–130, 139, 141, 148, 175, 181, 192,
    194, 196
Longueville, Duchesse de 69
Lorraine, Philippe, Chevalier de 129, 143,
    145, 146, 149–152, 157, 160–161, 164–178,
    183, 184, 186–187, 195, 198
Louis, Dauphin of France 107, 121, 146, 161
Louis XIII, King of France 2, 24, 44, 100
Louis XIV, King of France 44, 48, 61–62,
    67, 94, 96, 106, 118, 138, 146–147, 151,
    161–162, 164, 199
    Appearance 3
    Childhood 13, 23–26, 29, 160
    Dutch Wars 115, 121, 126–128, 132–137,
        139, 144, 149, 158, 180–181
    England War 139, 144, 148–149
    Fronde war 29, 32, 45–47
    Marriage 76, 92, 100–101, 107, 128, 144
    Mistresses 56, 66, 77, 103–107, 109–110,
        113, 144, 147, 149, 154–155, 164, 167,
        178–179, 189
    Personality 24, 26, 100, 102, 117, 133, 143
    Prospective brides 4, 39, 46, 56, 59, 63–66,
        72, 74–76
    Relationship with Charles II 24, 51, 57,
        73, 95, 108, 115, 122, 126–127, 132–134,
        136–137, 139, 143, 147–148, 158, 167,
        170, 174, 180
    Relationship with Henrietta Anne 24–26,
        55–57, 60, 63, 74, 78, 95, 98–105, 107–
        110, 114–116, 118, 120–121, 123–127,
        129–131, 133, 135, 137, 139, 143–144,
        148, 154–155, 161, 165, 167, 171–172,
        174, 177–179, 183, 185, 188–189, 198,
        200
    Relationship with his brother Philippe 100,
        110, 114, 120, 143, 157, 164, 167–168,
        170–172, 174, 177–179, 185, 192, 198
    Secret Treaty with the English 134,
        136–137, 143, 148, 158, 160, 170–171,
        174, 179–181, 183, 185, 192
    Versailles project 97, 117, 127, 155–156,
        183, 185, 188
Louvre Palace 21–23, 27, 29–30, 32, 34–35,
    38, 40–41, 43–48, 52, 55, 58, 72, 75, 120,
    123, 139
Lovell, Richard 52, 54
Lully, Jean-Baptiste 116–117, 133, 146

Malicorne, Monsieur 143
Mancini, Anne Marie, Duchesse de
    Bouillon 56, 133
Mancini, Hortense, Duchesse de Mazarin 56,
    67, 73–74, 91, 182
Mancini, Laura, Duchesse de Mercoeur 56
Mancini, Marie, Princess of Colonna 56,
    66–67, 86, 179
Mancini, Olympe, Comtesse de Soissons 56,
    86, 109, 113–114, 122–123, 130–131
Mansart, Jules-Hardouin 97
Marcillac, Prince de 119
Marie de Medici, Queen of France 2, 26
Maria Theresa of Austria, Queen of
    France 63, 66, 72, 76–77, 96, 100–102,
    107, 109–110, 113, 116, 124–125, 128, 138,
    144, 148–149, 199–200
Marsan, Comte de 175
Martinozzi, Anne Marie, Princesse de
    Conti 56
Mary II 90
Mary Stuart, Princess of Orange 1, 3–4, 6,
    21, 29, 35, 37, 49–52, 59–60, 70–71, 74, 79,
    81, 85–86, 88–89, 94, 181
Mary, Queen of Scots 3, 27, 43
Mayerne, Sir Theodore 5, 12–13, 15,
    152–153, 162
Mazarin, Cardinal 25–28, 30, 44–46, 51, 56,
    57, 66–67, 69, 73–74, 78–79, 82, 86, 89, 91,
    93–94, 100, 143
Mecklebourg, Madame de see Chatillon,
    Elisabeth Angélique, Duchesse de
Medici, Cosimo de 75
Mignard, Pierre 119, 147
Molière 106, 116, 125, 146, 155, 182
Monaco, Catherine de Gramont, Princesse de
    see Valentinois
Monck, General George 67–68, 70–71

Monmouth, James Scott, Duke of 151–156, 180
Montague, Walter, Abbot of Pontoise 50–54, 60, 92
Montagu, Ralph 160, 165, 183, 190, 192, 195, 200
Montalais, Anne-Constance 109–110, 113–115, 143
Montbazon, Duc de 160
Montespan, Françoise-Athénaïs de Rochechouart, Marquise de 97, 114, 116, 120, 133, 147, 149, 154, 164, 167, 178, 189
Montpensier, Anne Marie Louise de 25–26, 35–36, 38–39, 42–47, 57, 59, 67, 72–74, 77–78, 107, 172, 188–189, 199
Montrose, James Graham, Marquess of 62
Moresini, Zuane 193
Morton, Anne Countess of see Dalkeith
Motteville, Madame de 32, 34, 98, 131

Nocret, Jean 97

Oatlands Palace 17–20, 41
Orange, Prince William of 4, 59
Orange, Prince William of (later William III) 90, 126
Orléans, Anne Marie d' 161
Orléans, Élisabeth Marguerite d' 26
Orléans, Elizabeth Charlotte of the Palatinate, Duchesse d' 198
Orléans, Françoise Madeleine d' 75
Orléans, Gaston, Duc d' 25–26, 75, 104
Orléans, Henrietta Anne, Duchesse d' see Henrietta Anne
Orléans, Marie Louise d' 110–112, 121, 139, 146, 155, 162, 184, 187, 199
Orléans, Marguerite Louise d' 26, 75
Orléans, Philippe I, Duc d' 60, 87, 91, 104, 106–107, 109–110, 120, 131, 138, 142, 154, 163, 180–181, 183
    And the Chevalier de Lorraine 129, 143, 145, 149–152, 161, 165, 167–173, 175–178, 184, 195, 198
    Appearance 76–77
    Childhood 24–26, 143
    Henrietta Anne's death 185, 187–188, 190, 194–195, 198–199
    Improvements to Saint Cloud 78, 97, 119, 184
    Jealousy 86, 92, 101, 103, 113–114, 129, 135, 145–146, 148, 150, 152, 154, 169–171, 174–175, 177–179, 184–185
    Personality 24–25, 57, 64, 75–77, 89, 94, 96–97, 119, 143, 149, 179, 199
    Relationship with Charles II 76, 122, 143, 194, 197
    Relationship with Henrietta Anne 24, 55, 57, 64, 75–79, 81, 86, 89, 92–97, 101, 112–115, 119, 129, 135, 139, 145–146, 149–151, 157, 161, 164, 167–173, 175–179, 182, 184–185, 188, 190, 195, 198
    Relationship with Henrietta Maria 76, 162
    Relationship with his brother Louis XIV 78, 100–101, 113, 146, 151, 157, 168, 172–173, 174–175, 178–179, 185, 198
    Relationship with his mother 24–25, 75–76, 81, 101, 135, 139
    Relationship with his children 111, 121–122, 124, 146–147, 162, 182
    Rumours of homosexuality 57, 75–77, 106, 119, 125, 129, 150, 177
    Second marriage 198
    Wedding 93–95
Orléans, Philippe Charles d', Duc de Valois 121–122, 125, 146–148, 199
Orléans Longueville, Charlotte Louise d' 69
Ormond, James Butler, Marquess of (later Duke) 53–54
Oxford 6–13, 16, 19, 22

Palais Royal 23, 26, 29, 47–49, 52–55, 58–60, 62, 64–65, 72–73, 76, 80, 94, 111–113, 115–116, 123–124, 129, 131, 133, 138, 143, 145, 147, 149–150, 152, 154, 160, 164, 175–176, 183
Palatinate, Prince Edward of the 83, 176, 185
Palatinate, Prince Karl of the 84
Palatinate, Princess Louise Hollandine of the 61, 62
Palatinate, Prince Maurice of the 19, 21, 24, 52
Palatinate, Prince Rupert of the 7–8, 12, 19, 21, 23–24, 39, 42, 52, 61–62, 84, 180, 182, 195
Paris 2, 9, 18, 21, 26–32, 35 40, 42 49, 51–54, 56–61, 63, 67, 70, 72, 76, 78–79, 81, 84, 89–93, 95–97, 100, 107–108, 113–114, 116–117, 119, 122–125, 128–129, 131–132, 141–143, 145, 147, 149, 152–154, 159–162, 164–165, 170, 172, 178, 181, 183–184, 187, 199
Paulett, Lady 16
Pepys, Samuel 84–85, 87, 89–91

Peronne, Madame 13
Philip IV, King of Spain 46, 63, 66, 133, 138,
Pons, Bonne de 104
Pyrenees, Treaty of 66, 68

Rambouillet, Marquise de 58, 62
Richelieu, Cardinal 106
Richmond, James Stewart, 1st Duke of 8
Rochester, John Wilmot, 2nd Earl 195–196
Rohan Guémené, Louis, Chevalier de 160–
    161

Sabran, Marquis de 14
Saint Aignan, Duc de 116
Saint Albans, Earl of see Jermyn, Henry
Saint Chaumont, Suzanne Charlotte de
    Gramont, Madame de 146–148, 150–151,
    164–165, 168, 172, 175, 177–178, 184
Saint Cloud 59, 78, 95, 97–99, 117–119, 139,
    146, 149, 157, 161, 163, 184–185, 188–189,
    192, 199–200
Saint Denis 93, 137, 139, 148, 163, 199
Saint Germain, Palace 21–23, 29, 31–32, 34,
    47, 136–137, 143, 146–147, 172, 174, 177,
    183
Saint Simon, Duc de 116
Saint Simon, Gabrielle-Louise de 116
Sandwich, Edward Montagu, Earl of 90, 91,
    178
Savoy, Charles Emmanuel, Duke of 74–75
Savoy, Christine of France, Duchess of 44,
    63–65, 75
Savoy, Princess Margherita of 63, 65–66
Seguier, Pierre 64
Sévigné, Françoise Marguerite de 116, 133
Sévigné, Marie de Rabatin-Chantal, Marquise
    de 116
Shadwell, Thomas 182
Soissons, Olympe, Comtesse de see Mancini
Soissons, Prince Eugène Maurice de Savoie,
    Comte de 86, 87, 130,
Spain 4, 31, 46, 55, 63, 66–67, 133–134, 138,
    154

Stewart, Frances, later Duchess of
    Richmond 108, 152, 181
Stewart, Lord Bernard 8
Stewart, Lord George 8
Stewart, Lord John 8
Suze, Madame de 172

Tuileries 29, 31, 95–96, 109–110
Turenne, Henri La Tour d'Auvergne,
    Maréchal 44–45, 47–48, 68, 149, 165, 169,
    189

Valentinois, Catherine de Gramont, Duchesse
    de (later Princesse de Monaco) 106
Vallot, Dr 162
Van Dyck, Anthony 1–4, 8–9
Vardes, François René du Bec Crespin,
    Marquis de 109, 112–115, 117–120,
    122–124, 129–131
Vaux le Vicomte 105–106
Vendôme, Duchesse de 32
Versailles 97, 117–119, 127, 130, 137,
    154–155, 183, 185, 188, 194
Victoria, Queen 3
Vieuville, Duchesse de 131
Villeroy, Marquis de 175
Villers-Cotterêts 125, 149, 151, 169–171
Villiers, Barbara, Duchess of Castlemaine 16
Vincennes 76, 93, 124

Waller, Edmund 11, 16, 18
Walter, Lucy 151
Whitehall 1, 7, 27, 32, 65, 73, 79, 84–88, 157

York, Anne Hyde, Duchess of 79, 89, 134,
    162, 181
York, James, Duke of 3, 28–30, 35, 39–40,
    44–45, 48–51, 59, 68, 70, 79–81, 86–87, 89,
    128, 135–136, 149, 162, 180, 182
York, Lady Anne of 162–163, 181, 198

Zoccoli, Père 167–168